THE

Settle–Carlisle Railway

THE
Settle–Carlisle Railway

PAUL SALVESON

THE CROWOOD PRESS

First published in 2019 by
The Crowood Press Ltd
Ramsbury, Marlborough
Wiltshire SN8 2HR

enquiries@crowood.com

www.crowood.com

British Library Cataloguing-in-Publication Data
A catalogue record for this book is available from the British
Library.

ISBN 978 1 78500 637 1

Designed and typeset by Guy Croton Publishing Services,
West Malling, Kent

Printed and bound in India by Parksons Graphics

Contents

Dedication

I would like to dedicate this book to all those who fought, in the face of 'conventional wisdom', to oppose the closure of this magnificent railway and who have continued to support its renaissance.

Paul Salveson
Bolton,
April 2019

Acknowledgements

I am particularly grateful for the tremendous help given by members of the Friends of the Settle–Carlisle Line (FoSCL), the Settle–Carlisle Railway Development Company, the Settle and Carlisle Railway Trust (SCRT) and the Cumbrian Railways Association (CRA). Special thanks must go to Mark Rand, Richard Watts, Martin Bairstow, Bryan Gray and David Joy for taking the time to comment; and particularly to the archivists of The Settle-Carlisle Railway Trust and The Cumbrian Railways Association.

I am also deeply grateful for the assistance I have received from Nigel Mussett, Martin Pearson, Edward Album, Bob Swallow, Paul Kampen, Tony Freschini, Douglas Hodgins, Ruth Annison, Andrew Rosthorn, Harvey Scowcroft, Steven Leyland, Drew Haley, Ken Harper, Gordon Allen, Geoff Weaver, Vernon Sidlow, Dick Fearn, Marion Armstrong, Martin Bairstow, Brian Eaton and Solomon Ng.

I would stress that any errors in the book are entirely my own responsibility.

Foreword

As a teenager, living in London, the Settle and Carlisle line was a long way away, but already seemed familiar. The two terrible accidents, high in the hills, described compellingly by L.T.C. Rolt in *Red for Danger*, made the railway and the terrain it went through feel very familiar; and *North of Leeds* by Peter Baughan was similarly evocative of the railway, the story of its building, and the countryside it traversed. Then came the end of steam in 1968, and the 'Fifteen Guinea Special'; I persuaded my parents to buy me a ticket, and on a memorable day, I first saw the whole line from British Rail's last steam train.

I'd think it would be impossible for anyone with any sense of romance not to regard the line with affection, if also respect. It probably should never have been built, but for competition between Victorian railway companies, and when it was, it was an expensive and deadly job, across wild and inhospitable countryside. It was hard to run (and still is), because even though steam and unfitted freights have gone, the remoteness and the weather still conspire to make operations and maintenance costly and challenging. But also, the line is an incredible survivor: it nearly closed, having been run down for years by British Railways, perennially short of money and resource to keep it going, and only saved by luck, political chance, a huge community effort, and by a little official subterfuge.

But now its future is assured. Since 1968, I've made several trips along the railway, but none more enjoyable than on the train hauled by *Flying Scotsman* in March 2017 that reopened the line after Network Rail spent £30m or so restoring the railway after the Eden Brows collapse. If that had happened even fifteen years earlier it would have been the end, but the railway in Britain has turned a corner, and a line like the Settle and Carlisle is valued for the contribution to the economy of the area it goes through, for tourism and because connectivity brings growth, jobs and houses across Britain.

Paul's text is important because it describes all this, but it also focuses on people – the people who built it, operated and maintained it, and fought for it when it was under threat. Too many railway books deal only with facts and figures when there are heroes to be found, engineers and builders to admire (and grieve over, given the huge loss of life in construction), and drivers, firemen, guards and signallers to hear stories from.

It's a real pleasure to be asked to write a foreword to this compelling description and story of the line, written by someone with intimate knowledge and real enthusiasm for it. I read the text from cover to cover in one sitting; many of you will too. And then, of course, you have to travel on the line – for the first time, or again. Whenever you go, whatever the season, this text will help you enjoy one of the magnificent railway journeys of the world.

Sir Peter Hendy CBE, Chairman, Network Rail

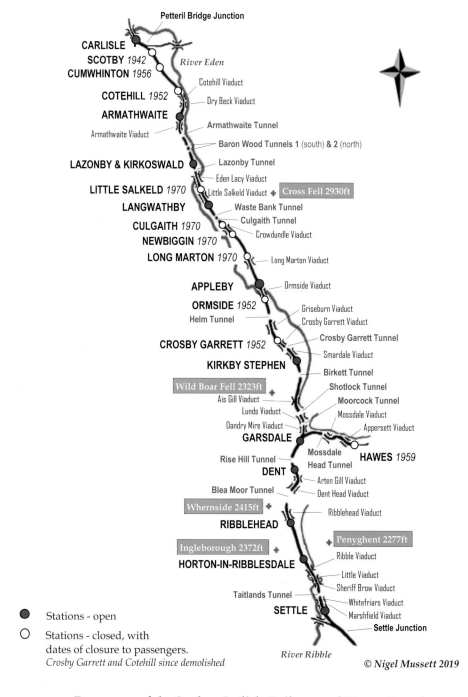

Petteril Bridge Junction

CARLISLE
SCOTBY *1942*
CUMWHINTON *1956*

River Eden

Cotehill Viaduct

COTEHILL *1952*
Dry Beck Viaduct

ARMATHWAITE
Armathwaite Tunnel
Armathwaite Viaduct

Baron Wood Tunnels **1** (south) & **2** (north)

LAZONBY & KIRKOSWALD
Lazonby Tunnel

Eden Lacy Viaduct

LITTLE SALKELD *1970*
Little Salkeld Viaduct ✦ Cross Fell 2930ft

LANGWATHBY
Waste Bank Tunnel

CULGAITH *1970*
Culgaith Tunnel
Crowdundle Viaduct

NEWBIGGIN *1970*

LONG MARTON *1970*
Long Marton Viaduct

APPLEBY
Ormside Viaduct

ORMSIDE *1952*
Griseburn Viaduct

Helm Tunnel
Crosby Garrett Viaduct

Crosby Garrett Tunnel

CROSBY GARRETT *1952*
Smardale Viaduct

KIRKBY STEPHEN
Birkett Tunnel

Shotlock Tunnel

Wild Boar Fell 2323ft ✦
Moorcock Tunnel

Ais Gill Viaduct
Mossdale Viaduct

Lunds Viaduct
Appersett Viaduct

Dandry Mire Viaduct

GARSDALE

Mossdale
Head Tunnel **HAWES** *1959*

Rise Hill Tunnel

DENT
Arten Gill Viaduct

Blea Moor Tunnel
Dent Head Viaduct

Whernside 2415ft ✦
Ribblehead Viaduct

RIBBLEHEAD

Ingleborough 2372ft ✦ ✦ Penyghent 2277ft

HORTON-IN-RIBBLESDALE
Ribble Viaduct

Little Viaduct
Sheriff Brow Viaduct

Taitlands Tunnel
Whitefriars Viaduct

SETTLE
Marshfield Viaduct

Settle Junction

● Stations - open

○ Stations - closed, with
    dates of closure to passengers.
    Crosby Garrett and Cotehill since demolished

River Ribble

© *Nigel Mussett 2019*

Route map of the Settle—Carlisle Railway and Hawes Branch

Map of the route. NIGEL MUSSETT

Introduction

Why another book on the Settle–Carlisle Line? It's almost certainly the most written-about railway in Britain, if not the world. The first book wholly dedicated to the line was Houghton and Foster's excellent work, *The Story of the Settle–Carlisle Line*, published in 1948. Many more have followed, including Peter Baughan's monumental work *The Midland Railway North of Leeds*, published in 1966. Others have covered different aspects of the line's operation, architecture and motive power. Each has its own particular merit, reflecting the deep affection that this line inspires.

I do have one claim to originality. As far as I'm aware, I'm the only person to have written a history of the line who actually worked on it. I was a guard at Blackburn depot in the 1970s and one of my regular turns was working freight trains to Carlisle 'over the Midland', as we still called it then. This experience gave me both a great love for the line and an insider's view of it. I describe my experiences in Chapter 6.

This book attempts several things. First of all, to provide an accessible overview of the line's history aimed at the intelligent general reader, bringing the story up to date. The railway enthusiast market is

The power of steam: A BR 9F heavy freight loco blasts away from Blea Moor with a Widnes to Long Meg freight, 9 April 1966.

A powerful view of Midland Compound 41103 piloting LMS Royal Scot 46133 (the 'Green Howards') on the southbound Thames–Clyde Express passing Garsdale. The 20A shed plate denotes that 41103 was a Leeds (Holbeck) loco, as was 46133. 9 September 1953. J. W. HAGUE, COURTESY DAVID BEEKEN

already very well catered for, but hopefully it will be of interest to them. Secondly, I wanted to bring in a strong 'social' element, highlighting the importance of the people who worked on the line, those who travelled on it and the men and women who fought so hard to save it.

I've peppered the book with quotes from a group of railwaymen who used to work over the line. In 1994, when I was working at Leeds University Adult Education Department, I ran an 'oral history' class for retired railway workers – 'Railwaymen Remember'. The group was led by Charlie Wallace, one of the most remarkable railwaymen I've ever been privileged to meet. His stories, and those of his colleagues like Fred North, Ron Stead, Harry Lewin and several others, would make a great book in their own right. I've only been able to use a few of their recollections here.

One dark feature of the line's history is the huge human cost of its building; not only the lives of construction workers but also those of their wives and children, who fell victim to disease caused by insanitary living conditions.

The line's fortunes have ebbed and flowed, perhaps the nadir being reached in the mid-1980s when even the most optimistic person would have been forgiven for thinking that the line was doomed to close. That this didn't happen was down to 'people power' – the highly effective mass campaign to resist the closure, which was crowned with success in 1989. Many of those campaigners have continued their work, positively promoting the line. A further blow came recently, in 2016, when a serious landslip led to the line's closure for over a year. If that had happened in the 1960s there is little doubt that the line would never have re-opened. The fact that it did is testament to the commitment that the line has within the railway industry and Government.

The line can look forward to a very positive future, playing an expanding role in passenger and freight, as well supporting sustainable tourism and rural development. That's something its original promoters would have welcomed and embraced.

This is a fun railway! Look out for Mickey Mouse tucked inside an alcove on one of the stations along the line. The cheeky mouse used to be located at Dent, but moved further south....

CHAPTER I

A Journey from Leeds to Carlisle

Passengers waiting at Leeds station for the Carlisle train, operated by Northern, often look a bit 'different' from the usual commuters coming into work, or businesspeople on their way to London. A lot of them will be geared up for a long walk in the hills; others will be carrying picnic hampers. This is, at least for some, a fun railway. Many people use it for enjoy-

ment – and the journey is a very big part of their day out. Get a good seat and enjoy the trip.

Departure from Leeds could involve running parallel with something a bit bigger – possibly an LNER service for London or a TransPennine Express heading for Manchester. Routes to Normanton, then Bradford and Wakefield split about a mile outside

The famous Flying Scotsman *prepares to leave Leeds for Carlisle on a railtour in the early 1980s.*

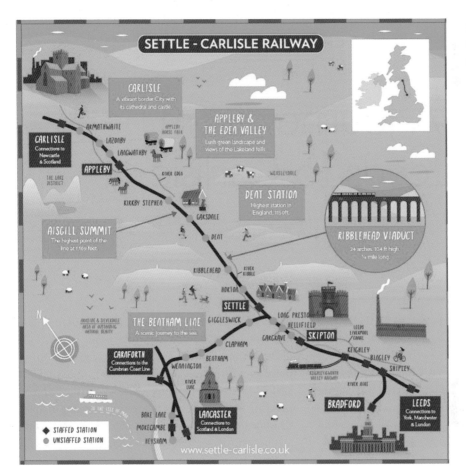

Sketch of the line.
SETTLE—CARLISLE RAILWAY
DEVELOPMENT COMPANY

the station, to the left. The Harrogate line diverges to the right about a mile further on. The Leeds–Liverpool Canal runs alongside the line most of the way to beyond Gargrave and is frequently visible from the train.

This section of the route, known as the Aire Valley Line, was electrified in 1995 and local services to Ilkley, Bradford (Forster Square) and Skipton are operated by modern Class 333 electric trains. We remain 'under the wires' as far as Skipton, passing Kirkstall Abbey on the right, followed by the new station at Kirkstall Forge which opened in June 2016. This section of line, as far as Shipley, dates back to as early as 1846.

The Ilkley line peels off to the right at Apperley Junction and we pass another new station – Apperley Bridge – which re-opened in 2015, before entering Thackley Tunnel after crossing the River Aire.

Beyond the north end of the tunnel the line from Guiseley trails in on the right. Before entering Shipley you may catch sight of the former Great Northern station, now the offices for a scrapyard, on your left. This was the start of the prosaically named 'Idle Branch' with its far-famed Idle Working Men's Club. You can buy the T-shirt.

Shipley is our first stop, using the relatively new platforms on the 'east' curve. It's one of the busiest stations on the line and is fully staffed. The line to Bradford (Forster Square) heads away to the west and the station now forms a complete triangle, with Bradford–Skipton services using the north-west side. It also has a station café, which is an added attraction to this pretty and well-used station. The buildings are classic Midland Railway and very well preserved, helped by the Railway Heritage Trust. Investment by West Yorkshire Combined Authority

Waiting for the 'right away' from Leeds (Wellington) station: Holbeck Royal Scot 46113 Cameronian at the head of the Thames–Clyde Express, 11 May 1959. J. C. W. HALLIDAY

A BR Deltic passes Kirkstall, in the Leeds suburbs, on a railtour bound for Carlisle in 1981.

LMS Jubilee Kolhapur on the morning relief St Pancras–Glasgow emerges from Thackley Tunnel between Leeds and Shipley, 22 July 1967. VERNON SIDLOW

An LMS Fairburn Tank leaves Shipley for Bradford on a portion of the St Pancras Express, 22 July 1967.

BR Britannia 70016 Ariel heads the summer Saturday afternoon relief St Pancras–Edinburgh round Shipley Curve on 22 July 1967. Platforms were provided in two stages, the first being completed in 1979 and the second in 1992. VERNON SIDLOW

Shipley station booking hall has been superbly restored and hosts an excellent café.

Bradford Forster Square: an LMS Fairburn Tank shunts parcels vans in the sidings. March 1967.

An LMS 4MT 2-6-0 shunts Crossley's scrapyard, Shipley, in June 1967.

(Metro) has seen construction of an accessible footbridge, booking office improvements and traditionally styled waiting rooms on the 'curve' platforms.

Bradford has always been an integral part of the Midland's service to Carlisle and the Lancashire coast, so it is worth making a brief diversion to Bradford and re-starting our journey from there. Forster Square station, once a real gem, is now much reduced. It was cut back from its original site by BR in the 1970s and the number of platforms reduced to four. Access is either by a lift from street level or down a cobbled access, which looks fine in the daytime but is less than attractive at night. The saving grace of Forster Square is the surviving Midland Hotel, finely restored and a good place for either a quick bar snack or a more relaxed meal in the dining room. It's the sort of place you might have expected to bump into JB Priestley. While you're there, make sure you explore the back entrance of the hotel with its superb tiled walls and railway posters. It's easy to miss.

Bradford is a bustling multi-cultural city; the city centre has had a lot of investment and Millennium Square facing the town hall is a great place to watch the world go by. If you've more time, the National Science and Media Museum is a great place to visit, but why not stay longer and enjoy a curry in one of the city's many Asian restaurants?

A modern-day scene at Shipley. A class 333 train electric calls at the station, on a service from Leeds to Skipton, using the new platforms. June 2018. MARTIN BAIRSTOW

Leaving Bradford behind, there's no trace of the former Manningham loco shed on the right but look out for the imposing Manningham Mills to the left, the scene of a prolonged strike in 1890–1 which led to the formation of the Independent Labour Party, forerunner of today's Labour Party. The one intermediate stop before Shipley is Frizinghall, well used by children from the Bradford Grammar School (whose old boys include railway historian Martin Bairstow). Look out for the scrapyard on the left and you'll see a couple of derelict diesel shunters, which once shuffled around Crossley Evans' yard.

The train eases round to the left to enter Shipley station on its way towards Skipton. But let's change here, have a coffee in the station café, admire the fine Midland Railway booking hall with its students' art work and be careful not to cause trouble – the British Transport Police have an office in one of the station buildings. Then there's the option to head across to Platform 2, through the busy car park. But look out for an unusual feature on a station: a site of special scientific interest. The SSSI is for a butter-fly meadow and is protected against all invaders, including some who wanted to remove it so the car park could be extended. This section of the line, as far as Skipton, opened in stages during 1847.

We pass the magnificent Salt's Mill on our right just before Saltaire. The mills and surrounding village were built by the Victorian philanthropist Titus Salt. Today they're home to the David Hock-ney Gallery and a range of shops and eating places. Saltaire is a World Heritage Site (acknowledged on the station signs) and it's a fascinating place to visit.

We emerge from Bingley Tunnel; train driv-ers once had to treat this with great care owing to the 'dip' through the station which could cause a goods train to uncouple through a 'snatch'. Today, most trains stop at this busy and attractive station, located in the centre of town. A local 'station friends' group has been busy developing new station garden areas at the station, reviving an old railway tradi-tion. Look out for the famous Bingley five-rise locks on the right as we head north, and the impressive Damart mills, before passing Crossflatts station as our train gathers speed.

Keighley is the next stop: the junction for what is now The Keighley and Worth Valley Railway. The line is one of preservation's great success stories and re-opened in 1968. Only a few people of vision, like the town's MP the late Bob Cryer, could have imagined what it would become and its importance for the local economy. If you're lucky you might catch a glimpse of steam. A former Midland Railway

When I was a young driver my father – a Holbeck driver in the '30s – advised me the best way to tackle the dip. 'Keep the buggers goin'!' he said. He insisted that the best plan was to keep steam on hard after slowing down before Bingley. I tried it out and we went storming through Bingley Tunnel, only to find we were signalled into the loop, with a 20mph speed restriction at the points. We hit them at something more like double that. We held the rails but I was a bit angry with my dad and told him so. He repeated his opinion, adding that I must have been a bit soft to worry about coming off the road. There wasn't any 'snatch' was there?'

Retired driver Fred North, speaking to author, 1994

signalbox controls access to the railway and you'll catch sight of it on the left as we leave. To the right is the new Keighley College building, which has been a real boon for the line, with students making good use of the train to get to and from college. Keighley is a classic West Riding wool town and Cliff Castle, within walking distance of the station, is well worth exploring.

We pass the busy commuter station of Steeton and Silsden (the 'Metro' boundary) followed by more rural Cononley before approaching Skipton. The line passes under the former Ilkley and Grass-ington branch. The Ilkley branch diverged from the Grassington (Swinden Quarry) branch at Embsay Junction as far as Rylstone; only a few yards of lifted track separates it from the Embsay Steam Railway. The branch to Rylstone sees frequent freight traf-fic, typically two or three a day, taking aggregates from Swinden Quarry to locations across the North of England.

Skipton station has retained much of its 'Midland' flavour and the main building is looking the best it has been for a long time. The booking office area is spacious with staff available throughout most of the operating day. The station café – Café Express – is a must. Not only does it do the best coffee in town, it's run by the Settle–Carlisle Railway Devel-opment Company (produce a copy of this book and they might give you a free brew!). Skipton has a

Preserved LMS 46229 Duchess of Hamilton *heads through the Aire Valley on a railtour.*

One of the most celebrated railtours in the 1970s was the pairing of LNWR Hardwicke and Midland Compound number 1000. The tour ran from York to Carnforth. Here they are at Snaygill on 24 April 1976, on the approach to Skipton.

A preserved 'Austerity' freight engine departs from Keighley for Oxenhope.

Celebrity Jubilee 45562 Alberta *at Skipton, surrounded by a couple of more shabby-looking LMS Black 5s. 12 August 1967.*
VERNON SIDLOW

Skipton station in the early 1980s, before electrification.

small train crew depot, with Northern drivers and conductors working as far north as Carlisle, south to Leeds and west to Morecambe.

The former Ilkley platforms are still in situ and, who knows, one day the Embsay Steam Railway may operate passenger trains into Skipton. On the right, north of the station, are the sidings for the electric multiple unit fleet – the Class 333 EMUs – which stable overnight ready for commuter services into Leeds and Bradford. Of more interest to the older railway enthusiast is the former steam shed (the code in latter days was 10G) on the left, now in industrial use. It is accessed along 'Engine Shed Lane'. The railway beyond Skipton opened in 1849 as part of the 'North Western Railway' to Lancaster, leaving the newer Carlisle line (opened in 1876) at Settle Junction.

Skipton itself is a thriving market town, and Skipton Castle is the jewel in the crown of the town's attractions. The canal wharf has been well restored with many good pubs and cafés in the area.

Leaving Skipton, the closed line to Colne curves away to the left and the trackbed is clearly visible. Trains may once again run through from Leeds via Skipton to East Lancashire and Blackpool, if campaign group SELRAP (Skipton–East Lancashire Rail Action Partnership) gets its way. I hope so. Gargrave is the next stop, with the former 'North

Western' station house in private occupation. Facilities are basic but the station serves a charming village and the Dalesman Café's egg and chips are strongly recommended; they have a good juke box with late '60s hits too.

We cross the Leeds–Liverpool Canal for the last time and continue climbing past the former station at Bell Busk, closed in 1959 and once a popular railhead for walkers heading to Malham. The gradient then falls towards Hellifield, allowing non-stop trains to develop a good speed before hitting the 'Long Drag' after Settle Junction. Immediately south of the station the former Lancashire and Yorkshire Railway (L&Y) line from Blackburn trails in. The route beyond Clitheroe is used for diversions and the summer 'DalesRail' trains. Cement once again goes by rail from Ribble Cement, with the sidings controlled by Horrocksford Junction (Clitheroe) signalbox. Hellifield developed as a strong railway community, with both the Lancashire and Yorkshire Railway and the Midland having loco sheds and large teams of workers. Many of the houses in which they lived still survive, including Midland Terrace on Station Road.

In my days as a guard at Blackburn in the mid-1970s, Hellifield was a regular train crew relieving point for long-distance freights from the south and west heading for Carlisle (see Chapter 6). One

BR Clan Pacific 72008 Clan Stewart *hauls a summer Saturday extra through Gargrave in July 1963. Only ten of these locos were built, for lighter passenger work.* PETER SUNDERLAND

Two Class 37 locos on a coal train head north through Bell Busk, c.1984.

A general view of Long Preston with passengers waiting for the northbound local train headed by LMS Black 5 45209. PETER E. BAUGHAN

The Midland Railway's 'Wyvern' crest is integrated into the ironwork on the station canopy, together with 'MR' lettering.

The ornate Midland Railway ironwork at Hellifield, restored with help from the Railway Heritage Trust.

A general view of the north side of Hellifield station in the 1950s. The loco shed is to the left. W. H. FOSTER

The years of transition: BR Peak diesel D14 at Hellifield, with LMS Black 5 44894 in the goods loop at Hellifield. PETER SUNDERLAND

BR 9F 92012 waits in the goods loop at Hellifield before heading north with a heavy freight, 10 August 1967. VERNON SIDLOW

particular job involved signing on at 23:36 to work the Brewery Sidings–Carlisle as far as Hellifield, where we were relieved by 'Carlisle men', always a friendly lot. We then had a six-hour 'short rest' at Hellifield, making good use of the old waiting room's benches before the southbound Class 40-hauled freight appeared. It was easy to imagine ghostly figures appearing outside on the platform, as in the Arthur Askey film *The Ghost Train*, set at a remote Cornish junction, although the scariest thing at this lonely rural junction was the snoring from some of the drivers.

Hellifield (formerly 'South Junction') signalbox is still staffed, controlling the section to Settle Junction. All trace of the former Midland steam shed, which after closure in 1963 housed some of the National Railway Museum's collection of locomotives, has disappeared. The Lancashire and Yorkshire Railway shed closed decades earlier. This still splendid station, complete with its Midland Railway canopies and their 'Wyvern' crests in the ironwork, has a tearoom which serves up a 'fireman's breakfast'. The café always seems well used by a mixture of enthusiasts and local residents including a group of young mums who gather for a cuppa after leaving the kids at school. The tearooms host monthly railway slide shows, which are well-attended.

Two LMS Black 5s at Hellifield waiting for the road, 10 August 1967. 45080 is on a Heysham–Leeds parcels train while 44713 heads a freight bound for the Blackburn line. VERNON SIDLOW

Long Preston is a basic station serving another pleasant village community. The post office has been expanded into a café and does excellent food. It's only a short distance from here to Settle Junction, controlled by a fine Midland Railway signalbox. The original 'Settle' station was here, but was

LMS Jubilee 45566 Queensland *heads south through Long Preston on a summer Saturday relief in the early 1960s. Note the ancient camping coach on the right.* PETER SUNDERLAND

Settle Junction signalbox – the start of the 'Long Drag'.

Settle station has a great team of 'adopters' who look after the gardens and other features.

relocated to the current site in 1876 when the Carlisle route opened. The tracks to Carnforth fall away from the junction whilst the Settle–Carlisle Line proper continues, hitting a 1-in-100 gradient, which it maintains for the next 12 miles (19 km). We are now on the 'Long Drag'.

The 'new' 1876 station at Settle is soon reached. It is a very fine example of the Midland Railway's Settle–Carlisle architecture, one of the two 'large' stations on the line (the other being Appleby). It is well looked after by the station staff and volunteers of the Friends of the Settle–Carlisle Line, who run the small shop inside the building. Just behind the station building is the railway's very own joiner's shop, also run by FoSCL, to produce signage and station furniture for the line. It is a unique and highly successful venture. Look out for the altitude sign, erected by the enterprising former station master Jim Taylor in the 1960s. He was also responsible for creating the superb gardens, now looked after by volunteers.

The station master's house is just to the north of the main buildings and now in private ownership. The former water tower on the east side of the station has been imaginatively restored by Mark and Pat Rand and now forms their home, complete with historic vehicles and buildings displayed outside. Tours round the water tower are available to the

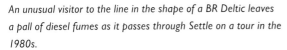

An unusual visitor to the line in the shape of a BR Deltic leaves a pall of diesel fumes as it passes through Settle on a tour in the 1980s.

LMS Jubilee Alberta *heads north through Settle on the summer Saturday St Pancras–Glasgow relief Thames–Clyde Express – the 10:17 from Leeds, which it would work as far as Carlisle. 10 August 1967.* VERNON SIDLOW

public during the summer period. Settle itself is a delightful Dales market town with a good supply of shops, pubs and cafés. The best day to visit is Tuesday – market day. The town hall is the base for the Settle–Carlisle Railway Development Company (see Chapter 8), formed after the line's reprieve, to promote a range of business opportunities along the line. It has proved highly successful, a model for others to follow.

The line continues across two viaducts – Marshfield and Settle – which offer glimpses of the town and parish church. The River Ribble runs parallel to the line, below to the left. A mile further on is the former Stainforth Sidings, which served the Craven Lime Works. Much of this is still visible, including the large Hoffman kilns, which are said to be unique survivors. We pass through Staincliffe Tunnel and then cross two more viaducts – Little Viaduct and the highly photogenic Sheriff Brow. The small community of Helwith Bridge still boasts a pub – The Helwith Bridge Inn – located close to the railway just by Ribble Bridge Viaduct. The pub was an essential part of railwaymen's route knowledge in the 1970s, after most of the signalboxes had closed. If your train was in trouble the pub was the natural place to call for assistance!

BR 9F 92223 brings the Long Meg–Widnes anhydrite train through Settle, 19 August 1967. VERNON SIDLOW

Helwith Bridge, 8 February 1977. A guard's view from the brake van of a northbound freight.

LMS Black 5 45061 north of Settle digs in for the climb to Blea Moor, 12 August 1967. VERNON SIDLOW

Just beyond Helwith Bridge is a sight to gladden railway people's hearts: a new freight connection into the Arcow Quarry. The sidings re-opened in January 2016 after a gap of several decades. The quarry sends out two full trainloads of aggregate each weekday, taking scores of lorries off the narrow Dales roads.

Horton-in-Ribblesdale is a pretty station, brought back to life after the 1960s closure by the Settle–Carlisle Railway Trust, with the buildings now in use as a holiday home. The altitude sign is similar to that at Settle, the handiwork of the much-respected station master Jim Taylor, before he gained promotion and moved down the line to Settle (see Chapter 10). The former station master's house is located just beyond the buildings. There is a fine view to the right of Pen-y-Ghent and many walkers use the train to access this and the other two of the 'Three Peaks' (Whernside and Ingleborough). Great views of Ingleborough open up to the left, particularly

when crossing Ribblehead Viaduct, a few miles further north.

The line passes the small hamlet of Selside with its characteristic railway workers' cottages. Though right alongside the railway, the hamlet never had a station, though it did boast a signal box. This reminds us that the main purpose of this line was to connect London and Glasgow – not to serve local communities unless they were large or vocal enough. A short distance further on to the right is the row of cottages called 'Salt Lake' after the navvy encampment set up during the line's construction, known as 'Salt Lake City'.

Ribblehead station is now home to a small museum and visitor centre; the station master's house, owned by the Settle–Carlisle Railway Trust, is a holiday home. Church services used to be held in the station waiting room. The nearby Station Inn is popular with walkers and railway photographers. Ribblehead was once a 'weather station' (see Chapter 3) and the station master was tasked with sending in regular reports to the Meteorological Office in wartime. The station was closed in 1970 and re-opened in 1986. For a while trains were only able to stop in one direction (southbound) only as the 'down' northbound platform was removed in 1974 to put in a siding for ballast traffic. The new platform was commissioned in May 1993. The meteorological role of the station has returned, making

Horton-in-Ribblesdale station.

The 'directional' sign at Horton, first created by former station master Jim Taylor.

The gardens at Horton are still well cared for.

Two LMS 8Fs 48506 and 48077 haul a heavy civil engineer's train of slab track for a relaying project in Scotland. Horton-in-Ribblesdale, 19 August 1967. VERNON SIDLOW

A Northern Class 158 heads north on a Leeds–Carlisle train in September 2018.

LMS Jubilee Kolhapur 45593 heads north on the afternoon relief St Pancras–Edinburgh in the summer of 1967. The train did not stop at Leeds station. It changed locos on the Holbeck Curve where the Jubilee took over from a diesel. 19 August 1967. VERNON SIDLOW

A guard's van view of the 7M86 St Blazey–Carlisle heading north, c.1978 with 'Salt Lake' cottages on the right, 8 February 1977.

Ribblehead station is today home to a visitor centre and café.

use of modern technology. You can see Ribblehead's weather live online at mylocalweather.org.uk/ribblehead.

The line crosses the Ingleton to Hawes road. Just up to the right, looking eastward, is the site of the navvy encampments at Batty Green. To the left, travelling towards Ingleton, you reach Chapel-le-Dale with its delightful chapel, St Leonards, whose prettiness hides a dark history. Navvies and their wives and children, many of whom died of accidents, smallpox and cholera, are buried here. There

Some of the most memorable experiences in my railway career included riding in the brake van over the 'Long Drag' on a clear winter's night when the snow lay thick on the ground. It was like going across the moon. I'd stand on the brake van veranda and see Whernside or Pen-y-ghent. Sometimes it was so bright you could almost read a book. But that line was lovely in all weathers, except when it was chucking it down!

Retired railwayman Ron Stead, speaking to author, 1994

is a fine memorial inside the chapel erected by the Midland Railway and the workers themselves (*see* Chapter 5).

We're on the approach to the famous Ribblehead Viaduct. Its location is truly spectacular, with dramatic views of the surrounding fells. The viaduct played a key part in the story of the attempts to close the line (*see* Chapter 7). The condition of the viaduct had, by the 1970s, deteriorated to the point that BR engineers proposed to build an entirely new structure. The high costs involved became part of BR's case for closing the line. Eventually, a cost-effective solution was found to safeguard the existing structure. (There is a web camera on the Ribblehead station master's house showing live views of the viaduct, courtesy of RailCam and FoSCL.)

The train slows for the crossing of the viaduct and the line becomes single-track. The conductor will often give a short commentary about the 24-arch viaduct and the view of Ingleborough across to the left, with Whernside ahead. There are many tales of various objects being blown off while crossing the viaduct. My favourite is the story of a platelayer walking his 'length' over the arches in a high wind and losing his cap – which was then caught by the

The weather station at Ribblehead, mid-1950s. The station master performs his meteorological duties. FOSCL

A BR Britannia 70050 Firth of Forth *calls at Ribblehead on a stopping train to Carlisle, April 1966.*

BR Britannia Pacific 70011 Hotspur *hauls a lightly loaded freight – probably the celebrated 'Limey' – across Ribblehead Viaduct on 10 August 1967.* VERNON SIDLOW

The same train heads away, showing the ancient limestone wagons that served the many quarries along the line. VERNON SIDLOW

A local stopping train crosses Ribblehead Viaduct in the early 1980s with a Class 47 at the front.

A Class 60-hauled freight train crosses the Ribblehead Viaduct. SETTLE–CARLISLE RAILWAY DEVELOPMENT COMPANY/COLIN BARKER

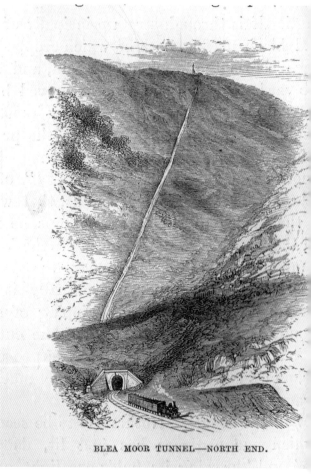

BLEA MOOR TUNNEL—NORTH END.

A fireman's view of Ribblehead Viaduct from the cab of BR 9F 92076, on a Long Meg–Widnes working, 9 April 1976.

An early artist's impression of Blea Moor Tunnel, from F.S. Williams' The Midland Railway.

wind current and blown back up, landing on the rail-wayman's head! Less fancifully, wagon sheets were routinely blown off while crossing the viaduct, and half a dozen brand new cars went over the edge one stormy night. Beyond the viaduct the line reverts to double track, with a passing loop on the 'up' (south-bound) side. The area is controlled by the remote Blea Moor signalbox, a relatively modern structure dating from 1941 when the former Midland box, subject to decades of storms and snow, reached the end of its life.

The line enters a deep cutting and then we plunge into the 2,629-yard-long (2.4 km) Blea Moor Tunnel. It is reputed by generations of railwaymen to be haunted. The continuous climb from Settle Junc-tion ends about half a mile inside the tunnel. Listen for the engine note to change.

We emerge into Dentdale, crossing Dent Head and then Arten Gill Viaduct. The place to sit is on the left, with the line offering lovely views of Dentdale and beyond. Dent station, the highest main-line station in England at 1,150 feet (350 metres) above sea level, is a short distance beyond. Look out for a glimpse of the sign. Notice too the dilapidated snow fences alongside the line erected to stop the snow drift-ing across the line. They don't work! The station buildings have been well preserved and the former snow huts on the left now provide holiday accom-

Ribblehead (Batty Moss) Viaduct under construction, from F.S. Williams' The Midland Railway.

BATTY MOSS VIADUCT.

Driver's view of Blea Moor Tunnel heading north, c.1978.

Dent Head Viaduct, blending into the landscape.

Arten Gill Viaduct on a snowy day in 1976.

BELOW: A steam-hauled railtour crosses Arten Gill Viaduct, c.1983.

The memorial to the navvies and their families who died during the line's construction, Cowgill churchyard near Dent.

LMS Black 5 44993 passes Dent on a local service in July 1960. PETER SUNDERLAND

The sign at Dent station proclaiming it as the 'highest main line station in England' at 1,150 feet (350 metres) above sea level.

LMS mixed-traffic 4MT 43016 brings a southbound freight through Dent, showing the signalbox, sidings, station and station master's house behind, July 1960. PETER SUNDERLAND

modation. Dent village is a long and arduous walk (coming back, especially) from the station. There is a (probably apocryphal) tale of an exhausted walker asking a local farmer why the station was such a long way from the village. The laconic response was, ''Appen they wanted it near to th'railway.'

Between Dent and the station is the small hamlet of Cowgill with its lovely church, St John's. A total of seventy-two people involved with the construction of the railway – navvies and their wives and children – are buried here, twenty-five of whom were buried in un-marked graves, too poor to afford a headstone. In 2016 a fine memorial was erected in the church (*see* Chapter 5).

LMS Black 5 44886 hurries a southbound fitted freight through Dent. The 'snow huts' are clearly visible in front of the signalbox. 22 August 1964.
PETER E. BAUGHAN

The preserved Midland Compound 1000 pilots LMS Jubilee Leander on a southbound railtour in February 1983, near Garsdale.

A short distance beyond Dent station is the 1,213-yard-long (1.1 km) Rise Hill Tunnel, after which the line runs along a ridge with Garsdale below. TV's 'Time Team' once did a dig above the tunnel around No. 2 air shaft, finding evidence of a navvy encampment and ground works for a steam winding engine. The month was June and they got wetter on top of Rise Hill Tunnel than anywhere else they had dug.

This section of line is level, allowing the Midland Railway to install what were Britain's highest railway water troughs, in 1907. Locomotives were fitted with a scoop which allowed the fireman to lower the device when the train hit the start of the troughs, forcing thousands of gallons of water into the locomotive's tender (see Chapter 3). Just 25 miles (40 km) away to the west were the world's lowest water troughs at Hest Bank, right alongside Morecambe Bay at sea level.

Garsdale is a classic railway hamlet, with a row of railway cottages adjacent to the station on the left – reflecting what a busy place this once was. The signalbox, on the down platform, is still operational.

BELOW: *A Northern Class 158 train prepares to depart for Leeds on a wet day in 2018.*

ABOVE: *A Northern Class 158 heads away from Garsdale on a southbound train.*

Railway village: a general view of Garsdale from the road.

The 'Little White Bus' provides a convenient link from the railway to Hawes.

It was from this signalbox on Christmas Eve 1910 that Alfred Sutton (see Chapter 10) made his tragic error in forgetting he had two locomotives on his line and signalled the Scotch Express through. The crash happened about a mile north of the station (Chapter 5). On the opposite platform is the well-restored waiting room and statue of the famous railway dog, Ruswarp (Chapter 9). The former Hawes branch platform is on the far side. Until 1954 trains left here for Hawes and Northallerton,

through rural Wensleydale. The Wensleydale Railway, currently operating between Leeming Bar and Redmire, has long-term aspirations to get back into Garsdale (formerly called 'Hawes Junction'). For now, the Little White Bus provides a handy bus link, meeting most trains.

Garsdale once had a small locomotive shed to service the North Eastern locomotives arriving from Northallerton. On the west side of the line are the remains of the stockade turntable that was

An elderly North Eastern D20 62388 waits in the side platform at Garsdale with a Wensleydale service while an LMS Black 5 heads a northbound local.
J. W. HAGUE, COURTESY DAVID BEEKEN

A view from the guard's brake van on a northbound freight through Garsdale, turntable on the left, 8 February 1977.

A snowy scene at Garsdale, 10 January 1959. In the bay platform is the train for Hawes, by then down to only two a day. The train's composition includes first-class accommodation and plentiful parcels space. J. C. W. HALLIDAY

Preserved LMS Jubilee Bahamas *heads a northbound railtour over Dandry Mire Viaduct in the 1980s. The chapel on the right still described itself as being at 'Hawes Junction'.*

LMS Duchess of Hamilton *emerges from Shotlock Hill Tunnel heading north.*

re-erected at Keighley in 1989, to turn locomotives arriving on the Keighley and Worth Valley line from Oxenhope. There is a legend that the stockade, provided to protect enginemen from the ferocious winds when turning their locomotive, was put in after a locomotive went into something of a spin and the turntable could only be stopped by the shovelling of large amounts of sand into the pit. True or false? Nobody really knows, but – like so many of the line – it's a good tale. What is true though is that a stockade of vertical railway sleepers was built around the turntable pit.

Beyond Garsdale the line curves to the left over the twelve-arch Dandry Mire Viaduct; the route of the Hawes branch can be clearly seen to the right. Dandry Mire was to have been crossed by an earth embankment but after two years of effort the bog had swallowed up everything the contractors could throw at it. Eventually the bog had to be drained

and the viaduct built on the bedrock far below – an unwelcome and costly setback. Two short tunnels follow in quick succession – Moorcock and Shotlock Hill – with Lunds Viaduct separating them. This is the scene of the terrible tragedy that befell the 'Scotch Express' on Christmas Eve 1910.

The line begins to fall shortly beyond, towards Ais Gill. This is the highest point on the line, at 1,169 feet (356 metres). Look out for the sign! The former signalbox has long disappeared but it was a welcome sight in steam days, marking the end of the 'Long Drag' from the north and often affording a brew from the signalman if the line was blocked ahead or the engine was short of steam. It is one of the most remote spots on the line.

There is a fine view of a waterfall to the left, while magnificent views of Mallerstang open up to the right. The waterfall is on County Beck – the one-time boundary between the West Riding of Yorkshire and

On the last day of steam – 11 August 1968 – LMS Black 5s 44781 and 44871 cross Ais Gill Viaduct on BR's 'End of Steam' special.

Preserved Southern West Country 34092 on the last few yards of the climb to the summit at Ais Gill.

I took charge of Ais Gill signalbox on a very snowy February night in 1937. I lodged at the school house by Grisedale Crossing with Tommy Harper, a platelayer, and his wife Mary. It was a terrible night and Tommy walked down to the box with me; he was on snow-sweeping duties. We walked down the road hand in hand it was that bad! We made it, but sometimes the weather was so bad I couldn't leave the box to go home.

Retired signalman Harry Lewin,
talking to the author, 1994

the county of Westmorland. Spare a thought for the sad fate of passengers on the southbound overnight express who died in the Ais Gill disaster of 1913, and the tragic figure of driver Samuel Caudle (Chapter 5), whose express ran into the back of a stationary train.

Dropping down towards Kirkby Stephen, the better view is to the right. We continue to fall on a 1-in-100 gradient, with stunning views across the dale to Mallerstang Edge, and glimpses of small farming communities such as Outhgill, with its tiny chapel – the smallest church in Cumbria – in whose

A lonely spot: the signalbox at Ais Gill, 1,169 feet (356 metres) above sea level.

A former LMS 'Crab' 2-6-0 hauls a short freight towards Ais Gill summit, 25 June 1960. P. HUTCHINSON

Preserved LMS Pacific 46229 Duchess of Hamilton *emerges from Birkett Tunnel heading a southbound special in the 1980s.*

graveyard is a memorial to those who died during the construction of this section of line. The ruins of Pendragon Castle are further along, again to the right. Merlin is reputed to have spent time here, as guest of the magnificently named Uther Pendragon. Birkett Tunnel takes us under Birkett Common and we soon reach Kirkby Stephen. This was originally 'Kirkby Stephen and Ravenstonedale' and for a short time 'Kirkby Stephen West' to distinguish it from its North Eastern cousin, Kirkby Stephen East – though both were actually located west of the ancient town, which once had a reputation for rebellion and lawlessness. Today, it has some nice pubs and genteel shops. There is an active preservation group based at Kirkby Stephen East, The Stainmore Railway Company. Their shop is open every weekend, staffed by volunteers.

The station is nearly 2 miles (3 km) from the town, though there is a segregated footpath to provide safe access. The signalbox here, a relatively modern BR flat-roof type, is still operational and is staffed 24 hours a day, 7 days a week. The station buildings are well looked-after and the main building is now two holiday lets, managed by the Settle–Carlisle Railway Trust. Just beyond the station is the former station master's house and a fine row of Midland Railway cottages. The footbridge was installed as recently as 1999, having previously been located at Guiseley.

ABOVE: *An LMS Jubilee approaches the summit of the line at Ais Gill on a northbound express in 1965.* PETER SUNDERLAND

A Northern Class 158 unit leaves Kirkby Stephen for Carlisle.

Kirkby Stephen – a well-preserved example of Midland 'S&C' architecture.

Promoting sustainable tourism!

A Northern Class 158 departs Kirkby Stephen on a Leeds service, December 2012.

We pass over the twelve-arch Smardale Viaduct, one of the line's most elegant structures and the tallest. Halfway along is a stone marking its completion, laid by Lady Crossley in 1875. As you can imagine, casual visitors are not encouraged to seek it out. Below the viaduct you may get a glimpse of the former North Eastern line from Kirkby Stephen east to Tebay, which itself crosses a fine viaduct nearby which can be glimpsed from the train.

We are now in the Eden Valley, one of the North's most magnificent rivers which flows into the Solway Firth. The Eden is one of very few English rivers which flow counter-intuitively from south to north. To the left, there are views of the Lakeland fells,

Smardale Viaduct: preserved ex-Southern Railway King Arthur Class 777 Sir Lamiel *and LMS Black 5 5407 head across the viaduct on a southbound special in May 1982.*

Midland Compound pilots LMS Jubilee Leander *towards Smardale Viaduct, February 1983.*

A diverted Class 47-hauled train heads south near Smardale, April 1983.

Preserved LNER K4 The Great Marquess *heads south over Crosby Garrett Viaduct.*

Preserved LMS 8F 48151 with Class 25 head across Griseburn Viaduct. The Class 25 provided electric heating for the train.

A Class 47 in the Eden Valley on a diverted London–Glasgow train in April 1983.

including Coniston Old Man, northwards to Blencathra. Crosby Garrett Tunnel is followed by a six-arch viaduct, which takes us above the small village which had its own station until 1953. The remains of the station are still visible and the station master's house is on the right. Notice Crosby Garrett church prominently perched on a hill behind the village.

More viaducts follow – Pott's Beck, then Griseburn – and Helm Tunnel follows soon after. Look out for lovely views to the right, towards Stainmore and Mickle Fell. Notice too that by now the geology has changed. Gone are the limestone walls so familiar in Yorkshire. Helm Tunnel marks the geological boundary after which the now verdant fields are

When you trained as a fireman on the Long Drag the most important lesson was how to deal with Helm Tunnel. You had to put 'the jet' on full otherwise you risked a blow back – the cab would be engulfed in flames, not a pleasant experience. The Helm Wind caused turbulence in the tunnel, probably made worse by lack of proper ventilation.

Retired driver and senior footplate inspector Charlie Wallace, talking to the author, 1994

separated by hedgerows and the buildings are of red sandstone, so characteristic of southern Scotland, towards which we are rapidly heading.

This area is notorious for the 'Helm Wind', the bane of the lives of generations of railwaymen, particularly platelayers who would struggle to stand in the face of the wind blowing its worst. The Helm is Britain's only named wind, blowing from the east and curling over Mallerstang Edge especially. When the conditions are right the streams running down the valley side can blow back upwards – a rare but spectacular sight.

Duchess of Hamilton crosses Ormside Viaduct on a northbound railtour in 1983.

A Class 47 diesel brings a stopping train in to Appleby, 1976.

'Milk for London' – *the rail-connected dairy at Appleby before milk supplies transferred to road.* PETER SUNDERLAND

LMS Jubilee 5690 Leander *performs a photographic 'run-past' at Appleby while running a southbound special, 1976.*

An LMS Black 5 45481 halts at Appleby with a southbound stopping passenger train to Hellifield, 24 September 1963. PETER E. BAUGHAN

We pass the site of Ormside station, another early closure in 1952 though the red sandstone buildings have survived. The station served a tiny village with a historic church. Ormside Viaduct is yet another impressive structure, with ten arches.

Our train will now be slowing on the approach to Appleby, once the county town of Westmorland. It has a fine church and a magnificent main street, with some delightful almshouses tucked away to the side. Like Kirkby Stephen, Appleby once had two stations, though in this case they were closer to each other. Appleby East was the North Eastern station whilst 'West' was the Midland's. There was a connection between the two lines, and this still sees occasional use. For many years after the North Eastern Line (Penrith to Kirkby Stephen) closed, the line remained operational for military traffic to Warcop. Today, the Eden Valley Railway Trust is working hard to re-open part of the line, which once crossed two famous viaducts – Belah and Deepdale. The Stainmore Railway Co has a base at Kirkby Stephen East.

The goods yard is now part of a training centre specializing in heritage buildings and equipment. At one time it had an unlikely resident: a former Great Western 4-6-0 4979 Wootton Hall, which was being restored after rescue from a scrapyard. It has now left the site and is undergoing further restoration by the Furness Railway Trust at the Ribble Steam Centre in Preston.

The station itself is one of the best kept on the line, with fine gardens and heritage features including the still-operational water column, used for steam specials. The water tower dates from only 1991 – the work of Appleby Round Table in support of the returning steam operations. The station booking hall has a range of small exhibits celebrating the line. The footbridge was installed in 1901 and was, for many years, the only footbridge on the line. The signalbox is of the LMS type and is still operational, controlling access to the Warcop branch and sidings.

Leaving Appleby, we cross the bypass that was built on the site of the North Eastern line to Penrith. After a short while some fine views of Murton Fell and Murton Pike open up, with glimpses of High Cup Nick, a walker's favourite. Further along, again on the right, is Knock Old Man followed by Great and Little Dunn Fells and Cross Fell beyond – the highest point on the Pennine Way. We cross the

The lovely booking hall at Appleby, restored with help from the Railway Heritage Trust. RAILWAY HERITAGE TRUST

five-arch Trout Beck Viaduct before Long Marton station, closed in 1953. Beyond here is the busy gypsum works at Kirby Thore, which sends out at least one train a day. Gypsum is mined at nearby Long Marton and brought by conveyor belt nearly 2 miles (3 km) long to the Kirkby Thore works. You can see the covered conveyor belt as it crosses the fields to the south of the works and passes under the railway line. The sidings, opened in 1993, are controlled by a modest Portakabin-style signalbox.

Newbiggin station, closed in 1964, is adjacent to a fine four-arch viaduct, which crosses Crowdundle Beck. Culgaith is another closed station (1970) with the buildings in private use, close by the level crossing and signalbox. Two short tunnels follow in quick succession – Culgaith and Waste Bank. Look out for the River Eamont below to the left, which joins the Eden shortly after. At Culgaith is the first of just two road level crossings on the line, the other being at Low House, north of Armathwaite.

LMS Duchess of Hamilton *shunts her train at Appleby whilst working a southbound special in 1983. The LMS design signalbox is on the right.*

LMS Duchess of Hamilton *passes the site of Long Marton station on a southbound special, 1983.*

Langwathby station.
RAILWAY HERITAGE TRUST

LMS Pacific 46229 Duchess of Hamilton *crosses Eden Lacy on a bright autumn day on a southbound railtour, 1983.*

A BR 9F heads away from Hellifield bound for Long Meg with anhydrite empties, 9 April 1966.

An LMS Fowler Tank 2313 on a southbound local from Carlisle to Appleby, leaving Armathwaite, 5 June 1962.
R. LESLIE

Langwathby is one of the stations that re-opened in 1986 and the building has been in use as 'The Brief Encounter' restaurant, which opened in 1996; it is currently seeking new owners. Just before the station on the left is the immense chicken process-ing works of Frank Bird & Co, at the southern end of which is the base station for the Lake District air ambulance. The helicopter may be seen on its pad. Little Salkeld was an early closure but the buildings have survived. Little Salkeld (also known as Dodd's Mill) Viaduct crosses Briggles Beck just south of the former station.

Shortly after, there is a once-famous railway location which has a much more ancient ancestry. This is Long Meg, named after the 18-foot-high (5.5 m) stone, surrounded by a stone circle of fifty-one 'daughters'. It is suggested that the circle was a druid's temple. Whatever, in more recent times a rich seam of anhydrite was discovered which was mined and used for chemical processes between 1955 and 1983. In the 1950s and '60s there was a regular train of anhydrite from here to Widnes, operated in the last years of steam by the powerful BR '9F' 2-10-0s. The rail operation ceased in 1975.

The same loco on the same train, on another sunny day, near Armathwaite. Note the '12A' shed plate on the smokebox door, indicating its home shed was Carlisle Kingmoor depot. 11 September 1961.
R. LESLIE

Another fascinating feature of this area are Lacy's Caves – five red sandstone chambers carved out in the eighteenth century – well worth a look.

Close to Long Meg the line crosses the Eden on Eden Lacy Viaduct. The next station is Lazonby and Kirkoswald, which serves a growing rural community. Lazonby is the larger of the two villages from which the station takes its name. The station buildings are occupied by Bell's Bakery, a flourishing example of local enterprise, whose products are available from the trolley on your train.

The train skirts the Eden Gorge, with fine views to the right. Three tunnels follow in quick succession – Baron Wood numbers 1 and 2 followed by Armathwaite. The railway is carried on an embankment south of the nine-arch Armathwaite Viaduct before the station itself. The signalbox was de-commissioned in 1983 and is now a museum run by FoSCL volunteers open to visitors and on selected days. Cold Fell is visible to the right, the northern limit of the Pennines. We cross Drybeck Viaduct before

reaching Low House Crossing, still controlled by a classic Midland Railway signalbox.

Beyond here is the high embankment known as Eden Brows, which gave railway engineers and operators a serious headache recently. In 2016 a major slippage took place, closing the line for over a year (see Chapter 9). The end of the embankment is followed by High Stand Gill Viaduct and then Cote-hill, which once had its own station. Whilst there is little trace of the station itself, there is a row of railway cottages adjacent to the line.

The last 'manual' signalbox on the line is Howe and Co.'s Siding, the 'fringe box' for Carlisle Power Signalbox. The sidings used to serve an alabaster works, which had its own fleet of industrial shunting locos. Two are preserved at the Ribble Steam Railway in Preston – *John Howe* and *JN Derbyshire* – both built by Barclay in Kilmarnock. The sidings were used to stable 'cripples' – typically, wagons that were defective, mostly having developed hot axle boxes coming down the 'Long Drag' at perhaps slightly higher speed than was judicious. Some years

Cumwhinton – a very well preserved but long-closed station, now a private home.

Preserved BR 9F 92220 Evening Star – the last steam locomotive built in Britain – leaves Carlisle
on a railtour heading over the Settle–Carlisle, 1976.

ago a 'hot box' was put off here, which was actually an ammunition van. The train crew thought the fire surrounding the axle box had been doused and it was left to cool down. The signalman on the night turn, normally a quiet shift, had a very rude awakening when the van exploded in the middle of the night. Fortunately it had been left some distance from the signalbox and there were no injuries.

Cumwhinton station closed in 1956 but is very well preserved and in use as a private house. The last station on the line was Scotby, closed in 1942 but also still occupied.

The line passes under the M6 motorway and the historic railway from Newcastle, opened in 1837, appears to the right. Before joining the 'West Line' (as it is still known by railway people) at Petteril Bridge Junction we pass, on the left, the site of the Durran Hill loco sheds. When the line opened these were the main locomotive facilities for the Midland Railway in the border city.

Petteril Bridge Junction marks the end of the Settle–Carlisle Line as such. The line contin-ues past London Road Junction where a connection onto the West Coast Main Line at Upperby curves away to the left, followed by another freight connection to the Maryport line shortly after. The former goods lines that by-passed the main station also diverged to the left and are out of use. The tracks were decommissioned in 1984 following the derailment of a freight train, which wrought havoc with the track. BR engineers decided it wasn't economic to repair the damage and they have lain silent every since.

Carlisle is a fine city, well worth spending a day exploring. Pride of place must go the wonderful cathedral, in my view the finest in the North of England with a ceiling that can only be described as stunning. Modern artwork and historic paintings and artefacts can be seen at the Tullie House Museum and Gallery whilst the historic castle is nearby. The market hall, though 'modernized' in recent years, has retained some of its traditional features. The guild hall in the city square is now the tourist information centre.

Carlisle station – the bay platforms for Leeds services.

A former ScotRail Class 158 waits to leave Carlisle for Leeds.

A pair of former LMS Black 5s arrive in Carlisle from Scotland on a summer Saturday relief in July 1966.

Petteril Terrace, Carlisle. Midland Railway houses provided for company employees when the Settle–Carlisle was built.

The Glasgow and South Western Railway had a loco shed on the south side of the city. They provided these good-quality terraced houses for their workers.

Grimy Black 5s prepare to head south on summer Saturday reliefs in July 1967.

As a railway centre, Carlisle was served by no fewer than eight companies before the 'grouping' in 1923. The Midland came in from Leeds, whilst the North Eastern arrived by the 'West Route' from Newcastle. The West Coast Main Line, operated by the London and North Western, arrived from Lancaster while the Maryport and Carlisle (look out for the railway warehouse still bearing the name) came in from the coast. The North British Railway arrived from Edinburgh and operated the Silloth branch whilst the Glasgow and South Western arrived from Kilmarnock and Dumfries. Perhaps pride of place went to the Caledonian Railway, with their magnificent blue 'Cardean' locomotives, the epitome of late Victorian elegance. Evidence of the pre-grouping presence is still to be found in the many houses provided by the railway companies for their employees, including 'South Western Terrace' and 'Caledonian Buildings'.

Today, Carlisle still has a multiplicity of operators, with Virgin, ScotRail, Northern and the TransPennine Express each providing regular services to the city. An even wider range of freight operators runs through Carlisle, including DRS with its major depot at Kingmoor, north of the station, Freightliner, GB Railfreight and others. Steam-hauled charter passenger services are mostly operated by Carnforth-based West Coast Railways.

The station is operated by Virgin Trains. It has seen considerable investment in passenger facilities recently and a welcome innovation is 'Milepost 301', a cosy real ale bar next to Platform 6, which happens to be where most Leeds trains arrive and depart from. Why Milepost 301? That's a question I will leave to you, dear reader. Hope you enjoyed the journey.

CHAPTER 2

An Impossible Dream?

Why build a railway across some of England's most inhospitable terrain? The construction of the Settle–Carlisle Line was a remarkable example of Victorian railway politics. It was born out of a conflict between the Midland Railway and the London and North Western Railway, two of the largest and most powerful railway companies of the second half of the nineteenth century. Whilst the LNWR from the start had its roots in London, at their Euston terminus and headquarters, the Midland was more of a 'provincial' railway with its HQ and main workshops based in Derby. Ironically, the LNWR had its own main engineering works at Crewe, a mere 30 miles (50 km) or so from the centre of the Midland empire.

The Midland Railway's ambitions

The Midland built its 'London extension' to St Pancras in 1868, though it had been operating through services to London King's Cross over Great Northern Railway metals since 1858. So from a business point of view, once the Midland had secured its own route to London, developing its business to the North was a logical next step. The most sensible option was to use the existing 'Little' North Western Railway route from Skipton via Giggleswick and Clapham to Ingleton and then on to Low Gill where it would join the Lancaster and Carlisle's route to Carlisle and then on to Glasgow. The Midland had effectively taken the line over with a 999-year lease in 1859, before absorbing it completely in 1871. The problem was getting beyond Ingleton. The Midland reached Ingleton by 1861 but railway politics prevented it going further. A bizarre situation emerged with Ingleton having two stations – Midland and LNWR – separated by a steep valley that was bridged by a nine-arch viaduct. The LNWR ran a small number of trains along its section of line to Low Gill and Tebay and the Midland ran trains to the south-east from its station, via Clapham to Skipton. For a while, through passengers were expected to trudge from one station to the other. Fortunately the situation didn't last long and through trains began running in 1862. Connections were steadily improved and by 1866 the service had increased to a still-modest four trains a day.

Resolving the Ingleton problem meant that potentially the Midland could develop through services from its new London terminus to Scotland, via Skipton and Clapham and on via Ingleton, Tebay and Carlisle to Glasgow. This involved using LNWR tracks beyond Ingleton to Carlisle, and Caledonian metals north to Glasgow. Negotiations between the Midland and LNWR had begun as early as 1864 but ultimately foundered on the issue of fares and goods charges.

Meanwhile, a separate company – The North of England Union Railway – had deposited a bill in 1865 for a railway that would branch off from Settle and head through Garsdale and Hawes and on to Darlington, using North Eastern Railway infrastructure from Hawes. It was a highly optimistic project and suffered from being under-capitalized. However, it presented the Midland with an opportunity to snub the LNWR. The company took over the promotion of the bill and subsequently withdrew the original proposal. They re-submitted the bill in 1866, which involved building a main line railway, with a ruling gradient of 1-in-100, running directly from Settle to Carlisle with a branch to Hawes.

This hugely ambitious proposal was a direct challenge to the LNWR's supremacy. The Midland was highly astute in winning support from other companies, including the North Eastern Railway and the Lancashire and Yorkshire (L&YR). The latter had an agreement with the LNWR to send its Manchester to Scotland traffic via Preston and Shap, but the agreement was to end in 1876. The 'Lanky' thought they might get a better deal from the Midland, running trains over the new Midland route north from Hellifield. There was an Anglo-Scottish dimension to the controversy: the Caledonian Railway, which operated the direct route to Glasgow via Beattock, was closely allied to the LNWR. However, the North British and Glasgow and South Western Railways were no friends of 'The Caley'. The G&SWR had a rival route from Carlisle to Glasgow via Dumfries whilst the North British ran from Carlisle to Edinburgh over the famous 'Waverley' route via Hawick. They both welcomed the Midland's proposals.

A strange tale of railway politics

Parliament deliberated on the Midland's proposal at length. Many, including MPs, viewed the LNWR as 'the unacceptable face of capitalism' and had little desire to do anything that would protect its monopoly. The Midland Railway (Settle and Carlisle) Bill was passed on 16 July 1866.

But the Midland's troubles had only just begun. The company began purchasing land and doing preliminary surveying work but some savvy commentators were pointing out the folly of building an expensive new mainline railway at a time of recession, which had hit the British economy in the late 1860s. Secret talks were started between the Midland and the LNWR to see if a solution could be found that would be in each other's interests. In other words, to abandon the proposed direct route from Settle and route the Midland expresses via Ingleton – which is what the Midland had aspired to originally.

Agreement was reached between the Midland and the LNWR in November 1868, which allowed the Midland running powers over the LNWR from Ingleton to Carlisle. A bill was then presented to Parliament in April 1869 which provided for the abandonment of the proposed Settle route and confirmed a joint leasing arrangement between Low Gill (south of Tebay) and Carlisle. Common sense seemed to have prevailed.

However, it wasn't as simple as the Midland had hoped. Its erstwhile allies, including the Scottish companies, were alarmed at this 'cosying up' to the LNWR and by implication their Caledonian rivals. The small North of England Union Railway, which had promoted the original bill for a line from Settle to Hawes and Darlington, claimed they had been cheated.

The outcome was a situation quite exceptional in railway promotion. Martin Bairstow, in *The Leeds, Settle & Carlisle Railway*, sums up what happened:

> Basically, the companies petitioning against the Abandonment Bill objected to having been used by the Midland to force the LNWR into negotiation. The case for abandonment was overwhelming. But the decision lay with a committee of MPs who didn't like being used either. They expressed their feeling by rejecting the bill. The Midland was committed to building the Settle–Carlisle.

Surveying and constructing the line

The surveyors and land agents were told to re-start their work in readiness for actual construction to begin in November 1869.

The story of the building of the line alone has taken up several books. It was an exceptionally difficult project, involving the construction of a high-speed main line railway through extremely inhospitable country.

Frederick Williams, in his marvellous work *The Midland Railway: Its Rise and Progress*, published in 1877 and sub-titled *'A narrative of modern enterprise'*, devotes considerable space to the origin and construction of the line. Williams observes:

> A railway for merely local purposes might indeed have been made by running up and down steep gradients ... but such a line would have been useless for the very purposes for which the Settle and Carlisle was to be constructed. An ascent would also have to be made over the country to a height of more than 1,000 feet (300 metres) above the sea, by an incline that should be easy enough for the swiftest passenger expresses and for the heaviest mineral trains to pass securely and punctually up and down....

The Midland's engineer for the line was a young man called Charles Sharland, born in Tasmania (see Chapter 10) and recognized as an intelligent and resourceful engineer. As soon as he was appointed, he set off to walk the potential route – a difficult trudge of over 70 miles (112 km), all the way from Settle to Carlisle. He completed his trek in a very creditable ten days. He and his colleagues were less fortunate some months later when he was surveying the central section of line, staying at the former Gearstones Inn near Blea Moor. It snowed for three weeks continuously and the snow lay 'eighteen inches above the lintel of the door – a door six feet high.' Williams tells us that the engineer and his team of six men, the landlord and his family were able to survive on eggs and bacon, though supplies were running low at the end of the third week. They managed to escape by tunnelling through the snow.

The actual construction work was beset with problems. At Dandry Mire, just north of Garsdale, it proved necessary to build a viaduct instead of a simpler (and cheaper) embankment, owing to the boggy ground conditions. Other problems abounded and it became clear that some of the contractors had been over-optimistic in their tender prices. The firm of Ashwell had the contract for building the first section, from Settle to Ribblehead. The firm ran out of money and had to ask the railway company for assistance. The project was running seriously behind time and the Midland cancelled the contract in October 1871 and took on direct responsibility for that part of the project.

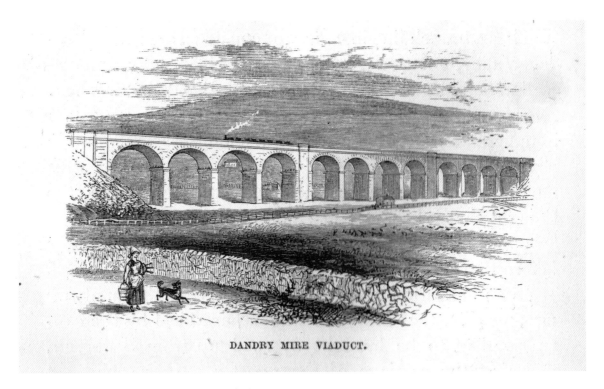

DANDRY MIRE VIADUCT.

Dandry Mire Viaduct, from F.S. Williams' Midland Railway.

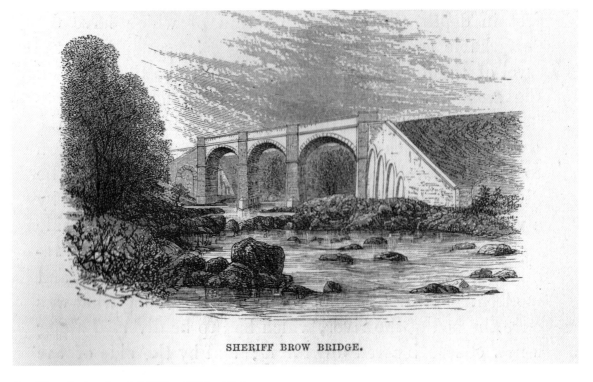

SHERIFF BROW BRIDGE.

Sheriff Brow Viaduct, from F. S. Williams' Midland Railway.

The newly placed memorial in the churchyard at St Leonard's Chapel-le-Dale was erected in 2000.

The original memorial tablet in St Leonard's Church, Chapel-le-Dale, funded by the navvies themselves.

The memorial in St John's Church, Cowgill (near Dent).

If I have had one work in my life that gave me more anxiety than any other, it was this Settle and Carlisle Line.

James Allport, General Manager of the Midland Railway, August 1876

Four contracts were awarded with the line divided into sections. At the peak of construction work as many as 7,000 men were employed. They were recruited from near and far, sometimes giving rise to brawls. The great days of railway building had gone – this was the first major railway-building project for some years and it took time to re-assemble the teams of 'navvies' with the skills, and strength, to build this railway. The workers were sometimes recruited from local farms, but men came from Ireland, Wales, Scotland and other parts of the North of England, often bringing their wives and children. They lived in shanty towns with names such as Inkerman, Sebastopol, Salt Lake City and Belgravia. The navvies were strong on irony.

Some of the remaining earthworks of the shanty town at Batty Green, near Blea Moor and adjacent to the Ribblehead Viaduct, can still be seen. The shanty towns were not, perhaps, quite the lawless places that outraged Victorian morality (and subsequent

ARTEN GILL VIADUCT.

ABOVE: *Arten Gill Viaduct under construction, from F. S. Williams'* Midland Railway.

Construction of Smardale Viaduct, from F. S. Williams' Midland Railway.

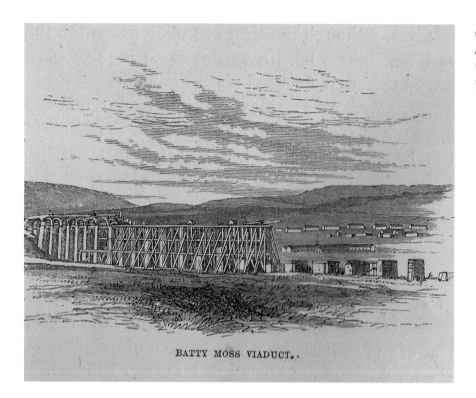

Construction of 'Batty Moss' (Ribblehead) Viaduct, from F. S. Williams' Midland Railway.

BATTY MOSS VIADUCT.

modern TV sensationalism) might have made out. They had Sunday schools and shops as well as the drinking houses. The Midland, and its contractors, did have a sense of responsibility and worked with both the local constabulary and religious organizations to maintain a semblance of order.

The biggest threat was less the bare-knuckle fighting, which admittedly went on, but work-related deaths from explosions, rockfalls and other mishaps. In the Batty Moss area alone, men were dying at the rate of one a week. In 1871 there was an outbreak of smallpox at Ribblehead, which was eventually contained (see Chapter 5).

Some people did well out of the misery and death: a former navvy opened an undertaker's business and claimed to have delivered 110 bodies to the graveyard at St Leonard's Chapel-le-Dale (Chapter 5). A memorial inside the chapel commemorates those who lost their lives in building the railway. The total number of deaths has never been satisfactorily established, but it was certainly well into the hundreds. The graves at Chapel-le-Dale were from just one section of the line's 71-mile (114 km) length.

Men, women and children who died during the construction of the Settle–Carlisle railway line were remembered at a dedication of a new memorial stone. The stone was put up following the discovery of 72 unmarked graves at St John's Parish Church, Cowgill, which belonged to the workers and their families. The Reverend Peter Boyles researched the graves after he discovered them and found that the workers lived in a camp high up above Dent for six years. Their living conditions were as extreme as their working conditions: the camp was makeshift and at high altitude, in the middle of a peat bog.

Westmorland Gazette, 22 August 2016

Frederick Williams and some colleagues were given a tour of the construction work in 1870. They arrived at Settle at around lunchtime and found teams of navvies having a quiet siesta. Their journey continues through Stainforth and Helwith Bridge, Selside until they reach Blea Moor and Batty Wife Hole. Contrary to subsequent myth, they didn't encounter a scene of lawlessness and vice.

An early and highly impressionistic view of Blea Moor Tunnel, from F. S. Williams' Midland Railway.

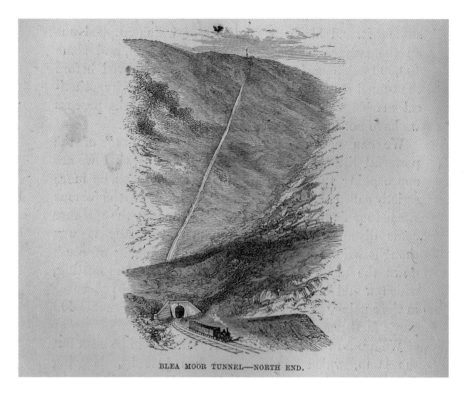

BLEA MOOR TUNNEL—NORTH END.

The town of Batty Wife had, when we visited it, a remarkable appearance. It resembled the gold diggers' villages in the colonies. Potters' carts, drapers' carts, milk carts, greengrocers' carts, butchers' and bakers' carts, brewers' drays, and traps and horses for hire, might all be found, beside numerous hawkers who plied their trade from hut to hut. The Company's offices, yards, stables, storeroom and shops occupied a large space of ground. There were also the shops of various tradespeople, the inevitable public houses, a neat-looking hospital, with a covered walk for convalescents, a post office, a public library, a mission house, and day and Sunday schools.

Frederick Williams, *The Midland Railway: Its Rise and Progress*, 1877

Williams could be describing a typical refugee camp of today. But perhaps the biggest challenge was the weather. He continues:

Despite all these conventionalities, the spot was frequently most desolate and bleak…. Though many of the men had been engaged in railway making in rough and foreign countries, they seemed to agree that they were in 'one of the wildest, windiest, coldest and drearest localities' in the world.

The inhabitants of Batty Green were engaged in the two most demanding parts of the line's construction, Ribblehead ('Batty Moss') Viaduct and Blea Moor Tunnel, whose entrance stands about a mile north of the viaduct. Today, little remains of the shanty towns that once were home to the thousands of workers and their families who were engaged in building this most difficult of British railway engineering projects. Stripping away the romance and sensationalism, we can say that they – and their families who lived there with them – were heroes whose contribution has never been given its full recognition.

The target date for opening the line was 1873, though it was nearly three more years before trains began to operate over the full length of the line. The first goods train operated on 2 August 1875, though the first passenger train wasn't to run until 1 May 1876.

CHAPTER 3

Operating England's Highest Main Line: 1875–1989

The Settle–Carlisle has always been a huge challenge for railway operators, from the original Midland Railway pioneers to today's passenger and freight companies and infrastructure managers Network Rail. The fact that it is England's highest main line railway, rising to 1,169 feet (356 metres) above sea level at Ais Gill, gives only a clue to the difficulties of operating the line. The core 73-mile (117 km) section from Settle to Carlisle has fourteen tunnels and twenty-one viaducts. The famous Ribblehead Viaduct is the longest, but is one among many. The entire railway was a remarkable feat of Victorian engineering, built for speed with a ruling gradient that is no more than 1-in-100. However, the climb in both directions is a long one, much more than the original Lancaster and Carlisle mainline over Shap engineered by Stephenson, with steeper gradients. Even now, the Settle–Carlisle is a challenge for heavy freight trains as well as steam specials.

Driver's view of Ribblehead Viaduct, approaching from the south, March 1977.

A Class 66 diesel loco hauls a southbound coal train over Ribblehead Viaduct, June 2012.

An LMS 8F hauls a northbound freight past the signalbox at Ais Gill summit. The summit sign of 1,169 feet (356 metres) above sea level is to the left. 22 August 1964.
P. HUTCHINSON

It's no wonder in steam days the line was often called the 'Long Drag'. Even before the climb starts in earnest after Settle Junction the gradients are demanding. There's a story dating back to the early 1960s about a diverted Crewe–Carlisle freight train which took on a local driver as route conductor at Blackburn for the unfamiliar Settle route. The Crewe fireman worked hard over the demanding Clitheroe line and when he reached Hellifield he turned to the route conductor and said, 'Bloody hell, I can see why they call it "the Long Drag".' To which he was told, 'We haven't even started yet, lad!'

The line is prone to extreme weather – snow and torrential rain that has often washed away the tracks, including recently at Eden Brows, near Armathwaite (Chapter 9). This necessitated a lengthy closure of the line, which had a major impact on local communities dependent on the line for visitors as well as getting to work.

Early services and opening of branches

The line, as we have seen, opened to freight traffic on 2 August 1875. Passenger trains began operating several months later, on 1 May 1876. A typical week-day would see eight freight trains in each direction. The time allowed from Carlisle to Settle Junction for freight trains was a seemingly generous 4.5 hours, though that included an allowance for taking water at several points en route.

A few days before the line officially opened for passenger trains a trial run was made which covered the route from Skipton to Carlisle in just over 2 hours, at an average speed of 43mph. Clearly, this was no backwater railway but a route built for speed, despite the terrain.

The first day of passenger operation saw only limited celebrations: it had been a long wait and local Dales people probably couldn't believe it had finally happened. The first 'express' service left

A Midland Railway express near to Settle Junction, before the outbreak of the First World War. CUMBRIAN RAILWAYS ASSOCIATION

St Pancras at 10:30am. A journalist writing for the *Railway News* joined the inaugural service in London, impressed by what he saw: '... a train such as had not before been seen in this, or indeed, in any other country, for the perfection of its appointments, and for the luxurious ease and comfort provided for the passengers.' Yet there was a lack of public display along the line itself. Contemporary accounts suggest that a large crowd turned out at Skipton to see the first train depart from the town's new station, but 'all ceremony was dispensed with'. Perhaps the railway had been so long in the making, with many lives lost in the process, that the opening was almost an anti-climax, particularly since freight had been running over the line for several months.

From the start, the Midland used its premier rolling stock on the route, part of the longed-for London–Glasgow/Edinburgh corridor. Pullman cars, introduced by the Midland Railway just two years earlier, took pride of place on the 'Scotch expresses'. For the less exalted passenger, the Midland provided third-class accommodation on all its services over the line.

The July 1876 edition of *Bradshaw's Guide* gives a clear picture of services along the line in its opening year. The Pullman sleeping car express left London St Pancras at 21:15 the previous evening, departing

A Midland Railway express near Shotlock Hill Tunnel. MARTIN BAIRSTOW COLLECTION

Leeds at 02:08. Interestingly, the train split at Skipton, with Edinburgh and Glasgow portions running separately northwards, both non-stop to Carlisle where they handed over to North British and Glasgow and South Western locomotives respectively. The fastest timing for the 86.8 miles (140 km) from Skipton to Carlisle was an even 2 hours, in both directions.

A stopping train left Skipton at 07:15 for Carlisle, while a semi-fast train from Leeds left Skipton at 11:23 calling at Settle and Appleby only. The main

A Midland 4-4-0 halts at Ormside on a southbound local passenger train in 1946. Ormside station was closed in 1950. W. H. FOSTER

Some Victorian gentlemen started the tradition of 'train timing' – recording the times and speed of trains. This is a log, dated 21 June 1889, of a journey between St Pancras and Carlisle. The log shows the numbers of the locomotives that hauled the train, including loco number 168 to Carlisle. The journey took just under 8 hours. The train was piloted by loco 1308 from Normanton to Hawes Junction, not calling at Leeds.

daytime northbound train was the 10:30 from St Pancras, which departed from Leeds at 15:10, conveying the Midland Railway's state-of-the-art 'drawing room' car. As with its overnight equivalent, the train split at Skipton going forward as separate trains to Edinburgh and Glasgow. A further stopping train left Skipton at 16:45 calling at principal stations to Carlisle. The southbound service was, to a degree, a mirror image of the northbound 'down' timetable, with an overnight Pullman sleeping car

LMS 2MT 41205 brings a local passenger train – the famous Hellifield–Hawes 'Bonnyface' into Ribblehead, on a summer's day in 1950. D. IBBOTSON

'Bonnyface' at Ribblehead with an LMS 2MT tank loco. SCRT

train from Edinburgh (with through carriages from Inverness) leaving Carlisle at 00:08. It was followed by its Glasgow equivalent leaving Carlisle at 00:18. They joined the two trains at Skipton for the onward run to St Pancras via Leeds and Derby. A stopping train then left Carlisle at 07:36 arriving in Leeds at 12:35.The daytime Pullman 'dining car express' left Carlisle, again in two separate portions, at 13:05 and 13:15. The Pullman arrived at St Pancras at 21:05 that evening. Another stopper left Carlisle at 16:10 followed by a semi-fast train at 20:05.

Some local services on the line operated for only part of the route. The best known –the Bradford to Hawes 'stopper' (and return) – was known for generations as 'Bonnyface'. Another locally named train was the pick-up goods known as the 'Limey', which served many of the local limestone quarries along the route.

The Settle–Carlisle Line was managed by an important but unseen body officially called the 'District Control Office', with centres at Carlisle, Leeds and (for many years) Skipton. Traditionally, Carlisle 'Control' covered as far as Ais Gill with Leeds having responsibility for the southern part of the line to Skipton and on to Leeds. In LMS days Carlisle Control Office was given responsibility of the line as far as Skipton. Generations of railway workers – drivers and firemen, station masters and signalmen in particular – would be in fairly regular contact with 'Control', whose word was law. Highly skilled men, often drawn from signalling grades, would ensure the smooth running of the railway, making sure that services were staffed and resourced with the appropriate motive power. If a particular train was struggling on the 'Long Drag' and risked delaying other trains, Control would instruct the signalman at, say, Blea Moor, to 'put the train inside' to allow a faster train to pass. If a train crew was working a late-running train and 'their day was up', they would ring Control and ask for relief.

Generally, a day in 'Control' would not be too demanding. Yet the real importance of Control was when something did go wrong: such as a derailment, adverse weather or, less seriously, a locomotive failure. Houghton and Foster spent a day in Carlisle Control office in the late 1940s and their description in *The Story of the Settle–Carlisle Line* is vivid

An LMS Black 5 44993 heads a northbound summer extra passenger train through Dent while a freight is 'waiting for the road'. July 1960. PETER E BAUGHAN

The Midland Railway had an active marketing department. This poster from the 1880s promotes the scenic Eden Valley.

and perceptive: 'All along the line the signalmen, stationmasters, inspectors and others who are working out the halt and passage of trains look to Control for guidance and information. At all points such as 'Ask Control', 'Control want you', 'Tell Control', are as ceaseless as they are urgent.' Today, there is still a 'Control' but remotely located in Manchester (with Northern's Control in York). The remaining signalboxes along the line are still in regular contact to ensure traffic is properly regulated.

An important aspect of the line's operation from the beginning was the close attention given by Midland Railway timetable planners to ensuring good connections with their services to Bradford, Colne and elsewhere. But again, the day-to-day planning of the service and ensuring wherever possible connections were made, was down to the men (for it was entirely staffed by men until recently) in Control. Very often trains would be double-headed up the long steep sections, usually from Carlisle to Garsdale and from Leeds to Ais Gill. The operation to detach the 'pilot' locomotive had to be done quickly and efficiently, despite often-difficult weather conditions. The prize for the footplatemen was a welcome cup of tea with the signalman.

A celebrated feature of the daytime 'Scotch expresses' for many years was the 'refreshment stop' at Normanton, between Leeds and Rotherham. The small railway town, once known as the 'Crewe of the Coalfields' was provided with what

> I used to love watching a pair of Midland 'Compounds' coming up from Garsdale on the ' Thames–Clyde Express'. One would be detached at Ais Gill and the Leeds men were very quick. The fireman would jump off to uncouple as the train was still moving and the pilot engine would be off and into the loop almost without the train stopping!
>
> *Retired signalman Harry Lewin, in conversation with the author, 1994*

A Midland Compound 1018 near Lunds Viaduct in 1946. W. H. FOSTER/MARTIN BAIRSTOW COLLECTION

E.L. Ahrons called 'palatial refreshment rooms ... devoted for many years to the good Samaritan's task of filling up the insides of passengers to and from Scotland.' The full dinner service at Normanton ceased in 1893 when the Midland began running dining cars on its Scotch expresses which were available for third-class passengers as well as first. Ahrons lamented the reduction of the Normanton dining rooms to that of a mere buffet supplying light refreshments, making the place resemble 'the Sahara desert furnished with a beer pump.'

On the core section from Settle Junction to Carlisle were a total of twenty stations (inclusive). The station at Settle Junction (originally named Settle and serving the existing Skipton–Lancaster line) was closed shortly after the new line opened, with a fine station provided in Settle itself which survives virtually intact from when it opened. What is now Ribblehead station was originally Batty Green, while Hawes Junction, notorious in the annals of railway history for the 1913 disaster, became Garsdale. Longwathby became Langwathby, and Knot Hill was changed to Cotehill.

There was some originating traffic; Houghton and Foster commented that 'all originating traffic on the Settle–Carlisle is of the good earth', a state-ment as true today as it was when they wrote in the 1940s. In the nineteenth and early to mid-twentieth centuries the small goods yards handled cattle, sheep, dairy products and minerals, notably limestone. There were occasional special events such as the cattle and horse fairs at Appleby and Kirkby Stephen when the railway brought in large quantities of both livestock and passengers.

The branches

Northwards from Leeds, the main Midland Railway branches began at Apperley Bridge where the Ilkley line diverged. The branch from Guiseley joined the 'main line' just south of Shipley and is still operating, with electric trains from Bradford to Ilkley. At Shipley, the branch to Bradford Forster Square diverges, with both north and south curves. The platforms on the main line itself were a much later addition. At Keighley the branch to Oxenhope opened in 1867 and now forms the popular Keighley and Worth Valley Railway. Skipton was a major hub with the line from Ilkley via Embsay reaching the station by crossing the main line south of Skipton at Snaygill and curving round into what became known as the 'Ilkley platforms'. To the north of the station the branch to Colne veered away to the left. At Hellifield the Lancashire and Yorkshire Railway's branch from Blackburn trailed in to the left (in the direction of northward travel). This line opened in 1880 and became a key part of the Midland's route to the North, permitting through expresses operated by Midland engines to handle expresses from Liverpool and Manchester.

The 'North-Western Railway' (often termed the 'Little North Western' to distinguish it from its bigger sister the London and North Western) diverges from the Settle–Carlisle at Settle Junction and heads west towards Wennington where the line splits with routes to Carnforth and Lancaster/ Morecambe. This route pre-dates the opening of the Settle–Carlisle.

Hawes Junction – later to become Garsdale – was the junction for the Wensleydale line to Northallerton, which opened, after much delay, in 1880. The

Hawes Junction in Midland Railway days. CUMBRIAN RAILWAYS ASSOCIATION

A sign of the times: the closure notice for the Northallerton–Garsdale line, displayed at Hawes on the last day trains ran, 10 January 1959. J. C. W. HALLIDAY

A snowy day at Hawes, shortly before the line closed to passengers, 10 January 1959. J. C. W. HALLIDAY

An elderly Midland 4-4-0, no. 470 at Hawes in 1946. W. H. FOSTER

Midland owned and operated the line as far as Hawes where it became part of the North Eastern Railway's empire. The line closed on 14 March 1959.

Appleby was the interchange for the Midland and North Eastern Railway's services. The North Eastern line from Barnard Castle via Kirkby Stephen to Penrith used a separate station at 'Appleby East', though there was a physical connection to the Midland main line just south of the station. The line from Kirkby Stephen (East) to Tebay passed underneath the Midland at Smardale with no connection.

The Settle–Carlisle Line joined the North Eastern's route from Newcastle just outside Carlisle at Petteril Bridge Junction. It preceded the Settle–Carlisle by many years, opening in 1837 and becoming the first railway to link the east and west coasts of England.

Working the line

The Settle–Carlisle Line provided substantial employment in an area that was overwhelmingly agricultural. Skilled workers for the new railway were often recruited from other parts of the Midland Railway empire, from as far afield as Gloucestershire, the south Midlands and South Yorkshire. Footplate staff and firemen, as well as the highly skilled drivers, came from other Midland depots and often were able to step up the promotional ladder. For example, the driver involved in the Ais Gill disaster of 1913, Samuel Caudle, moved to Carlisle from Gloucestershire (see Chapter 5). In steam days, the starting grade was 'cleaner', followed by 'passed cleaner', which allowed you to fire a locomotive on the main line. The next grade was fire-

Durran Hill loco shed in its Midland Railway heyday. CUMBRIAN RAILWAYS ASSOCIATION

Station staff at Garsdale, on a cold January day in 1949. J. C. W. HALLIDAY

man, then 'passed fireman', which meant you could drive a locomotive. The ultimate achievement was to be booked as a driver. This could take decades and some 'passed firemen' (including some at Carlisle sheds) never made it to driver status before they reached retirement age. The 'rules' exam was rigorous and the more conscientious drivers would organize quiz sessions in the local pub to test each other out!

Footplate staff who worked over the line were mostly based at Carlisle (Durran Hill), Hellifield,

> Very often the drivers would ask their wives to question them on 'Rules and Regulations' – and they became better than the men! When I became a Footplate Inspector I passed some wives and failed their husbands!
>
> *Retired footplate inspector Charlie Wallace, talking to the author, 1994*

Carlisle had several lodging houses – Upperby, Durran Hill and Kingmoor. Kingmoor had a lot of Scotch lodgers. They were big, hefty men. In the middle of the mess room there was a table with a big bowl of fat. They'd ladle some up to make a fry up and then sling the fat back in when they'd finished. God only knows how old that fat was.

Retired driver Fred North, talking to the author, 1994

On our way back from Carlisle, after lodging, we were on the lookout at certain signalboxes for something to take home, such as rabbits and the like. When the signalman had any, he would hang them in pairs over the rail round the box so we could see them from a fair distance approaching. The price was fixed as a rule, at 2s 6d a pair.

Bill Addy, West Riding Engineman (1984)

Skipton and Leeds (Holbeck). In Midland and LMS days, footplatemen from as far afield as Saltley (Birmingham) and Derby had Carlisle work and lodged at the company hostels in the city. Some goods trains were worked by Stourton (Leeds) footplatemen and guards. In post-war years there was a hostel at Upperby (now a hotel), Durran Hill and another at Kingmoor, which catered primarily for Scottish crews. Carlisle footplatemen working south would lodge at Leeds and even as far south as London. Hellifield had its own lodging house, which was very popular amongst crews, whilst some of the larger establishments were disliked for reasons varying from noise, the quality of food and even in some cases vermin. It was common, in pre-war years, for drivers and firemen to share the same bed.

Bradford's Manningham shed had some work on parts of the south end of the line. In later years, Lower Darwen (Blackburn) men worked through to Carlisle. Footplatemen were organized into their own trade union, the Associated Society of Locomotive Engineers and Firemen, which was formed in 1880 by a group of locomen at Leeds (Holbeck) depot.

Every train would have at least one guard, and in some cases two. Premier passenger trains would have at least two, as we know from the Ais Gill disaster of 1913 when two passenger guards were involved in the drama on the sleeper car train which stalled just before Ais Gill summit, leading to the rear-end collision with a following train. Again, there was clear segregation between the grades of guard. A goods guard, probably recruited from the 'lower' grade of shunter, would look enviously

A Midland Railway guard with his family, c.1900. CUMBRIAN RAILWAYS ASSOCIATION

During the 1950s there was a regular cattle train from Stranraer via Carlisle to the south, carrying cattle from Ireland. A Stourton (Leeds) guard was booked to work the train from Carlisle to Leeds, and on this occasion was stopped at Kirkby Stephen. A signalman further north had spotted one of the cow's legs hanging out of the van. The train reversed into the cattle dock at Kirkby Stephen so the crew could open the van door and ensure the cow was back in safely. Unfortunately the guard didn't check to see if the cattle dock gates out onto the road were shut. All the other cows in the van made a bid for freedom and the only one that was rescued was the cow with the sore leg!

Retired guard Ron Stead, in conversation with the author, 1994

Selside signalbox, with resident female signaller. Selside was one of the signalboxes on the line that had female signallers who joined the railway during wartime. SCRT

Pride in the job: a signalman at Horton-in-Ribblesdale, c.1949. W. H. FOSTER

at his passenger guard colleagues who were finely attired and proud of their calling. The line of promotion beyond the grade of guard could be to running a small station, or to other operational roles such as an inspector, based at Carlisle, Hellifield or Skipton.

Like their locomotive colleagues, the guards – passenger and freight alike – were often staunch trades unionists, but members of a different body. The Association of Railway Servants (ASRS) had been formed in 1873 and became the National Union of Railwaymen in 1913, recruiting in most 'wages' or blue-collar grades. It became the RMT – the National Union of Rail, Maritime and Transport Workers – in 1990, through a merger with the National Union of Seamen. Clerical staff had their own union: the Railway Clerks Association, which became The Transport Salaried Staffs Association in 1951.

The new line was signalled by a large number of signalboxes and again, the Midland recruited from other parts of their network. Alfred Sutton, the tragic character from the Hawes Junction calamity, moved north to gain promotion. He was typical of several signalmen who moved to the Settle–Carlisle Line to get promotion from lower-graded boxes elsewhere on the network. Just as with other posts, there was

a hierarchy of signalmen: boxes with relatively few movements were graded at a lower level than busy signalboxes such as Hawes Junction, Hellifield South Junction and the Skipton boxes. Some signalmen progressed to positions within the Control office, or to station-master roles. Carlisle Control was an important centre that would have employed around twenty-five staff working three shifts, seven days a week. Control's job was all embracing, ensuring trains were fully resourced in terms of staff and locomotives and regulating trains so that priority was given to 'key' trains. Whilst a signalman had sway over just a few miles of track, Control could take a strategic view of the line's operation and direct signalmen, when necessary, to detail a slow-moving train 'inside' to allow a faster train to pass.

The job came into its own when something went wrong. In the case of a derailment Control would ensure that services were, if possible, diverted and crewed appropriately. When serious incidents occurred they would have prime responsibility for getting emergency services to the site.

One of the most important responsibilities along the line was that of station master. Yet again, a rigid

Cumwhinton station staff c.1900, showing the station master with his top hat. CUMBRIAN RAILWAYS ASSOCIATION

A fine view of Ribblehead station staff and families in the early 1900s. MARTIN BAIRSTOW COLLECTION

hierarchy applied. A station master at a quiet spot such as Crosby Garrett would have had less staff, not many passengers, fewer goods to deal with and would be on a lower rate of pay. Yet he would still be an important figure within the village community, along with the vicar and school teacher. The role of the station master was often complex. At a station such as Appleby he would have responsibility for a

Station master Jim Taylor at Settle in the 1960s, waving off a train.

range of staff, including signalmen and station staff who dealt with passengers as well as goods. They were in the front line when anything went wrong. The station master at Hawes Junction, Mr Bunce, was one of the first on the scene following the Christmas Eve crash in 1910, taking charge of the initial rescue operation.

The busier stations employed clerical staff who often regarded themselves as a 'cut above' some of their colleagues. Stations such as Skipton and Carlisle, and to a lesser extent Settle and Appleby, would have had a number of clerks dealing with passenger receipts and goods transactions, as well as staff wages. Every station would have a booking clerk, though at small stations the role could be combined with other duties. Larger stations such as Carlisle would have a Chief Clerk who was lord of all he surveyed.

Most stations would have at least one, and possibly several, porters, whose jobs included assisting with most aspects of station work. Young lads wanting to get a foot on the professional railway ladder would often start as a 'junior porter' and move through the ranks as vacancies arose. This could be to shunting or possibly guards' jobs, or to signalling roles; these would require several weeks' training before being 'passed out'.

Stations such as Settle and Appleby commanded a higher salary and were sought-after positions. Traditionally there was internal promotion along the line with, for example, a station master at Horton-in-Ribblesdale applying for a vacancy at Settle, as in the case of Jim Taylor in post-war years. Recruitment to the post of station master came from a variety of grades, including clerical grades and sometimes passenger guards. There was seldom any crossover from the footplate grades to 'white-collar' duties.

The men who kept the railway running were often the least rewarded. The track workers – or 'platelayers' – had a hard and dangerous job that was traditionally poorly paid. Some of the early platelayers would have been sourced from the line's construction workers, though most departed to get more lucrative contract work elsewhere. Other platelayers would have been recruited 'from over the railway fence', i.e. from amongst farm workers. They would come under the control of the District Permanent Way Inspector, who would typically have risen from the ranks of platelayers, through various grades. A number of gangs would be located along the line, in charge of specified lengths of track, or sections. There were gangs located at most points along the line. In later years, from the 1960s, mobile

A gang of platelayers on the line, possibly Dent c.1930s. SCRT

Not much sign of health and safety hi-vis vests! A group of platelayers stands back to allow LMS Jubilee 45565 Victoria pass by on a freight. Ribblehead, c.1949. W. H. FOSTER

gangs were introduced and based at places such as Appleby, Armathwaite, Little Salkeld and Kirkby Stephen.

On the north end of the line, section supervisors were located at Appleby and Kirkby Stephen, covering local gangs of between eight and ten men. As well as routine maintenance they would have responsibility for snow clearance, responding to accidents and other incidents that arose, including clearing stray livestock from the line.

An often ignored – and dangerous – job was that of the humble 'lampman', who had the important and often challenging job of keeping the oil in signal lamps full and serviceable. The job had to be done regardless of the weather and involved using a ladder to access the signal lamp perched behind the signal arm's coloured lens. Larger depots such as Skipton and certainly Carlisle would have a range of more specialist grades including the much-lampooned 'wheel-tapper', whose job was to check train wheels and ensure the vehicle was in a safe condition to run. In more recent years the job was redefined as 'rolling stock technician'!

It was very much a man's world. In the early years of the Settle–Carlisle Line, the only female employees would have been in refreshment rooms at the larger stations, such as Carlisle and Skipton, or running the railway lodging houses at Carlisle, Hellifield and Leeds. They must have had a challenging job looking after some of their guests.

Some female workers were drafted in to work in traditionally male-only grades during the First and Second World Wars. These jobs included engine cleaning, ticket collection and portering during the First World War, though most women had to relinquish their jobs at the end of the war in 1918. In the 1939–45 conflict the role of women widened and some signalboxes along the line had female signal-

> Some of the lodging houses were very comfortable. The house at Carnforth was run by a nice lady – Mrs Marshall – who kept the place immaculate. The food was good too. It was normal for footplatemen to take their families there for holidays in summer! Mrs Lockhart was stewardess at Carlisle Kingmoor lodging house. It was a rum place. On my first visit she told me to be careful if I went into town, as there were 'a lot of bad women in Carlisle'. Unfortunately, I didn't find any!
>
> *Retired Leeds driver Fred North, talking to the author, 1994*

lers. The most notable was the small box at Selside where all three 'regular' signallers were female. Unlike after the First World War, several women retained their jobs and retired in the 1950s and '60s.

During the Second World War many railwaymen went into the forces and saw action overseas. Charlie Wallace was stationed in France and stayed on after the Dunkirk evacuation, responsible for sabotaging the railway infrastructure so the advancing German army couldn't use anything. 'We were told to abandon the depot before the Germans got within reach. Everything was to be destroyed including the ancient Great Western 'Dean Goods' that we'd worked on. We threw two Mills bombs into the firebox, and got out of the way quickly!' When he came to be evacuated his train – amongst several taking remaining troops and refugees to the Channel – was attacked by the Luftwaffe and about 500 men died.

Charlie was badly injured and spent the rest of the war as a prisoner of war. Whilst the Settle–Carlisle Line escaped attack, Leeds itself wasn't so lucky and at least one locoman died in a bombing raid.

The line in its heyday – and decline

The years just before the outbreak of the First World War saw the line flourishing, with two sleeping car expresses in each direction: three daytime London to Scotland expresses as well as a direct express from Liverpool and Manchester to Edinburgh and Glasgow, reaching Hellifield via Blackburn and Clitheroe. No passenger trains ran on Sundays apart from the four overnight expresses (two in each direction).

In 1930 the LMS decided to name several of its premier services. For the St Pancras to Scotland services, the Glasgow daytime express became the 'Thames–Clyde Express' while the Edinburgh equivalent, inevitably, was called the 'Thames–Forth Express'. In 1957 this became the famous 'Waverley', running via the 'Waverley Route' from Carlisle via Hawick, which closed in 1969. Right up to the late 1970s, the 'Thames–Clyde Express' offered a high standard of comfort with a full restaurant car service from London to Glasgow.

Dinner on the Thames–Clyde Express: It was Summer 1974, a student with time to spare – the London Midland region was short of dining car staff, so why not? A week's training and duty assigned – Circuit 721 1S68 08:00 St Pancras to Glasgow, train number 1M86 – 09:50 return the next day: the Thames–Clyde Express, the premier train over the Settle and Carlisle line for 100 years. So reporting for duty on 27th May and under the direction of Chief Stewards George and Arthur, both from the highest LMS tradition, three months were spent serving all the meals offered by the BR restaurant car service except dinner, the only meal not covered by the two-day circuit. Over the S&C it was lunch

An LMS express passes over Arten Gill, c.1928.
SCRT

An LMS Jubilee on a local train, near Selside in the 1930s.
MARTIN BAIRSTOW COLLECTION

Midland Compound 1075 emerges from Culgaith Tunnel on a
passenger working in the 1930s. D. IBBOTSON

The down Thames–Clyde
Express passes Blea Moor
in February 1976.

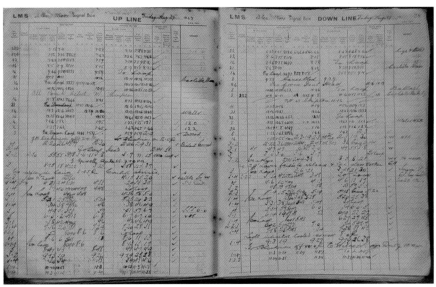

An excerpt from Blea Moor
Train Register Book, 1949.

with the call going out on leaving Leeds or Carlisle and usually finished by Ais Gill, leaving the crew to enjoy the scenery over the rest of the route during staff lunch. The main course was always roast beef – who would have thought you could be sick of it after a couple of weeks, so it was a good job our chefs would find tasty alternatives for us.

Ian Ambrose, former part-time restaurant car attendant, now Network Rail manager

As well as the premier expresses, the line maintained a strong flow of freight traffic. The Train Register Book for Blea Moor in 1949 (rescued from oblivion by the author when calling in at the box as the guard of a Carlisle-bound freight to 'sign the book') shows a constant stream of freight trains punctuated by local or express passenger services and the occasional 'special'.

The line played an important role during the First and Second World Wars. It provided a vital alternative route for the West Coast and East Coast main lines, both to handle additional passenger and freight traffic but also in the event of either line being blocked by enemy action. The post-war years saw the line continue as an important through route. Most northbound freight was re-marshalled at Carlisle, at the huge Kingmoor marshalling yard just north of the city. Southbound freight would often be re-marshalled at Leeds (Stourton Sidings) and in later years at Healey Mills yard, near Wakefield.

> The signalmen at Dent and Garsdale, during the intensive bombing of Manchester and Merseyside, could look across from their high position and see the glow in the sky from the fires. Also, they could tell when an air-raid was imminent by the large number of planes which passed overhead.
>
> *Bill Addy,* West Riding Engineman *(1984)*

During the 1950s, enterprising BR management introduced bargain-fare 'Starlight Specials' between London (Marylebone) and Glasgow, which were routed via the Settle–Carlisle. Car sleeper trains were also introduced in the late 1950s, including a Glasgow to Eastbourne and Stirling to Sutton Coldfield service. This brave attempt by BR to meet the challenge of the motor car was, ultimately, unsuccessful.

In the post-war years the line continued to generate considerable amounts of local traffic – mostly but by no means entirely, minerals. Horton-in-Ribblesdale had several rail-served quarries and it is pleasing to see that one has recently re-opened after a gap of many years (Chapter 9). Just before the First World War, Horton was sending out about 50,000 tonnes of limestone a year. This was down to 23,000 by the mid-1950s and the quarries ceased using rail in the 1970s. The busiest goods yard on the line (excluding Carlisle and Skipton) was Lazonby, which was still handling nearly 300,000 tons of

An LMS 8F loco hauls a heavy freight train through Skipton heading north.

The timetable of that year (1952) boasted of no less than 35 goods departures during any 24-hour period (from Carlisle Durran Hill Sidings). Amongst the destinations were Birmingham (Water Orton), Somers Town (London) and Ancoats (Manchester).

Peter Brock, Calling Carlisle Control *(1990)*

BR 4MT no. 75041 on the up 'Limey' passing Blea Moor signalbox, April 1966.

freight in the early 1960s. This would have included minerals (gypsum, limestone, coal, coke and lime) as well as livestock and general merchandise.

A sign of the transition from steam to diesel and new forms of freight operation was the introduction of the 'Condor' express freight service from Glasgow to London. The train was hauled by two 'Metro-vick' diesels and was entirely containerized. It was routed via Settle and was worked throughout from Carlisle by Kingmoor crews.

By 1960, on the eve of publication of the infamous Beeching Report, the line was down to carrying one overnight express in each direction (with a stop at Appleby), the two daytime Anglo-Scottish expresses (the Thames–Clyde Express and the Waverley) and three local trains in each direction, one of which terminated at Garsdale – the former 'Bonnyface', which as we have seen traditionally ran to Hawes.

Infrastructure

Building the line required careful attention to infrastructure ranging from track capacity, sidings, loops and refuge sidings to signalling arrangements (signalboxes, length of block sections) and locomotive facilities. As we have seen, the line was built as double-track throughout, though in the early months of the line in 1875 parts of the line were operated as a single-track railway. However, by the full opening on 1 May 1876 the line was a fine example of a modern, well-resourced railway with trains operating at high speeds, certainly into the mid-1970s on some sections of line.

The signalboxes provided were of the classic Midland Railway style, several of which still survive

The front cover of BR's London Midland region staff magazine, February 1961, featuring the 'Condor' freight service.

LMS Jubilee 45562 Alberta prepares to leave Skipton with the 10:17 Leeds–Carlisle on a summer Saturday in 1967.

A trio of Midland Railway fire buckets, still in use at Shipley in 1967.

A general view of Armathwaite station in the 1930s; little had changed since it opened in the late 1870s. PETER E. BAUGHAN

A well-preserved example of a Midland Railway warehouse at Kirkby Stephen.

A guard's view from the brake van of Horton signalbox and sidings in 1978.

Griseburn Ballast Sidings signalbox, looking north in 1977.

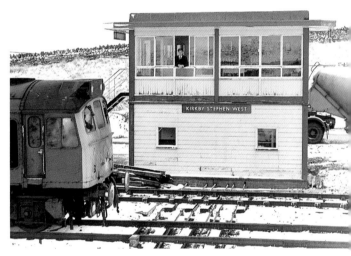

A Class 25 pauses at Kirby Stephen to receive the signalman's instructions, c.1979. SCRT

on the line today (e.g. Settle Junction, Garsdale, Howe & Co.'s Siding). The signalboxes fulfilled two prime functions, the first of which was to ensure there was capacity on the line that could be safely managed, using the 'block system' whereby only one train could be allowed on a specific section of line at any one time. If you skimped on the number of block sections you would drastically reduce your track capacity and cause delay. The other important function was to control access to sidings and manage junctions, such as those at Skipton, Hellifield, Garsdale (Hawes Junction) and Appleby. Most stations had a goods yard, typically with two or three sidings, including cattle dock and warehouse. Again, some of the warehouses have survived, such as those at Langwathby, Armathwaite, Kirkby Stephen and Appleby.

Garsdale: the highest water troughs in the world! W. H. FOSTER

BR 9F 92076 in the 'up' loop at Blea Moor on a Long Meg–Widnes train, 9 April 1966.

The wartime Railway Executive built hundreds of rugged 'Austerity' 2-8-0 locos for heavy freight work. Here one of the class crosses Arten Gill Viaduct with a heavy load of rails for the Civil Engineer's Department, 22 August 1964. PETER E. BAUGHAN

Two BR 9Fs pass at Blea Moor on anhydrite workings, 9 April 1966. The Lower Darwen (Blackburn) crew coming up from the south swapped trains with their Carlisle (Kingmoor) colleagues who would take the train on to Long Meg.

A famous feature on the line was the turntable at Garsdale (formerly Hawes Junction), which was provided primarily to 'turn' assisting locomotives which detached there to head back south to Carlisle (or occasionally to Hellifield). The turntable itself is now preserved on the Keighley and Worth Valley Railway at Keighley station (*see* Chapter 1).

The line was provided with several refuge sidings allowing slow-moving freight trains (and, occasionally, passenger workings) to allow faster trains to pass, and for the locomotive to take water. The remote location of Blea Moor had both 'up' and 'down' loops provided during the Second World War to replace the 'dead-end' refuge sidings.

A special feature of the route's infrastructure was the provision of water troughs south of Garsdale, provided in 1907. This arrangement allowed for locomotives to take water without stopping. A trough was placed between the tracks; the locomotive crew, when approaching the trough, would lower a scoop from the tender. Timing was everything: lowering the scoop too soon could damage the apparatus, but leaving it too late would result in insufficient water going into the loco's tender. Leaving it too late to take up the scoop could also cause

The troughs at Garsdale were the only ones on the Carlisle road. There was also a turntable. It is such a remote place, high in the mountains and there was a branch line to Hawes, so facilities to turn and water engines were provided. I don't think I can remember a time when there was no wind blowing there.

Bill Addy, West Riding Engineman *(1984)*

ABOVE RIGHT: *Holbeck (Leeds) loco shed, October 1967, days before closure to steam. The last surviving LNER B1 61306 is visible.*

A 'Peak' diesel at the head of a Nottingham train stands by the water column at Skipton, 1976.

problems. The water troughs at Garsdale were the highest on any railway in Britain and frequently froze during the winter months.

Construction of the line required the building of new locomotive facilities. The Midland already had its premier northern loco shed at Leeds (Holbeck) whose locos provided much of the motive power for the line. Skipton's role was enlarged following the opening of the Settle–Carlisle Line, and provided some 'assisting' power for the Pullman expresses. An entirely new loco shed was built at Hellifield, with the Lancashire and Yorkshire Railway having its own facilities for locos bringing in trains from Blackburn. At Carlisle, a new loco shed was built at Durran Hill, south of the station, with some good quality housing built nearby for the locomen and their families. The depot closed in 1936 with locomotive maintenance transferring to the LMS's depot at Kingmoor, the former Caledonian Railway loco shed for Carlisle. The staff were mostly redeployed to Kingmoor, with some to the former London and North Western shed at Upperby. However, Durran Hill reopened in the latter stages of the Second World War as a sub-shed of Kingmoor, finally closing in 1959.

The smaller depots at Hellifield and Skipton were still important facilities for both freight and passenger workings in the 1950s and '60s. Skipton's steam shed closed in 1967 though there is now an important depot at the town servicing electric trains for the Aire Valley network. Hellifield shed closed in 1963.

Many locations along the route had water columns to allow locos, hauling both passenger and freight trains, to take water during their arduous journeys over the 'Long Drag'. A small number have survived, such as the example at Appleby. The former water column at Settle is preserved in the water tower complex.

Locomotives and carriages: the steam era

The Settle–Carlisle was a special line and it required some quite special locomotives. The Midland Railway's locomotive engineers at Derby were in no doubt that this new main line, with steep gradients and potentially high speeds required a distinctive kind of locomotive. Matthew Kirtley was Chief Mechanical Engineer at Derby in the 1870s

A Midland Railway 2-4-0 loco at Lancaster Green Ayre shed in the early 1900s. CUMBRIAN RAILWAYS ASSOCIATION

Preserved Midland Railway 4-2-2 'Spinner' designed by S.W. Johnson, at the 'Rocket 150' celebrations on the Liverpool and Manchester Railway in 1980.

and designed the Class 800 with perhaps an eye to the new railway that was under construction. They were of 2-4-0 wheel arrangement and a total of forty-eight were built between 1870 and 1871. Eight of them, numbered 812–819, were based at Leeds (Holbeck) whilst a further three were allocated to Skipton, specifically for use on the Carlisle route when it opened in 1876. Houghton and Foster commented:

> Although these 800s were pigmies compared with, say, modern Stanier engines, they did great work. Not only was their performance first rate, but they were also as hard as nails and they fought the weather and 'the hump' gallantly.

The 800s underwent some modifications during the reign of S.W. Johnson at Derby, who took over Kirtley's mantle and became one of the world's most celebrated locomotive engineers. The 800s were fitted with new cylinders and larger boilers, but Johnson had his mind on something much more ambitious for the rapidly expanding Midland empire. Initially, he stayed with the 2-4-0 design with a new Class 1302 which included an allocation at Carlisle Durran Hill. Hellifield shed also received a stud of the Class 1302s for work over the Carlisle road.

In the early 1880s Johnson introduced larger 4-4-0 passenger locomotives and ten were dispatched to Durran Hill shed. A larger version of these locomotives emerged for the Derby workshops a few years later, known as the 1808 series. Several were based at Hellifield and were amongst the most handsome locomotives ever to grace a British railway. They were painted in the stylish Midland Red livery (otherwise known as Crimson Lake) with black and yellow lining and burnished brasswork.

Johnson and his successor, Deeley, gradually perfected the 4-4-0 design, introducing new types with greater power towards the end of the century. In 1900 yet another new 4-4-0 class with larger boilers and the more modern Belpaire firebox were introduced, becoming the 700 series. Several were based at Holbeck to work the accelerated Carlisle services. The real breakthrough came in the early 1900s when the first three-cylinder compounds were introduced. A further series was built by Deeley in 1903. In addition to the Midland Compounds (one of which, no. 1000, is preserved as part of the national collection) Deeley developed a rugged, two-cylinder 4-4-0 engine with high boiler pressure. These were dedicated to the Settle–Carlisle Line and all ten (990–999) were based at Durran Hill.

The 1920s saw some significant changes, with the Midland being absorbed into the new London

In the summer of 1902 one of the original Compounds, number 2632, was sent to Durran Hill shed for trials on the Settle–Carlisle section and was later joined by 2631. The results were sensational, and apart from weight haulage some startling maximum speeds were recorded during the descent of Ribblesdale. The compounds were so successful that a further twenty-nine were built between 1905 and 1906 by Mr Deeley.

C.C. Dorman, Carlisle (Citadel) Railway Scene (1972)

Midland and Scottish Railway, one of the biggest joint stock companies in the world. Yet the Derby influence continued and a further twenty Compounds were built under the LMS regime. The greater flexibility in the locomotive fleet resulting from the 'Grouping' encouraged the LMS management to try out different locomotives on the Settle–Carlisle as loadings were increasing to the point where double-heading was the norm. Whilst this was common Midland practice, it was highly uneconomic tying up two sets of both motive power and footplate crews. Some London and North Western and Caledonian classes were tried but performance didn't compare with the Compounds. One LNWR type tested on the route was the large Claughton locos. Despite the poor test

results, a substantial number were 'cascaded' to Holbeck and Durran Hill when the LMS introduced the three-cylinder Royal Scot class to the West Coast Main Line. The Claughtons became the standard power for expresses on the line, though the popular 4-4-0s continued on less demanding duties. In 1930 a number of the Claughtons were rebuilt and became known as 'Baby Scots', continuing well into the 1960s as express passenger locos. Several were based at Holbeck for Carlisle duties.

For many years the staple freight locomotive on the line was one of the family of Derby-built 0-6-0s. These gradually developed in power with the final phase being the ubiquitous 'Derby Four' designed by Deeley. Hundreds were built and could be found all over the Midland empire from Swansea to Carlisle. They were popular with Midland enginemen (but not their brothers on the LNWR or Lancashire and Yorkshire!) and were regarded as 'do anything' locos. They would often be used for short passenger workings or for longer-distance holiday excursions. In the 1920s, some of the Horwich-designed 2-6-0 'Crabs' were based at Holbeck and used for some of the faster 'fitted freights' over the line.

The most decisive change in LMS locomotive policy came with the appointment of William Stanier as Chief Mechanical Engineer. He had a Great

An LNWR Claughton 4-6-0 undergoing maintenance, probably at Crewe North, c.1920.

Preserved LMS 'Derby Four' 4F no 4027 in storage at Hellifield loco shed, 1967.

LMS Jubilee 5690 Leander *heads a charter special on the S&C.* PETER KIRKHAM

One particular driver was infamous on the Midland. He was best avoided if you wanted a quiet life. On one occasion he was on an express coming back from Carlisle and hit Settle Junction at 80 – the limit was 60. There was an enormous shower of sparks and the loco went over onto one set of wheels – but luckily righted itself. Arrival in Leeds was 15 minutes early, on the line's fastest-timed train. After all his wild adventures on the railway, he was killed crossing the road outside Holbeck shed.

Charlie Wallace, talking to the author, 1994

Western background and brought many aspects of 'Swindon' design with him, including taper boilers. He designed a new 5XP 4-6-0 three-cylinder locomotive with a combination of power and fast running. They became known as the Silver Jubilee class (or just '5Xs' to locomen) and several were based at Holbeck, with some remaining through to the shed's closure in 1967. Although the Jubilees had some teething problems, they put in some outstanding performances on the Settle–Carlisle. The most famous example was 5660 *Rooke*'s run, which ran a test train from Leeds to Carlisle in October 1937. With a trailing load of 302 tons, Driver Harry North of Holbeck did the 113 miles (182 km) from Leeds to Carlisle in 117 minutes, with an even faster performance on the return journey. This included climbing the long gruelling section to Ais Gill in 'even' time, averaging 60mph on the climb. The line was

engineered for speed and it was an ideal route to test locomotive performance to its limit.

At the same time as the introduction of the Jubilees, Stanier was busy producing two 'standard' classes for mixed traffic and freight, both of which were to do sterling service on the Settle–Carlisle. Some members of the class (45690 *Leander* and 45699 *Galatea*) still see regular work over the line on special trains. The two-cylinder mixed-traffic '5MT' locos – the 'Black 5s' ¬– were a Stanier design but were constructed under contract at railway workshops around the country. Swindon even built a few! Similarly, the Class '8F' heavy freight locomotives were a Crewe design but many were built at other independent workshops, or LMS shops at Derby, Horwich and elsewhere. The introduction of both these immensely successful designs in the mid to late 1930s could not have come at a more vital time. During the Second World War Britain's railways needed strong, reliable engines requiring minimal maintenance. Stanier provided them.

As well as the Jubilees, Stanier was working on bigger plans for express passenger locomotives. The high point was the 'Coronation Pacific', dedicated to heavy West Coast Main Line work. However, a halfway house between the Jubilee and Coronation class emerged in the shape of the Royal Scot rebuilds from the earlier Fowler design. They had high boiler pressure, three cylinders and double chimneys. And they looked superb. Two of these powerful re-builds – 6170 *British Legion* and 6103

A Black 5 shunts a heavy freight train at Horton while another member of the class waits at Horton's up 'home' signal.

LMS 8F 48151 heads through Settle on a northbound 'Dalesman' special, June 2018.

An LMS Royal Scot rushes through Settle on a southbound express, c.1960. SCRT

An LNER A3 Pacific 60038 Firdaussi heads the southbound Thames–Clyde Express past the summit at Ais Gill, July 1960.
P. HUTCHINSON

Royal Scots Fusilier, were based at Holbeck from 1943. After the war, more of the 'rebuilt Scots' were allocated to Holbeck and did great work on heavy express services, running through from Leeds to Glasgow. Two of the class – 46100 *Royal Scot*, and 46115 *Scots Guardsman* – are preserved, with the latter returning to its old stamping ground on specials in the early 2000s.

The 1950s and early 1960s were essentially a period of stability in motive power on the line, with freight being very much the mainstay of the Stanier 8Fs and Derby 4s on lighter work. However, the new BR-built Britannia Pacifics were introduced to the line, with several based at Holbeck to work the Thames–Clyde Express to Glasgow. An even more surprising development came in 1961 when BR introduced some of the former LNER A3 Pacifics to top-notch work on the line. The crews at Holbeck had seen them heading King's Cross expresses on the 'GN' (Great Northern) out of Leeds Central but had never worked on them. They proved immensely popular but their stay was relatively short-lived, with all going back to their native climes on the Eastern Region in 1963.

By then, the impact of BR's Modernization Plan was starting to be felt. A batch of the new diesel-electric Peak locomotives was allocated to Holbeck for work on the former Midland routes to London and Carlisle/Glasgow. The 'Scots' were

> The first we saw of the diesel was the Condor – a new fast fitted freight from London to Glasgow. It was worked by a pair of Type 2 Metrovicks. We didn't have the job at Leeds – it was worked by Carlisle and Birmingham men. Generally we viewed the diesels with suspicion. If a steam locomotive went wrong, we'd make do somehow. With a diesel the slightest thing could render it a complete failure. A lot of the older men wouldn't go near a diesel, they thought they'd make fools of themselves. One driver said he'd pack the job in before going on a diesel and he meant it.
>
> *Retired driver Harry Thurlow, talking to the author, 1994*

withdrawn by 1963 and dumped at nearby Farnley Junction shed, making a sad sight. However, the Jubilees continued doing some passenger work, particularly seasonal extras. As late as 1967 Holbeck was turning out highly polished members of the class (notably 45593 *Kolhapur* and 45562 *Alberta*) to work summer Saturday expresses to Carlisle. It was very much the swansong of a great class and the end of a fine tradition. The crews were very much playing to the audience of railway enthusiasts who came from all parts of the country to travel on the 10:17 Leeds to Carlisle, with speeds as high as 93mph being recorded on the long down-hill run to Carlisle. Holbeck closed to steam on 7 October 1967.

LMS Jubilee Alberta *drifts into Skipton on the 10:17 Leeds–Carlisle (a summer Saturday relief from St Pancras to Glasgow). An LMS Black 5 arrives on the southbound platform on a Morecambe–Leeds working, in July 1967.*

LMS 2MT tank loco takes a break from shunting at Skipton, June 1966.

While railway enthusiasts have a passion for locomotives, the majority of passengers are probably more interested in what they are sitting in than what is pulling them. And again, the Settle–Carlisle Line had some distinctive features. In 1874, just two years before the opening of the Settle–Carlisle, the Midland Railway took the radical step of abolishing second-class. Henceforth there would be only first and third.

At the same time, the Midland began a much-needed programme of carriage construction to address existing shortages and cope with expansion. The long-established railway tradition of four-wheeled coaching stock was on the way out in favour of longer carriages with bogies, giving more space and a much-improved ride. The Midland was well ahead of the game. Thomas G. Clayton was the company's Carriage and Wagon Superintendent and he was well aware of the importance of passenger comfort. A new first-class carriage was introduced in the early 1870s, 28 feet (8.5 metres) in length with four compartments. An interesting contemporary observation, which seems lost on modern-day carriage designers, was that they had wider windows, 'in order that travellers may more easily see the country through which they pass'.

New carriages were ordered for use on the Settle–Carlisle Line but a much more revolutionary plan was afoot. During 1872 the Midland's visionary General Manager, James Allport, had toured America looking at Pullman car design. This was the world standard in passenger comfort. Allport met George Pullman and a very positive business relationship developed between the Midland and the American entrepreneur. In 1873 the Midland agreed to buy some of the luxury vehicles. They were constructed at the Detroit works and then dismantled and shipped to Derby for re-assembly. The first Pullman carriage to emerge from Derby was a sleeping car, named 'Midland', in early 1874. The carriages were introduced during 1874 on a new Bradford–London service. The 1876 opening of the Settle–Carlisle Line was highly fortuitous, giving the company time to iron out technical issues and prepare the new, luxurious trains for intensive service between London and Scotland.

The Midland Railway entered into partnership with its Scottish neighbours – the North British and Glasgow and South Western – to build a new fleet of luxury carriages, which became known as the 'Midland–Scotch Joint Stock'. They marked a sea change in comfort, with plush seats (in both first and third class), toilets and steam heating. It was still the norm for many services in the 1870s to have four-wheeled carriages with wooden seats, no toilet facilities and only foot-warmers (if you were lucky) to keep you from freezing in winter months.

Another feature of even the most up-to-date carriages was the gas lighting, which was to prove so disastrous in the accidents at Hawes Junction (1910) and Ais Gill (1913) when collisions led to gas explosions and horrific fires (*see* Chapter 5). Electric lighting became the norm in the post-First World War years as the LMS introduced new standardized fleets of good quality carriages which continued to provide the mainstay of services on Settle–Carlisle expresses well into the 1950s, before BR introduced the highly successful 'Mark 1' coaches which replaced the former LMS stock. By the 1950s the Pullman trains of the 1870s and the later Midland–Scotch Joint Stock were a very distant memory. Yet the Midland set the standard for some of the most luxurious trains in the world. As Peter Baughan in *North of Leeds* commented, writing in the 1960s, the Midland '...in conjunction with its northern allies, had been able to pioneer a degree of comfortable travel, with magnificent carriages, that was perhaps second to none, and which will probably not be bettered in certain respects.'

Battling the weather – snowdrifts, high winds and floods

Winter brings in its train the difficult and arduous task of keeping the railway open during the heavy falls of snow which are so frequent in this district....

LMS Railway Magazine, January 1928

It was a tough life working on the Settle–Carlisle Line; you were, and still are, always on the alert for severe, even extreme, weather. It was normal for the line to be blocked by snow, though sometimes trains were 'snowed-up' for weeks with the line effectively closed.

The first winter to bring major problems was 1881 when a blizzard struck the line on 3 March. The line became blocked with some ten locomotives 'snowed up' in drifts. The Midland mustered no fewer than 600 men to cut through the drifts at Dent Head. More heavy snow came the following year. In early December a southbound express became stuck in a drift near Garsdale (then Hawes Junction) and had to return to Carlisle. Three expresses were marooned, with many passengers offered hospitality in the nearby railwaymen's houses. Another express was stranded at Dent. Amongst its passengers were Robert Ferguson, the MP for Carlisle, and Robert Alison of Scaleby Castle, who was a director of the Midland Railway. The passengers were plied with cups of tea and cakes made by the station master's wife and left Dent the following afternoon. The station master received a letter of commendation from the company, saying that the Midland Railway was 'glad to find that you and your wife did all you possibly could for the passengers who

A 1906 view of Ribblehead in the snow. FOSCL

BR 'Peak' D16 is snowed up in 1979 while hauling the Thames–Clyde Express. FOSCL

An LMS 8F is snowed up at Dent during the harsh winter of 1962–63. FOSCL

were delayed by the snow storm', with a cheque for £5 enclosed. (See the account in 'Settle–Carlisle: A History of Snow!' by Ken Harper, Ron Herbert and Peter Robinson, in the January 2014 edition of *BackTrack*. A copy of the letter can be found in W.R. Mitchell's *One Hundred Tales of the Settle–Carlisle Railway*).

One particularly severe snowstorm saw Dent station 'so buried that only the chimneys of the station building were seen.' (*LMS Railway Magazine*, June 1928).

Particularly bad years for snow disruption were 1895–6, 1908, 1911, 1928 and 1931. However, the year 1933 saw events of an altogether more extreme nature: during the Great Blizzard of February, the line was blocked for nearly a week, with drifts up to 20 feet (6 metres) deep.

More bad winters followed, including during wartime -- 1940, 1941 and 1945. The year 1947 saw a particularly hard winter and snow blocked the line on several occasions and the line was closed for two months. Soldiers, having spent years fighting Hitler, came home to find themselves drafted into clearing snowdrifts in sub-zero conditions. Many prisoners-of-war were also drafted in. It wasn't quite the Eastern Front but it must have seemed like it. Inspector J. Slindon, who led the snow-clearing operation in

1947, gives a detailed account in *Railway World*, February 1981. He describes the remarkable sight that greeted them at Dent:

> The sight ahead amazed us: looking towards Dent there was a sea of snow, the overbridges in Shale Cutting were out of sight and Dent head's home signal, which was on a 27-foot post, had only about a yard sticking out of the snow....

The line finally opened for normal working at the end of March. Mr Slindon made the comment that they were losing about a hundred shovels a day, mostly a result of the prisoners of war and soldiers 'going on strike' and throwing the shovels over viaduct parapets to have an excuse to stop the back-breaking work. Who could blame them?

> Conditions are almost indescribable, and at times the blizzard forced the gang of men with the railway snow plough to a standstill. Twice the plough has literally been forced off the lines by the terrible wind and sheer weight of snow.
>
> *Report in* The Carlisle Journal, *28 February 1933, quoted in 'Settle–Carlisle: A History of Snow!'*

The effect of the snow on the Dales communities was terrible, with many farmers losing livestock. All roads were impassable and the railway managed to bring basic necessities to many isolated farms and villages when the line was only partly open.

The line was again severely affected by heavy snow in the winter of 1962–3. *The Craven Herald* described the events in an article published some years later:

> Strong winds created drifts of more than 20 feet as heavy snowfall was followed by gale-force winds. Railway workers and special snow ploughs dug out trains stuck in drifts and worked tirelessly to keep the track clear. The Settle–Carlisle Line was closed for four days following a blizzard that saw 52 people stranded on the Edinburgh Waverley express to London St Pancras.
>
> *Craven Herald*, 30 January 2010

The next particularly hard winter was in 1979. Weather alerts were issued in the last week of 1978 and the snow ploughs were made ready, which by this time would be diesel-propelled. Heavy snowfalls continued throughout January and February. The worst day of all was 15 February when the line became completely blocked and a freight train had to be abandoned at Mallerstang. A group of Leeds schoolchildren were stranded at Dent but were collected by the snow plough from Lostock Hall (Preston) which took them to safety in Skipton. Tragically, two track workers were killed while clearing snow at Hellifield.

Whilst the efforts of the railwaymen succeeded in re-opening the line, more heavy snow came

> During this grim week some of the track workers on snow duty at signalboxes had slept 'on the job' and had never been to their homes for three or four nights, so snow ploughs were used to convey provisions from Carlisle to these isolated locations. Bacon, eggs, beans, bread, milk, biscuits and even cream cakes were sent....
>
> *'Settle–Carlisle: A History of Snow!*

down on Saturday 17 March. The evening Glasgow–Nottingham express was stuck for nearly two hours north of Appleby and had to be rescued by the snow plough. The hundred passengers on board included a mother nursing a newborn baby who urgently needed hot water for the bay's food. She was well looked after by the station staff at Appleby once the passengers had been taken back to safety. The line was kept open despite further snow, and it was not until 21 March when the snow plough team were told to stand down.

In general, winters in recent years have been mild. But arctic conditions returned in early 2018 when many railways in the North of England and Scotland were hit by the 'Beast from the East'. The Settle–Carlisle was badly affected. Snow ploughs were hard at work in early March and the line was closed for several days. Further snow returned on 17 March but trains were able to continue running. The heavy snow of 2018 didn't have quite such an extreme impact as in 1947 and 1963 but some small communities were cut off for over a week and even towns like KIrkby Stephen had essential supplies suspended for several days.

The snow ploughs: a vital part of the railway toolkit

From the earliest days, the line has had its own dedicated snow ploughs, based at Carlisle, Hellifield and Skipton. Two ploughs were located at each depot and were built out of old locomotive tenders. It was essential to have them operating in 'pairs' so that they could charge into snow drifts with considerable force, usually with at least two locomotives sandwiched between the two ploughs. Each plough was fitted to carry the men involved in snow-clearing duties. The LMS staff magazine for January 1928 describes the conditions:

> Both are fitted with comfortable seating arrangements with a table in the centre, also a coal stove, this being used for heating purposes and for keeping a constant supply of hot water for coffee and tea, and for cooking or keeping food warm.

LMS Black 5 45209 with snow-clearing train, 1947. FOSCL

Another view of D16 snowed up during the 1979 blizzards. FOSCL

A Class 66-hauled freight forges through Appleby in blizzard conditions, March 2018. PAUL SUMMERS/FOSCL

A Class 37 diesel loco on snow plough duties at Dent Head, 1983. KEN HARPER

Serious railway work – the snow plough in March 2018.
PAUL SUMMERS/FOSCL

The snow plough heads through Garsdale in horrendous conditions in 2018. PAUL TEMPLEMAN/FOSCL

The LMS magazine article gives a fascinating insider's account of the arrangements when the calls comes:

> ... all concerned set to work to get them away as expeditiously as possible. The running foreman will probably have the ploughs marshalled ready to leave as soon as the trainmen come on duty. Two no. 2 class freight engines fitted with permanent back cabs are used; these are placed chimney to chimney between the two ploughs, the effective part of each plough being at each end.

The composition of the snow plough team was interesting. In addition to the two sets of train-men (driver and fireman) the entourage included an inspector from the locomotive department, a permanent-way inspector, and – perhaps the most important job of all – a cook! In addition, there would be a strong team of permanent way staff ready with their shovels once the initial clearance had been done by the ploughs. To have seen a snow plough in operation, in the days of steam, was one of the most spectacular sights imaginable. Faced with, say, a cutting blocked by drifts which could have been as high as 20 feet (6 metres), charging into the drift

The author up to his knees in snow, 1983.

required courage and sheer bravado on the part of the enginemen. It was not unusual for the plough to derail on impact with the drift. A remarkable film of the process – *Snowdrift at Bleath Gill* – was made on the Stainmore Line by the British Transport Film Unit in 1955.

During the heavy snow of March 2018 the line saw snow ploughs hard at work once again, with railway staff working extremely long hours to try and keep the line open.

Snow ploughs in action, Armathwaite, 4 March 2018. GORDON ALLEN (NETWORK RAIL)

Snow plough at rest, Bog Bank, south of Lazonby, March 2018, with Network Rail supervisor Phillip Cavaghan taking a break. GORDON ALLEN

The station master at Ribblehead performing his meteorological duties. W. H. FOSTER

Ice can be a major problem in some of the tunnels. During the harsh winter of 2017–18 Network Rail worked hard to remove large icicles that had formed on tunnel roofs and sides. The picture shows ice inside Waste Bank Tunnel. GORDON ALLEN

Snow plough close-up. GORDON ALLEN

Network Rail and DRS staff confer before their next round of snow plough duties. Armathwaite, 4 March 2018. GORDON ALLEN

On the snow plough! Near Armathwaite, 4 March 2018. GORDON ALLEN

Keeping an eye on the weather

Having good intelligence on weather conditions has always been an extremely important aspect of operating the line. In the 1920s there was a weather reporting station, complete with anemometer, located at Crosby Garrett, which sent out weather reports up and down the line, particularly to the Control offices. The instrument was fitted to the top of a telegraph pole and measured wind speed in miles per hour. *The LMS Railway Magazine* for October 1928 noted, 'The weather reports are made by the signalman on duty and forwarded by the stationmaster to the various district controllers, locomotive superintendents and others interested.' The Crosby Garrett facility was eventually closed in 1938 and a more sophisticated arrangement was installed at Ribblehead, which reported both to the railway and to the Meteorological Office. Again, it was managed by the station master. This arrangement continued until the station was de-staffed in 1967. Part of the station master's duties was to let off a helium-filled balloon and see how long it took to reach the clouds! With the coming of modern weather-forecasting techniques, even had BR not removed staff from the station, it seems unlikely the arrangement would have continued for very long. However, 'Ribblehead Station' is still a weather reporting location for the Meteorological Office to this day.

Some parts of the line had 'snow fences' provided to minimize the danger of drifting in cuttings. Those near Dent were still visible until recently, though they had long since ceased functioning effectively through many simply rotting away and not being replaced. Climate change is resulting in fewer severe winters as far as snow is concerned, though the risk of disruption through heavy rain is possibly worse than it has ever been. Torrential rain can cause enormous damage, and even death. As recently as 1996 severe rain led to a landslip; a train was derailed, resulting in the death of a member of train crew (*see* Chapter 5). The most recent catastrophic event was the landslip at Eden Brow, near Armathwaite, in 2015 (*see* Chapter 8). On this occasion there were no casualties but a significant part of the high embankment shifted as a result of prolonged rain. Network Rail had no option other than to close the line 'for as long as it would take'. It took over a year.

CHAPTER 4

The Creation of a Railway Community

The building of an entirely new railway required careful attention to human needs and resources. Whilst staffing at Leeds and Skipton involved an incremental increase in staffing at existing depots, the challenges of providing locomotive staff at Hellifield and Carlisle would have been considerable. Similarly, operating and permanent way staff throughout the line route would need to be either recruited or transferred. The last thing the railway would have wanted would have been an entirely 'rookie' staff, with no experience of running a railway. Existing staff across the Midland Railway (and probably other companies) were enticed to transfer, often with promotion. Samuel Caudle, the Carlisle driver on the ill-fated overnight express that crashed into the rear of a stationary train near Ais Gill in 1913, had started his railway career on the Midland in Gloucestershire. Alfred Sutton,

A busy scene at Appleby as station staff attend to a northbound local service headed by LMS Jubilee Seahorse, 24 September 1963. PETER E BAUGHAN

Midland Railway houses at Petteril Terrace, Carlisle.

A fascinating picture at Blea Moor, c.1900. Was this the signalman's wife? Railway workers' housing is on the opposite side of the track. SCRT

LMS Black 4 44933 passes Garsdale on a summer Saturday holiday special returning south from Heads of Ayr. An LMS 4F is waiting in the side platform to head south with a freight. July 1963. PETER SUNDERLAND

signalman at Hawes Junction of the night of the Christmas Eve disaster of 1910, had transferred from a lower-graded post further south.

In the Victorian railway hierarchy a station master at some lowly station such as the likes of Woodlesford or Cromford could make a good promotional move by transferring to a busier station like Settle, where he would become a respected member of the community.

The Midland Railway was able to offer good quality accommodation at most stations, and well-designed terraced cottages along the route. Many of these are still occupied and in private ownership, commanding high prices. They can be seen at Hellifield, Settle, Garsdale, Selside, Kirby Stephen and elsewhere. Carlisle has some good examples of smaller and medium-sized houses close to the site of Durran Hill loco shed, at Petteril Terrace.

The houses were built to a standard design described by David Jenkinson as 'Derby Gothic'. Jenkinson pointed out in his brilliant *Rails in the Fells* (1973) that the design was not unique to the Settle–Carlisle and could be found on most parts of the Midland network as far afield as southwest England and outer London. Yet the design has blended in with the landscape of the Dales, and most of the buildings have survived the demolition hammer that was so prevalent in the 1970s.

The houses provided essential accommodation for station staff, signalmen and permanent-way workers. There was the inevitable hierarchy: station masters were typically provided with substantial detached houses such as those at Settle and Kirkby Stephen; the 'lower grades' were housed in what were still quite comfortable terraced cottages. Particularly good examples of these can be seen at Garsdale and Kirkby Stephen. At Hellifield, 'Midland Terrace' on Station Road typifies basic railway housing for staff employed at the station and loco shed.

The Dales people – and incoming workers – were relatively fortunate in having the Midland as their employer. It was a classic example of Victorian paternalism, infused with a strong Quaker ethos; it took the welfare of its employees seriously – spiritual as well as temporal. Religious services were actually held in the station waiting rooms at Garsdale and Ribblehead.

LMS Jubilee 45705 Seahorse *at Appleby on a northbound stopping train. Local railway staff head for home in the rain. 24 September 1963.* PETER E. BAUGHAN

Railway workers houses at Kirkby Stephen – the station master's detached house is at the end.

A similar juxtaposition of terraced houses with the detached station master's residence at Horton-in-Ribblesdale.

Moorcock Cottages today.

'Midland Terrace' at Hellifield.

Railway people

The LMS staff magazine is a useful source of information about the lives of railway workers, both individuals and as a group. There were regular reports of social events but also obituaries and retirement notices for members of staff. It sheds light on the very common migration of skilled or semi-skilled railway staff from different parts of the Midland Railway empire to take up essential posts on the new Settle–Carlisle Line.

The January 1927 'Northern Edition' of the LMS railway magazine notes the retirement of Mr J. Down, signalman at Bell Busk, between Skipton and Hellifield. He had begun his railway career as a porter at Desford, Leicestershire, in May 1878 and transferred to Giggleswick as a signalman in May 1880. He then moved to Bell Busk in January 1882, which he held up to his retirement at the end of 1926. There was an interesting comment on railway discipline at the time: porters came under the supervision of the local station master and it seems that the particular one that Mr Down had at Desford was something of a martinet. The young porter discovered a bottle of gin on the platform in a basket, but the bottle was leaking. He tells the story that he found a milk can near at hand and poured the gin into that receptacle. The station master was not impressed, however, and insisted that the hapless porter take the blame, deducting 1s from his wages.

Hellifield was an important railway community, growing from a tiny collection of houses before the railway into a substantial village with the coming of the line. The 'new' Settle–Carlisle railway branched off just a couple of miles north of Hellifield and the new depot provided an important base for the railway. Railway staff formed the bedrock of the local community, often taking the lead in local politics. Mr Edwin Newman, passenger yard foreman for Hellifield, was made a Justice of the Peace in 1928, reflecting his active role in village affairs, including being a parish councillor for eighteen years and an active member of the Labour Party and National Union of Railwaymen. Like Mr Down, he had transferred to the line from elsewhere on the Midland network. He joined the railway at Bradford as a carriage cleaner in 1895 and moved to Hellifield the following year as a lampman. He was promoted to passenger shunter (carriages, that is...) before taking up the passenger yard foreman job in 1924. His biography tells us that he had been a member of the NUR since 1896 and was a delegate to the 'All-Grades Movement' in 1906. The following year he acted as a witness to Lord Cromer's enquiry into social conditions on the railways.

Although Carlisle is an ancient city, as the nineteenth century progressed its role as a major railway centre grew, with railwaymen playing a key role in civic life. This became more pronounced by the time the Labour Party emerged as a major political force in local and national politics, in the early twentieth century. Ritson Graham, a Midland Railway footplateman who started his career at Durran Hill, becoming Mayor of the city, was not untypical (*see* Chapter 10).

Railway people formed the core of many small communities. Railwaymen, and very often their wives, would play an active part in the local community – be it church, chapel or wider local community activities. Very often the railwaymen would be the only workers who were organized into trades unions and they would often provide the mainstay of support for the Labour Party in places such as Appleby, Hawes, Kirkby Stephen and Settle.

There was a lighter side to railway life as well, with many railwaymen, particularly signalmen, having their own 'sidelines'. Several signalboxes were well known to drivers for their 'retail offers' – typically rabbits that would be available at competitive prices. In the 1950s the going rate was 1s 6d but by the 1960s it had increased to 2s 6d.

> We'd often stop to chase rabbits, and more than one driver carried a gun. One actually wore a poacher's jacket and wouldn't finish a turn without bagging a couple of pheasants or rabbits. He'd often carry a ferret with him as well.
>
> *Retired guard Ron Stead, talking to the author, 1994*

Spotlight on Hellifield

Hellifield, on the main line between Leeds and Carlisle, 231 miles from St Pancras, is said to be the "bleakest and healthiest station in the Pennines". The station, which still retains much of the attractive Midland Railway "Wyvern" embossed iron-work, is an exchange point for traffic between Lancashire and Scotland. There are two signal boxes with a total of 112 levers, also high and low level sidings.

Being in a completely rural area, the village (population 2,500), situated half a mile from the station, consists mainly of railway families. The Stationmaster/Goods Agent has charge of 80, including a small carriage cleaning staff. Other departments at Hellifield are the Motive Power – the depot is the last for the 76-mile stretch to Carlisle – and the District Engineer's whose new material depot, supplying sleepers, rails, etc., lies to the north of the station.

Staff shown in the picture strip are Stationmaster/Goods Agent A. Gee, Acting Station Inspector Leslie Duerden, Telegraph Clerk Peter Horner and Station Foreman Norman Preston.

Just after the war it was hard to get things like rabbits and eggs in Leeds. I was working as a guard on the Carlisle run, and most signalmen in the Dales would shoot rabbits and hang them on the signalbox veranda, like a market sale. It was 1s 6d a couple. The platelayers had a supply too; we'd often run 'short of steam' at places like Selside, Horton or Kirkby Stephen and buy a few.

Retired guard Ron Stead, talking to the author, 1994

Social life

Within the railway itself there was a social and cultural life that was remarkable, seen from today's perspective of isolated individuals glued to smartphones, PCs or televisions. Even relatively small locations would often have sporting teams, musical societies, first-aid classes and a series of social events spread across the year. This culture cemented a very strong railway identity and also offered railwaymen's wives, some of whom might not have done formal jobs, an opportunity to participate in social activities.

Skipton was the main centre of social life along the line. An important event in the inter-war social event was the annual staff ball in Skipton,

ABOVE: *Hellifield station featured in BR's staff magazine in the early 1960s.*

The station master's house at Hellifield – reflecting the importance of the job in this railway community.

usually held in the Devonshire Hotel Assembly Rooms. The 1926 event involved over a hundred members of staff and was described by the LMS magazine as 'a riotously convivial night of pleasure'. Staff travelled from up and down the line and reports said 'the organisers had an animated crowd, infected throughout the whole proceedings with a joyous and care-free spirit.' Hopefully the General Strike of May that year would have become just a memory.

Only a couple of weeks after the staff ball, presided over by the line's permanent-way superintendent, Mr H.L. Cooke, it was the annual inter-departmental dinner, again held at the Devonshire Hotel. That night's proceedings chaired by the station master, Mr Heggs, and featured the district goods manager, district controller, district locomotive superintendent and goods agent. The evening's entertainment was provided by railway staff themselves, all drawn from the accounts department. There was singing accompanied on the piano followed by a whist drive and, to round off the evening, dancing. Somehow it sounds a slightly more refined occasion than the 'riotous' staff ball!

The annual staff ball had shifted to 14 February in 1928, and the conviviality obviously continued, judging by the report in the LMS magazine:

> Happiness and mirth predominated from 8.00pm to 2.00 a.m. and a gay laughter-loving crowd romped through the 'Paul Jones', merrily danced the one steps, welcomed the more sedate waltz and boisterously encored the last figure of lancers.

The host for the occasion was Mr Cooke, the district controller, who welcomed the guests and stressed the importance of such occasions.

As well as balls and dinners, there was an active sporting culture at Skipton. Every Good Friday there was a football match between the 'operating' and 'loco' departments. The 1927 fixture saw the Traffic department beating the Loco team 3–2. Mr Cooke, of the Permanent Way department (whom we have already seen presiding over the riotous staff ball) presented the winning team with a cup.

Skipton also had a Railway Welfare and Athletic Club, managed by railway staff.

Appleby was an important railway centre. It had its own active social life, which hinged around The Midland Hotel, which is still doing good business to this day. On 2 March 1928 the pub was thronged with well-wishers for the retirement of Mr Walter Hewitson, sub-inspector of the engineer's department, after 52 years' service. He had been permanent-way inspector at Appleby for the last 32 of these. He was presented with an easy chair and timepiece by the now-familiar Mr Cooke, permanent-way superintendent from Skipton. Mr Cooke commented, 'The passing of Mr Hewitson breaks a link with the past, as he has been on that portion of line since it was first made.' Further tributes were made by colleagues including Mr Lomas, permanent-way inspector at Appleby and many more. The LMS magazine reports: 'Their words were marked by a feeling of goodwill and fellowship which was a feature of the gathering. In responding, Mr Hewitson said, touchingly, "This is one of the happiest moments of my life."'

A longstanding and very practical aspect of railway life was the 'Ambulance Class'. Most railway installations – all of the large and most of the smaller locations – would have an ambulance team who were often highly skilled in first aid. Having rapid access to skilled first aiders was essential for a dangerous job such as working the railway. Getting immediate and skilled first aid following, say, a shunting accident could make the difference between life and death. The ambulance movement on the railways was very competitive with highly structured annual competitions, culminating in each company's annual awards.

The 1927 LMS magazine records an event at Hawes Junction (now Garsdale) when an examination of the class was conducted by local GP Dr Moffet. The magazine records that 'twenty-three students presented themselves and passed'. There was a social side to the ambulance class too, part of the presentation of local awards. The magazine notes:

At a social evening on June 24th the awards gained were distributed by Mr Cook, district controller, Skipton. Advantage was also taken of the occasion to present a pocket watch to Dr Hughes as a small token of appreciation of his service as a lecturer. Mr Hammond, Station Master, Dent, made the presentation on behalf of the class. Dr Hughes paid tribute to the great help given by Mr Frewell, who acted as instructor. An excellent supper was provided by the ladies.

Whilst Skipton was undoubtedly the operational and also social and cultural 'headquarters' for the line, events took place up and down the line on a regular basis, aimed at more local audiences. Normally, a senior officer of the company, perhaps based in Skipton or Carlisle, would attend as the special guest and say a few words. As well as the ambulance class events at Hawes Junction, the small railway community of Giggleswick managed to muster twenty-seven guests for its fifth annual supper on 25 November 1926, at the Railway Inn. A Mr Thorpe of the Control office (Skipton) was

> There was a good social life. On Friday nights there was a 'tanner hop' at Garsdale station. On Sundays they used the waiting room as a chapel.
>
> *Retired signalman Harry Lewin, talking to the author, 1994*

in the chair and gave some words of thanks to the staff for their hard work and dedication. The LMS magazine records that 'Mr Jackson, Station Master, Giggleswick, responded. After supper a very enjoyable evening was continued by songs and recitals from various members of staff.'

Garsdale water tower served for many years as the local community and dance hall. The water tower was furnished with 'recycled' flooring from the ammunition complex near Gretna for the dance floor. Mrs Brown, mother of FoSCL's Garsdale volunteer Peter Brown had her wedding reception in the water tower. She once told a FoSCL volunteer, 'they ripped the heart out of our community when they knocked it down' (in 1971).

Garsdale water tower, undergoing demolition. W. R. MITCHELL

Life-long learning

The railways have always had a great emphasis on what educators now call 'life-long learning'. The Settle–Carlisle Line in many ways exemplified this tradition, which was to a large extent based on self-help and 'mutual improvement'. The Mutual Improvement Class (MIC) movement is a fascinating aspect of railway social history and its roots go back to the early years of the railways. By the end of the nineteenth century virtually every locomotive depot would have had its MIC class, attended by footplate staff young and old. Skipton, Hellifield and Carlisle each had their own MIC class, surviving well into the 1960s. A typical example of the curriculum is given in a report for Hellifield MIC in July 1928: 'Inspector Tolley of Derby gave a very interesting lecture on "Lubrication and Lubricators" after which a lively discussion took place.' A few months later Inspector Tolley was back up north to address a meeting of Skipton MIC on the slightly broader subject of 'The Standard LMS Compound Engine'. The report states that 'the theme was dealt with in a masterly and exhaustive manner, and at the end Mr Tolley was warmly thanked.' The LMS magazine for September 1938 records a meeting of Hellifield MIC, with Inspector Brown of Derby lecturing on 'Development of the Steam Locomotive'.

The MIC movement was primarily for locomotive staff. It was a good example of more experienced workers sharing their knowledge with their younger colleagues, and it was common for drivers themselves to offer lectures on subjects as diverse

Fireman's view from the footplate of a BR 9F heading down the line towards Selside, 9 April 1976.

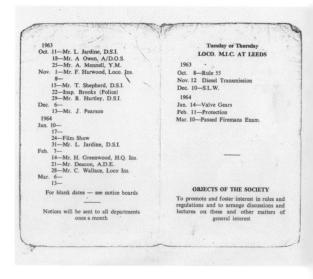

Leeds Mutual Improvement Class (MIC) rulebook and list of talks, 1962–3.

I used to go to the MIC when I was as young as 12 or 13. I went on a Sunday morning to Holbeck. One driver would usually speak – for example, on 'valve gears'. It was the only means of obtaining information and training. We went to other sheds' MIC classes too. Most classes sent notices of meetings to other MICs and each group had a secretary. We would go as far afield as Goole, Huddersfield or Bradford. Sometimes inspectors gave talks but often it was a driver.

Former driver (Holbeck and Copley Hill) and Footplate Inspector Charlie Wallace, talking to the author, 1994

Retired Leeds railwaymen, 1994: Charlie Wallace in foreground; Fred North (Holbeck) to his left;
Harry Thurlow (Farnley Junction) to his right. Harry was active in his depot MIC.

as valve-gears, firing techniques, new designs of boiler and other technical subjects which seem obscure to an outside reader but were part of the practical lifeblood of the footplate.

The unions

The Settle–Carlisle Line's workers, from the 1880s onwards, were organized into trades unions. The drivers, firemen and loco cleaners were mostly members of ASLEF – the Associated Society of Locomotive Engineers and Firemen, which was formed by Holbeck (Leeds) footplatemen in 1880. Most other 'blue collar' grades were members of the Amalgamated Society of Railway Servants (ASRS), which became the National Union of Railwaymen in 1913 and is today's RMT (Rail, Martitime and Transport Union). The ASRS organized particularly among guards and signalmen but also track workers, station staff and among some loco drivers.

There was a major strike on the Midland Railway in 1887, which led to a defeat for ASLEF and the loss of many of its members. In the 1930s, Skipton depot was split between drivers who owed loyalty to the NUR, and others who were strong ASLEF men. The clerical grades – and some station masters – were members of the Railway Clerks' Association, formed in 1899. There were branches of the RCA in Carlisle and Leeds, and in Skipton from the 1930s. ASLEF and the NUR had branches in Leeds, Skipton, Bradford, Hellifield and Carlisle. Carlisle and Leeds were sufficiently large centres of railway employment to justify both the NUR and ASLEF having several branches, from the early 1900s. The April 1934 issue of ASLEF's *Locomotive Journal* reports on a meeting of its Carlisle Joint Branches. It was

Carlisle NUR banner, c.1920s.

The new Leeds ASLEF banner.

addressed by the Society's regional organizer, Percy Collick. In a very wide-ranging speech he referred to union rule changes, promotion and resettlement arrangements, as well as the deteriorating political situation in Germany and Austria.

The *Locomotive Journal* of March 1911 reported on its Hellifield branch, where there was fierce rivalry between ASLEF and the ASRS (NUR from 1913). The report refers to disquiet amongst the

drivers at Hellifield in the aftermath of the Hawes Junction disaster of 24 December 1910. Industrial relations on the Midland were not good in the period before the First World War. Engine cleaners at Carlisle Durran Hill took strike action in 1913, not long after the national rail strike of 1911.

Each union had its own social dimension. The Carlisle branch of ASLEF organized a Christmas Ball each year, and the city's branch of the RCA held an 'annual dinner and concert' during the 1930s. Its *Railway Service Journal* reported on the 1934 event, held in March. Branch chairman Jack Graham presided and guests included the union president, and local aldermen. Several senior officers attended from railway management, both LMS and London and North Eastern Railway. The entertainment for the evening was provided by RCA members, including a violinist, baritone and ventriloquist! The Skipton branch of the RCA held its first annual dinner in February 1934. The district controller, Mr Cook (whom we have seen officiating at the Skipton staff annual dinner and other events), presided over the occasion. Mr Cook obviously enjoyed his parties. The RCA's *Railway Service Journal* records: 'After a substantial and most enjoyable repast, Mr R. Etheridge (Leeds) proposed the toast of "The RCA" to which Mrs H. Chadwick (Executive Committee member, Leeds) replied "The LMSR".' Guests included the district signalling inspector, goods agent and a Mr Alderson, 'late of the Nigerian State Railways'.

The LMS magazine for April 1938 carried a report on the Appleby and District branch of the NUR holding an annual dinner, after a lapse of some years. A total of fifty-five members were present and the branch secretary, a Mr Steele, proposed a toast to 'The Railways', which was replied to by a Mr Garner.

Strikes were rare. The most important national dispute was in 1911, when railway workers held a strike over union recognition, and the General Strike of 1926 saw the line closed for the duration of the nine days' strike, but the clear impression from contemporary reports is of a degree of harmony typified by the RCA's dinner in which the union proposed a toast to the company, and the LMS representative reciprocated by offering a toast to the union. Certainly there were conflicts, and the event that led to most bitterness was the aftermath of the Ais Gill (Mallerstang) accident of 2 September 1913, which left sixteen people dead. Carlisle driver Samuel Caudle was, in the view of most railwaymen and many members of the public across the country, treated shamefully by the company (see Chapter 5).

The line was affected by several national disputes after the Second World War. The most notable was the 1955 loco drivers' dispute, initiated by ASLEF but opposed by the NUR, which still had a substantial membership in the footplate grades. The strike led to considerable bitterness between members of the two unions, which lasted for decades after at some depots.

> There was rivalry between ASLEF and NUR. There was a major row in 1955. We saw the NUR as trying to bring everyone down to the same level…. The NUR and RCA carried on working during the 1955 strike, which lasted just under three weeks. I can remember an incident at Copley Hill (Leeds) shed during the strike. An NUR man brought an engine onto shed, it had worked in from Peterborough and the driver had been on duty a good 12 hours. He asked the storesman for some soap – you can imagine how dirty he was! The storesman refused; he didn't want to be seen helping a strike-breaker.
>
> *Charlie Wallace, talking to the author, 1994*

A changing social structure

The post-war years saw gradual but almost imperceptible changes taking place in the communities along the line. Carlisle maintained its role as a major regional centre with a modest but growing commuter market along the Settle–Carlisle Line. However, reduced service patterns may well have killed off some of that potential for several years, until growth returned in the 1990s. Today, Skipton is a thriving commuter town for Leeds and to a lesser extent Bradford, served by frequent electric trains. Hellifield has seen substantial new housing development whilst Settle and Appleby have become popular tourist destinations as well as attractive places to retire to.

Many of the railway workers' cottages in places like Garsdale have been converted into holiday homes, or sold off to private buyers. The social life that was so much a part of the railway has effectively gone, as the remaining railway workers live in more dispersed locations. However, a new 'railway community' has emerged with the dozens of community volunteers involved at stations along the line. Some are Dales 'early retired'; others have made a conscious decision to relocate to the area, with the line being a major attraction.

CHAPTER 5

Death and Disaster

The line has had more than its fair share of misfortune, some of which was avoidable, some down to chance and ill luck. Any description of accidents and the inevitable injury and death must start with the huge loss of life – and serious injuries – that accompanied the actual building of the line. The building of any railway in the nineteenth century was accompanied by serious injury and death, but the loss of life that accompanied the building of the Settle–Carlisle Line seems disproportionately high. An accurate assessment of the number of fatalities has never been reached. Churchyards along the route have numerous graves of the men who died building the line, the one at St Leonard's in Chapel-le-Dale being one of several. At St Leonard's alone there are records of nearly 200 who died building the line, or were associated with it – mostly wives and children of the navvies. A memorial inside the chapel is inscribed: 'To the memory of those who through accidents lost their lives in constructing the railway works between Settle and Dent Head', and adds: 'This tablet was erected at the joint expense of their fellow workmen and the Midland Railway Company 1869 to 1876'.

A more recent tribute was made in 1997 when a tablet was erected in St Mary's Chapel, Mallerstang, for twenty-five people involved in the railway's construction who are buried there. Of these, twelve

The memorial to the navvies and their families inside St Leonard's, Chapel-le-Dale.

were navvies; there was one 'wife' and no fewer than eleven were children, who died of disease due to the unsanitary conditions. In 2016 the vicar of Dent started to research twenty-five unmarked graves in St John's churchyard at Cowgill. The conclusion was that the graves were of navvies and their wives and children who had died during the construction of the railway in the Dent area. However, a total of seventy-two deaths recorded in the parish register are of men, women and children connected with the building of the railway.

A popular narrative has evolved over the years that the high loss of life was down to a combination of the navvies' own reckless lifestyle and the difficult conditions surrounding the building of a railway through one of the most desolate and bleak parts of the country. Of course there is some truth in both assertions but the responsibility of the Midland Railway and its contractors for this enormous human cost should not be ignored. If we take as a conservative estimate a figure of 300 deaths directly attributable to the construction project, we might not be too far off. What is remarkable is both the high human toll and the casual, to say the least, treatment of the navvies' deaths and the lack of any

ABOVE RIGHT: *The memorial to the navvies and their families who are buried at St John's church, Cowgill.*

The memorial at St Mary's Church, Outhgill.

ABOVE: *St Leonard's graveyard, where many navvies are buried.*

The funeral of some of the victims of the Ais Gill disaster, passing through Kirkby Stephen. CUMBRIAN RAILWAYS ASSOCIATION

accurate record of how many casualties actually occurred.

Deaths and serious injuries were caused by falls, explosions and falling masonry. However, the construction of the line was severely affected by an outbreak of smallpox in 1871. Again, estimates of the number of deaths vary – from nearly a hundred to a small handful. The disease arrived in May 1871 and affected the navvy settlements at Sebastopol and Jericho. It spread quickly, fed by the insanitary conditions in the shanty towns. The authorities sough to blame the victims, suggesting that 'most of the fatal cases in adults are due to intemperance', ignoring the appalling lack of sanitation in the places where the outbreaks occurred. A further outbreak of smallpox occurred in Ingleton, followed by another in Settle where a young man died. A smallpox hospital was opened at Batty Green, by the contractor Ashwell. Authors Mitchell and Mussett in *Seven Years Hard: Building the Settle–Carlisle Railway* noted, 'Within the first month, 35 cases were admitted, and of these 19 had been cured and discharged and only three had died....'

When the line opened for freight traffic in 1875 the line suffered a number of accidents. On 15 August, just two weeks after the line had opened, a freight train derailed at Culgaith following the collapse of an embankment. The train was wrecked but fortunately nobody was hurt. In the same month a plate-layer was killed in Blea Moor Tunnel as he walked down the track.

On 28 August a serious accident occurred at Kildwick, between Keighley and Skipton. An Ingleton to Leeds train ploughed into the back of an excursion from Skipton to Leeds, killing five passengers and injuring forty. At the time of the accident, the Midland Railway was still using the antiquated 'time interval' system, whereby signalmen could allow a train to pass after a certain amount of time had elapsed after the previous train had passed. By 1875 the Midland was beginning to phase the system out but unfortunately not quickly enough to prevent the Kildwick accident.

Hawes Junction, 1910

One of the most notorious accidents on the line occurred on Christmas Eve 1910, at what was then Hawes Junction (today 'Garsdale'). It was then an important railway operating centre, where 'assisting

Garsdale station today, showing the signalbox where the events of 1910 unfurled so tragically.

engines' from both directions would be turned, and trains would often stop to take water. On the night of 23 December traffic was busy and signalman Alfred Sutton signed on for duty at 20:00. He had a lot on his hands: there were five locos in the station area waiting for a 'road' to allow them to return to their respective depots. Two of them were standing at the signal on the 'down' mainline waiting to return north to Carlisle. Just after 05:30 Sutton prepared to allow two coupled engines to return south to Leeds, though he was 'offered' a southbound freight from Ais Gill, which was given priority. Meanwhile the London to Glasgow and Edinburgh express was heading north and was approaching Dent, some 5 miles (8 km) south of Garsdale. It was headed by two Midland locos, a 4-4-0 express engine piloted by 2-4-0 number 48. The train was composed of seven coaches plus a six-wheel brake van.

Sutton forgot that he had the two locos waiting at his 'down starter' signal and accepted the express from Dent. He pulled off all his signals on the down main line to allow the express to speed through, remaining unaware of the two locos already on his down line track. The drivers of the two locos that had been standing at the down starter – Scott and Bath – saw the signal clear and naturally assumed it was for them, allowing them to head for home to their depot at Carlisle Durran Hill. They set off, moving at a fairly leisurely pace. However, they were unaware that the Scotch express was thundering towards them, running under clear signals from Garsdale signalbox. Driver Oldcorn was on the leading engine of the express, with prime responsibility for signals. He had seen nothing untoward and was 'going for it' to make up some lateness. His train sped through Garsdale station and over Dandry Mire Viaduct, before plunging into Moorcock Tunnel. It was only as he emerged from the short tunnel that he saw the red tail light of the light engines. Probably at the same time, Driver Bath on the rear of the two light engines, chanced to look back and saw the headlights of the express approaching at speed. He sounded his whistle to alert his mate on the front loco and opened his regulator to try to minimize the inevitable collision, but was far too late.

Impact followed within seconds. The two light engines were pushed violently forward and the two leading passenger coaches telescoped into each other, with horrific consequences. To make matters far worse, the gas for the train lighting exploded when it came into contact with hot coals from the derailed locomotives. The explosion that followed claimed the lives of twelve passengers.

Railway accidents are seldom simple events to explain and many factors are often at work. On a superficial reading, the fault clearly lay with Signalman Sutton at Hawes Junction, who forgot he had two locomotives sat on his down line, only a few yards from his box. However, the crews of the two light engines were remiss in not complying with long-established railway operating rules (enshrined in 'Rule 55') which instructs that when a train (or light engine) is delayed at a signal for any length of time, the fireman should go to the signalbox and sign the Train Register Book so there is a clear record of the delay.

There was a full inquiry into the accident by Major Pringle of the Board of Trade. He censured Sutton for his part but also criticized the crews of the light engines for not making Sutton aware of their presence. One of his recommendations was that in such situations, when the fireman goes to the box to carry out Rule 55, he should ensure that the signalman places a 'collar' on the appropriate signal levers to prevent the signals protecting his train being pulled off. In terms of twentieth-century signalling, interlocking would have prevented the accident happening. Electric track circuits would have shown up the presence of the two light engines and prevented Sutton from clearing his signals. There were systemic failings at work, as well as human factors. To a very large extent, the history of railway signalling has been a continuous attempt to minimize the potential of human error causing accidents. Hawes Junction offered many lessons for the future safer working of our rail system.

Ais Gill, 1913

The next major accident took place less than three years later, within a few miles of Garsdale, on 2

September 1913. This serious accident in which sixteen people died became the subject of a major political controversy, with the Midland Railway accused of putting profits before safety.

Two southbound sleeping car expresses for London St Pancras were booked to depart Carlisle at 01:35 and 01:49 respectively; the first from Glasgow, and the second from Edinburgh. The first was particularly heavy, with ten coaches weighing 349 tons. It was hauled by Midland express engine number 993, driven by William Nicholson, and fired by James Metcalf of Carlisle's Durran Hill depot. The second (Edinburgh) train was lighter, with six coaches weighing 248 tons. The loco heading the second express was Midland 4-4-0 number 445. Samuel Caudle was the driver with fireman George Follows, also of Durran Hill. Caudle was a highly experienced footplateman, with thirty-seven years' experience working the Settle–Carlisle. Follows was a well-respected fireman, but unfamiliar with the particular type of loco he was assigned to that night.

Durran Hill shed had recently switched to a different sort of coal, supplied by Naworth Colliery, a few miles from Carlisle. The Carlisle locomen had

been complaining about its poor quality, which had caused problem with some locos' steaming abilities. It was a particular bone of contention as loco crews complained that if they had to 'stop for steam' they would be penalized by the company.

Driver Nicholson, of the first express, was aware that he would have a challenging task on his hands with such a heavy train, and asked for an assisting engine from the local Control office before he departed. Nothing was available so he had to make the best of it. His 01:35 train left Carlisle three minutes late but ran well as far as Ormside, just south of Appleby, along the easier-graded sections of the line. Once over Ormside Viaduct the line starts to climb, with the northern section of the 'Long Drag' beginning. The crew struggled to maintain speed and boiler pressure, labouring through Kirkby Stephen at about 20mph. Boiler pressure was dropping as the Naworth coal wasn't able to maintain pressure. As a locomotive's boiler pressure drops, so too does vacuum pressure which controls the brakes. The slower the train went the more the train brakes started to drag. By Mallerstang it was clear that the driver, Nicholson, couldn't persuade

English Electric Class 40 D200 heads towards Ais Gill summit, at the spot where the disaster happened.

his engine to go any further. It 'stuck'. Ironically, the summit of the climb, at Ais Gill, was just a couple of hundred yards away. The train ground to a standstill some distance beyond Mallerstang signalbox.

This need not have been a calamity. According to railway operating rules, in such a situation the train should be 'protected' by the guard going back and laying down detonators to prevent a following train running into its rear. By this time, the train was protected by the absolute block system, which meant that the signalbox in the rear (Kirkby Stephen) could not allow a train into the section without getting 'line clear' from Mallerstang box.

The train guard, Donnelly, walked up to the engine and asked Nicholson if he should go back to 'protect'. Nicholson told him it wouldn't be necessary as they would soon have steam sufficient to get them 'over the top' to Ais Gill and beyond. Donnelly went to the back of the train to inform the second guard, Oliver Whitley, of the situation.

Meanwhile, the second, lighter, train was heading south at good speed. Caudle passed Kirkby Stephen at about 45mph and made the fateful decision to get out of the cab to 'oil round' his locomotive. This was traditional Midland Railway practice, leaving the fireman to drive the train and observe signals. Although the fireman, Follows, was an experienced fireman he was having difficulty with the locomotive's injector, which fed water into the loco boiler. Caudle's absence and Follows' distraction were a toxic mix in the unfolding tragedy.

At Mallerstang, signalman Sutherland had placed his signals to danger and assumed the stationary express was protected, and would soon be on its way. He accepted the second express from Kirkby Stephen but wasn't in a position to allow it to proceed south towards Ais Gill as the first express was still in the section beyond Mallerstang.

As the second express steamed up the grade towards Mallerstang, Follows was still trying to get the injector to work and Caudle was making his way along the loco running board back to the footplate. Neither saw the Mallerstang 'distant' signal at caution. The distant signal is an important part of railway signalling – it tells a driver that if in the 'on' position the next signal should be taken as being at 'danger' and the train should prepare to stop at the 'home' signal.

Neither Caudle nor Follows noticed the Mallerstang distant being set at caution. However, Sutherland, in the signalbox, assumed that the train had seen the distant signal at caution and pulled off his 'home' signal to allow the express to creep forward past the box and stop at his 'starter' signal just south of Mallerstang. This was a fatal error, as Caudle saw the home signal as being 'off' and assumed, wrongly, he had a clear road ahead.

Signalman Sutherland realized that the second train was doing anything but 'creep' towards him. As the train thundered past his signalbox he frantically waved a red signal but to no avail. Things might have been saved if Caudle and Follows had seen Mallerstang's starter signal at danger but they assumed that this, like the home signal they had just passed, would be clear.

Sutherland sent 'train running away' to Ais Gill but there was nothing that he, nor his colleague Clemmet at Ais Gill, could do.

The first indication to Caudle and Follows that anything was seriously wrong was when Follows saw two red lights ahead. At first he thought it was the signals at Ais Gill, though in fact they were the tail lamp of the stationary express and the red lamp of the guard, Whitley.

The second train hit the stationary express at a speed of about 30mph. As with the Hawes Junction crash three years before, gas lighting made a bad situation infinitely worse. There was an explosion, exacerbating the impact of the violent collision. A fire quickly took hold of the train's wreckage, creating a deadly inferno. Fourteen passengers were killed almost immediately and two died later.

The alarm was raised by Sutherland; seven minutes after the collision, fireman Metcalf of the first train reached Ais Gill box to say there had been a crash. Within 30 minutes the station master at Hawes Junction, William Bunce, had reached the scene and did his best to help the dead and dying.

As with Hawes Junction and so many other railway accidents, it was easy to identify a scapegoat.

Aftermath of the disaster at Ais Gill; railway staff retrieving wreckage. SCRT

Caudle was held to blame by failing to see the danger signals, and was disciplined by the Midland Railway. He spent the rest of his railway career driving shunting engines. His treatment by his employers was mild compared to how he was dealt with by the law. He was put on trial for manslaughter and the case was heard at the Cumberland Assizes in Carlisle, where he broke down and wept. Although found guilty, the jury recommended clemency on account of the many mitigating circumstances. He was sentenced to two months' imprisonment, which many railway workers regarded as despicable. After spending a few days in prison, Caudle was given a free pardon by the Home Secretary. On his release, he was given a rousing welcome by Carlisle railwaymen.

Clearly, there was much more to it than one driver's mistake. If the Midland Railway had listened to their employee's complaints about poor quality coal, the first train would not have run into trouble in the first place. The practice of drivers going out of the cab to 'oil round' was a dangerous part of railway culture which the companies should, some felt, have prohibited.

The inquiry was held by Major Pringle, who had presided over the inquiry into the Hawes Junction crash three years earlier. Caudle was singled out as the main culprit but Sutherland was criticized for his mistake in prematurely clearing his 'home' signal to Caudle's train. The press criticized the Midland for a casual approach towards passenger safety. Pringle's report was seen as a 'whitewash' exonerating the company from blame. Arthur Henderson MP, chairman of the Labour Party, attacked the Midland's continued use of gas lighting at a time when other companies were moving to electricity, suggesting that 'the Midland company put profit before safety'. The National Union of Railwaymen, formed earlier in that year, fought a strong campaign to exonerate Caudle. Their new and charismatic general secretary, J.H. Thomas, took a personal interest in the issue and huge demonstrations of railwaymen were called. Questions were raised in the House of Commons. Thomas pointed out that drivers had been told that they would be penalized if they lost time even when a train's permitted load was exceeded. A notice to that effect had been posted at the Carlisle depot but was removed immediately after the accident.

Thomas laid into the Midland for its use of inferior coal and also their assertion, supported by Pringle, that it was no longer necessary for locomen

The substantial memorial at Kirkby Stephen Cemetery for the victims of the 1913 tragedy, with the church gravedigger.

to 'oil round' while the train was in motion, due to improvements in lubrication systems. Thomas responded:

> This is not true. The engine that Caudle had and every engine of the same class has had the 'well' for lubrication purposes stopped, and Caudle was most emphatic in stating his only object in leaving the footplate was to prevent the engine getting hot. There is not a driver on the Midland system today working this class of engine who does not have to leave the footplate every run to do similar work.

Quoted in P. Baughan, *North of Leeds*

The disaster had a huge impact on the Dales communities. The funeral procession through Kirkby Stephen was attended by several hundreds and a large memorial was erected by the Midland Railway in Kirkby Stephen Cemetery. Upkeep of the memorial is still the responsibility of the railway, through Network Rail.

Later accidents, 1918–1999

The last major accident to occur on the line before the Midland Railway's absorption into the London Midland and Scottish Railway (LMSR) occurred on 19 January at Little Salkeld. The 8:50 London to Glasgow express, headed by Midland 'compound' number 1010, ran into a landslide. The two leading coaches telescoped and seven passengers lost their lives. Strangely, a platelayer had walked the length concerned only 5 minutes earlier and noticed nothing unusual. Whilst no particular blame could be attached to anyone for this incident, clearly the practice of using wooden-bodied coaches, which telescoped relatively easily, resulted in a high loss of life. Interestingly, the same loco, number 1010, was involved in another accident at Little Salkeld some years later, on 10 July 1933. Whilst working a southbound express it collided with a goods train undertaking a shunting move.

On 6 March 1930 a serious collision occurred in Waste Bank Tunnel, Culgaith, during some engi-

Wreckage of the Thames–Clyde Express at Blea Moor, April 1952. SCRT

BELOW: *Another view of the crash at Blea Moor.* SCRT

neering work. A ballast train was stationed inside the tunnel and due to confusion between the ballast crew, signalman and driver of a stopping train, there was a head-on collision inside the tunnel. The loco hauling the passenger train was one of the former London and North Western 'Claughton' locos which had been drafted onto the line in the 1930s. The driver of the 'Claughton' was killed and a passenger also died.

Another accident involving a ballast train occurred at Griseburn on 29 November 1948. A 50-ton breakdown crane had been doing some work on the down (northbound) line. It had been inadequately secured and set off, out of control, on

The most memorable of all days at Blea Moor (for railwayman's daughter Nancy Edmondson) occurred on an April afternoon in 1952. Nancy was sunbathing on top of the pigsty when suddenly there was a tremendous crash. The up Thames–Clyde Express had derailed with one of its two locomotives toppling on its side and three coaches rearing up before crashing back sideways over the running lines. Apart from the signalman, who immediately summoned help, she and her mum were the only people on the scene and their home became a casualty clearing station. When rescuers eventually arrived they were appalled to find bodies littering the embankment but they turned out to be passengers who had given all possible help and were recovering in the sun.

David Joy, Rails in the Dales, 2017

the falling gradient towards Carlisle. It ran for 23 miles (37 km) before coming to a stand at Lazonby. Although it has the sound of a slapstick farce, one man was killed and another two were injured in trying to stop it.

An unusual accident occurred on 18 April 1952, when The Thames–Clyde Express from Glasgow to St Pancras derailed at speed. The train's locomotive was 46117 *Welsh Guardsman* piloted by Midland Compound 41040. The brake rodding on the Compound's tender fell apart and trailed along the track. When it came into contact with points the rodding became entangled with the pointwork causing the 'Scot' and leading coaches to derail. Remarkably, no passengers were killed but twenty-nine were injured. By then, improved couplers minimized the risk of carriages 'telescoping' which had been such a disastrous feature of previous accidents.

A more serious accident, also caused by a defective locomotive, took place on 21 January 1960 near Settle station. The overnight Glasgow to St Pancras express was heading south behind Britannia Pacific 70052 *Firth of Tay*. It was a dreadful night, with station master Taylor reporting 'blizzard' conditions. As the train climbed towards Ais Gill the driver heard a 'knocking' sound coming from the engine and 'stopped to examine' at Garsdale. He found nothing amiss. It was bitterly cold with snow

falling heavily. He failed to see that the locomotive's right-hand slide bars had fallen off. He decided that the best solution was to proceed to Hellifield at reduced speed and get a fitter to make a proper examination. The train set off at 40mph and eventually the piston rod fractured and drove into the ballast. This caused the opposite track to be pulled out of alignment, by a stroke of very bad luck just as a northbound freight train was passing. Although the goods train came to a stop it was foul of the southbound express, still travelling at about 40mph. The sides of the passenger train were ripped open by the goods wagons, with two of the carriages having their sides completely ripped out. Five people were killed and nine injured.

The inspecting officer, Brigadier Langley, criticized BR's maintenance of the Britannias, with the discovery that the failure of slide bars was a common occurrence. He also censured the driver for proceeding at what he considered too high a speed. Station staff at Settle were warmly applauded for the speed with which they responded to the accident, in such appalling conditions. Tragically, this accident arguably claimed a final victim in recent years when a Settle man, who in his boyhood witnessed the accident, threw himself in front of a train on the anniversary of the accident many years later.

Railway work, particularly on the track, has always been hazardous. One of the most awful tragedies in recent years occurred in 1979 during the heavy snow. On 15 February, two track workers involved in snow clearance duties were killed by a passing train at Hellifield.

The most recent fatal accident occurred on 31 January 1995. I happened to be travelling on the line, with the intention of catching the connecting bus from Garsdale to Hawes where I'd have lunch with friends before heading home later in the day. The weather was atrocious, with a steady downpour of rain from the moment we left Leeds. By the time we had left Settle the water was over the head of the rails at Staincliffe. It seemed only a matter of time before the line would be closed for safety reasons so I took the decision to get off at Horton and take the next train back. It was a wise decision.

Remarkably, trains kept running but the torrential rain led to a landslide at Ais Gill. A Class 156 Super-Sprinter formed the 16:26 Carlisle to Leeds service but could only proceed as far as Ribblehead, as the line south from Ribblehead was blocked by flooding. The train crew were instructed to return to Carlisle. Near Ais Gill Summit, the train hit a landslide. It derailed across both tracks, and the cabin lights went off, plunging it into darkness. The driver, who had been injured in the collision, managed to contact Crewe Control Room to tell them of the incident. The conductor escorted passengers into the rear vehicle, which was foul of the up line. He then returned to see his driver who was still in the cab. Another Class 156 had left Kirkby Stephen on the 17:45 Carlisle–Leeds train. About a quarter of a mile before the derailed train, the driver saw its red lights and started to make an emergency brake application, but the train was unable to stop before hitting the derailed northbound train. The resulting collision killed the conductor of the derailed train, and injured thirty passengers, some seriously.

Whilst tributes were rightly made to Stuart Wilson, the conductor who died in the accident, the inquiry found that the collision, and his own death, could have been avoided if he had carried out protection duties immediately following the derailment. As the driver was injured, the conductor should have made his way with all haste to lay detonators on the up (southbound) line to prevent any oncoming train hitting the derailed train. In his entirely understandable desire to look after his passengers and injured mate, he – tragically – failed in his duty. There may have been some misunderstanding in the chaos surrounding the derailment. The inquiry heard a transcript of the call made by the driver of the derailed train to Crewe Control, informing them of the derailment. The call ended with Control saying, 'We will take care of all of that, driver.' This may have given the false impression that the southbound service would be warned at Kirkby Stephen of the blocked line, obviating the urgency of protecting the train.

Further recommendations were made about the inadequate communications between control rooms and use of the National Radio Network. A 'group call' to all trains in the vicinity of the incident could have been made by Control and might have alerted the second train to the obstruction in time to prevent the collision.

On 16 January 1999 a similar incident occurred on the line at Crosby Garrett, north of Kirkby Stephen, though fortunately there were no serious casualties. Very heavy rainfall led to a landslide, which caused a Carlisle-bound passenger train to derail just outside Crosby Garrett Tunnel, blocking the up line. The driver – Carlisle man and former mayor, John Metcalfe – ran ahead to put down detonators to alert any oncoming train. His prompt action potentially saved lives, as the detonators alerted the driver of a southbound coal train that the line ahead was obstructed. The freight train slowed down but still hit the passenger train, propelling it back into the tunnel. Professional action by the driver and guard of the passenger train reassured passengers, some of whom received minor injuries.

The crew led the passengers to safety and from here the story takes a positive turn. There was a footpath providing access from the line down to the village, from where road transport was being arranged. The crew saw that the village hall was illuminated and discovered that a buffet had been arranged for a local event that evening. The canny railwaymen asked the organizers to let their somewhat shaken passengers join in the feast and the villagers responded with alacrity. A potentially unhappy situation was transformed into something much more convivial, with the villagers' hospitality being hugely appreciated by passengers and train crew. The upshot was that Railtrack's zonal director, Richard Fearn, wrote to the village hall thanking them for their kindness and asking if there was any way in which Railtrack could make a gesture of thanks to the village community. The hall committee responded by suggesting that the village hall roof was in a poor state of repair and any help in providing a new one would be welcome. Railtrack made good their promise and Mr and Mrs Fearn were invited to a celebratory luncheon after the new roof had been installed.

CHAPTER 6

Working the Settle– Carlisle: a Young Goods Guard in the 1970s

Writing this book brought back many fond (and some less fond) memories of working the Settle–Carlisle Line when I was a goods guard at Blackburn depot in the mid-1970s. While many people have written about the Settle–Carlisle Line, few of them have actually worked on the line. Peter Baughan, author of the epic work *North of Leeds*, was a railway employee, based in the Parliamentary Office at Euston, where I subsequently did a short stint in my

railway career. Dick Fawcett's book *Ganger Guard and Signalman* is a wonderful autobiographical account of one man's life on the line.

My sojourn at Euston was comfortable and enjoyable, but could never compare with my time working loose-coupled (and fully-fitted) freight trains over the Settle–Carlisle Line. The experience merits more than a passing nod, to give the reader a sense of what it was like to work over the line in

A Class 40 heads a southbound freight near Settle Junction, 9 February 1977; a view from the brake van veranda.

those years just after the end of steam but before 'modernization' had changed the nature of railway operations so dramatically. Apart from the diesel loco at the front of the train, the life of a goods guard on the S&C in the 1970s had not changed much since the line's opening a century earlier.

I started my railway career at Horwich Loco Works in September 1974, as a temporary job after leaving university. My passion for railways went back to early childhood, having been brought up within 100 yards (90 metres) of Bolton loco shed. If I was going to do a job to keep my young family fed, I might as well do something on the railway. And to have worked in the former engineering centre of the Lancashire and Yorkshire Railway had a romantic charm. But the romance of much railway life often pales in the face of hard reality. Working in the Spring Smithy at Horwich Loco Works was hard, dangerous and not well paid; romantic, it wasn't. And I've never enjoyed being stuck inside. So I kept an eye out for operational jobs, ideally a guard or maybe a signalling vacancy. I didn't have to wait long. The London Midland Region's Blackburn depot was recruiting guards to cover a number of vacancies caused by a substantial increase of work. Long-distance freight trains were being diverted from the West Coast Line Main line via Blackburn and the Settle–Carlisle as electrification north of Crewe went ahead.

I applied and was told to report to guard's training school at Lancaster in September 1975. There were five other 'new recruits', me being the only one who was already working for BR, albeit in a very different job. The traditional promotional ladder for a guard was, at the very least, to have worked as a porter or shunter before being elevated to the role of guard. By the 1970s those arrangements no longer worked and BR struggled to retain staff. In that wonderfully disparaging phrase used by 'old hand' railwaymen, guards were recruited 'from off the street' with no prior railway knowledge.

The course lasted about six weeks and I was privileged to have been taught basic railway operational principles by two venerable 'movements inspectors' who had spent a lifetime running trains.

We were instructed in basic railway rules, operating principles and other essentials of running trains. Although we'd be working passenger trains, none of our training concerned itself with such modern notions as 'customer service'. But I was taught how to set up a buckeye coupler, use a shunting pole and understand the essentials of brake forces. Throughout my railway career I've never had to lift a buckeye, and wagon shunting by the mid-1970s was becoming less common. I was never very good at using the pole, I have to admit.

We were given a basic examination in rules and regulations before being 'passed out' at the end of the eight-week course. The next stage of my induction was to sign on at Blackburn depot and start 'road learning' so that I'd be able to take over as a guard as quickly as possible. At the time, Blackburn depot was a busy place. It had absorbed displaced drivers and guards from Rose Grove (Burnley), which had closed a few years earlier, as well as Accrington, which had finished in the late 1960s. The core 'Blackburn men' were mostly from Lower Darwen steam depot, which had closed in 1966. This amalgam of three different depots, with their own ways of doing things, could have been a recipe for trouble. In fact, everyone got on pretty well with each other. It was a totally male domain, overwhelmingly white. By the mid-1970s there was a small number of Asian railwaymen, but only two made it to the guard's grades. One, Abdul Qureshi, was an entertaining and confident guy whom everyone liked working with. Some others who were less able to adapt to the environment didn't have an easy time.

The first routes I had to learn were Preston to Colne and the intermediate sidings such as Burnley goods yard, Blackburn Taylor Street and Whitebirk Colliery. We also did Blackburn to Manchester for the various passenger turns on that line, and – tantalizingly, Blackburn to Hellifield. But not beyond. Quite a few freight jobs at Blackburn involved taking a diesel down to Lostock Hall Junction and taking over a Carlisle-bound freight after the electric had 'hooked off'. We would work the train as far as Hellifield where Carlisle men would relieve us.

The majority of these trains were 'part fitted' – in

ABOVE: *Heading north – near Newsholme, south of Hellifield, a gang of platelayers are working on the track.*

LEFT: *Blackburn guard Abdul Qureshi with driver Brian Holmes, 1975.*

other words, the first twenty or so wagons would have continuous brakes leaving the remaining twenty-odd wagons with no brakes, other than the brake van at the rear. It was a challenging job managing those loose-coupled wagons, even when you had a 'fitted head' at the front. Of course even more demanding was a train that had no fitted head at all and was solely dependent on the loco brake and the guard using his skill on the handbrake in the brake van at the back.

By then, some goods trains were running 'fully fitted' with no need for a brake van, though a guard was required. He was supposed to ride in the 'back cab' of the diesel loco though most drivers welcomed the company of having the guard ride in the front cab with him. Longer distance trains would also have a 'secondman' – what was traditionally termed

'fireman' – whose job was to act as the driver's assistant. In reality, their role was virtually pointless and BR eventually won an agreement from ASLEF to remove the 'secondman' completely.

The route from Blackburn to Hellifield was hilly and undulating. In some ways it was more difficult for a guard working that section of line than the S&C itself, as there were several dips where the line descended quite steeply and then began to rise with equal severity. In those situations it was easy to get a 'snatch' if you weren't careful. In other words, the wagons would bunch up and when the driver put on power to get up the oncoming gradient the wagons would suddenly stretch creating a domino effect which would be felt – often with serious consequences – in the guard's brake van. I knew quite a few guards who had been badly injured by a nasty

A view of Blackburn secondman Joe Entwistle taking a break on his loco.

'snatch', sometimes caused by them not using their handbrake effectively – or by an insensitive driver putting on power too quickly. Good route knowledge was vital to know when to expect a potential snatch and to use the handbrake to keep the wagons 'on the stretch' all the time.

A typical guard's brake van hadn't changed since the 1870s. There was no lighting other than what you could provide with your handlamp, which was mainly intended to give signals to the driver and to enable you to pick your way down the side of the train. By the 1970s the old paraffin-lit handlamps had been replaced by powerful battery-operated 'Bardic' handlamps. As well as an absence of any electric lighting, there were no toilet facilities. So a four-hour trip to Carlisle involved either strong bladder control or taking your chance on the veranda. For major bowel movements the guard would 'do his business' inside the van on a sheet of newspaper then hurl the parcel onto the lineside. Primitive? It certainly was. But there were compensations: to stand on the rear veranda of a goods train on a summer's day heading up to Ribblehead was sheer bliss.

The one source of heat and light in a brake van: the traditional stove!

Passing Horrocksford Junction signalbox, between Clitheroe and Hellifield, 9 February 1977.

Hellifield station in the 1970s: A BR 'Peak' passes on a northbound express.

Heating was provided by a small stove, which ran off coal. It was always important to have a good supply of coal for long trips, such as Carlisle to Severn Tunnel Junction. You weren't just preparing the train for your part of the run; you had to think of the poor buggers who would take over for the remainder of a long journey. Traditionally, yard staff would prepare vans at places like Carlisle and they would ensure that there was a good supply of coal and that the lamps for the rear of the train were filled with paraffin. However, by the 1970s you couldn't depend on any of this and had to make sure you were well stocked with coal and the lamps were filled before giving the driver the 'right away'.

The stove, once well alight, gave off a powerful heat and you could keep your billy can of tea or coffee warmed up nicely on the top of the stove. Sometimes the stoves could be difficult to get going and a supply of paraffin was always useful to get the fire blazing, with the help of newspaper and a bit of kindling. Woe betide a guard who handed over his train and the fire was out. This once happened with me, shortly after I'd 'passed out', on a cold winter's evening working down from Hellifield to Blackburn. I was relieved by a Crewe guard, who was not happy at finding a cold van for his two-hour run to Basford Hall.

After a few weeks I 'signed the road' for all the routes I'd been instructed to learn. My first job – 3 February 1975 – was 'Target 17' – the Burnley 'trip' goods where we pootled around East Lancashire with our loco 25.248. The following day I worked a fully fitted goods up to Hellifield – 6S82 Penyffordd–Gunnie cement train. My first 'proper' freight train in the traditional sense – with a brake van – was the following day, working 7P77 Brewery Sidings to Carlisle, again as far as Hellifield, with driver Fred Shorrock, an old hand Bolton driver, always noted for his immaculate appearance. The train was heavily loaded with fifty-three wagons totalling 929 tonnes, about the limit for our Class 40 diesel. We reached Hellifield at 02:30 and returned quickly at 02:45 with 7M55 Mossend–Bescot, relieving the Carlisle men who took our train northwards.

I was put in the spare link, which meant I could do any job that came along, providing I had the route knowledge. So I found myself doing a mixture of passenger trains up to Colne and back to Preston, the Manchester line, some local shunting jobs and – my favourite from the start – freights to Hellifield. One Hellifield job – described above – involved signing on at 23:36 and relieving the Brewery Sidings (Manchester) to Carlisle freight at Blackburn and working it to Hellifield. The journey typically took

Members of the Blackburn Signing-on Point Ramblers on Ingleton Viaduct, May 1976.

Blackburn Driver Abraham Tattersall ('Ab Tat') in the cab of a Class 25 loco.

about an hour. So we'd usually arrive about 01:00 and then have a five-hour wait for the returning Carlisle–Brewery, which we again just worked to Blackburn. Fortunately the old waiting room was converted to a train crew mess room and still had long upholstered benches. So with luck, we (my driver and I) would get about five hours' sleep before our return working arrived.

The drivers I worked with were a good bunch. One or two were wary about this kid who was a 'new starter' but I managed to establish a rapport with most of them. Each had their own tales to tell and I only wished I had written some of them down. Many were self-educated intellectuals with extensive knowledge of music, literature and art. One of the former Lower Darwen men, Jack Bradley, was a crossword ace and could polish off the *Times*, *Telegraph* and *Guardian* crosswords – the

full ones – in between jobs. Raymond Watton was an accomplished musician. Several drivers had their own 'sidelines'. Johnny Holland kept bees and we were well supplied with delicious honey in the mess room. Some others such as Leo Kay, a former Rose Grove man, had a smallholding. Before my time, but the stuff of legend, was 'Knicker Jack' who ran a ladies' lingerie stall on Blackburn market. One of the eldest of the Rose Grove men was 'Ab Tat' – or Abraham Tattersall – never to be seen without a fag in his mouth and a great practical joker.

Many other drivers were involved in the 'MIC' – the Mutual Improvement Class movement, whose history stretched back to the dawn of railways and the culture of working class self-improvement. The MIC classes were held in the Ambulance Room in the bowels of Blackburn station, and invariably covered technical issues relating to the new diesel traction, as well as the more abstruse aspects of railway rules and regulations. This was a serious business and every depot had its own MIC, which competed at regional and national levels for coveted prizes.

As well as the more formal 'out of hours' activities I was involved in a very enjoyable activity that involved walking disused railway lines. We formed the 'Blackburn Signing-on Point Ramblers' in 1976, which generally did a walk every month or two, mostly in the North of England but occasionally further afield, such as Abergavenny to Brynmawr. There were about a dozen of us, a mixture of guards and drivers. The latter included Raymond Watton, John DeLuca and George Whittle whilst the guards had Les Scott, Jimmy Leadley, myself, and a few more. It was great fun and the sort of thing today's railways should encourage more.

There was a strong drinking culture on the railway that survived well into the 1970s. For a driver and fireman working a steam locomotive, in a hot and physically challenging environment, a couple of pints would soon be sweated off. However, the drink culture persisted after the end of steam and there were some frightening instances of drivers having had a drink and falling asleep at the controls. Eventually, BR went for a total ban on drinking on duty, and ensured it was rigorously enforced. It wasn't before time. During my time, if we were at a 'foreign' depot with time to spare before the next job, we'd adjourn to the nearest pub or local staff association club, where you'd join dozens of other drivers and guards doing the same thing. The 'staff club' at Victoria was a regular haunt, as was the railway club on Gresty Road, Crewe. At Preston there

was a choice of the 'top house' or 'bottom house' adjacent to the station. Blackburn itself offered the option of the Ribble Club, part of the local bus depot, or the more risky Adelphi, which had a reputation as a rough house. When we worked to Healey Mills (Wakefield) we would adjourn to The Horse and Jockey at Horbury Bridge, whereas Carlisle offered a choice of the Platform 1 Bar, Caledonian and other nearby hostelries. One driver was well known for bursting into song as he approached Petteril Bridge Junction, on the Carlisle outskirts, using the tune of 'California here I come' but substituting 'Caledonian here I come' followed by a litany of other local boozers.

When I began road learning north of Hellifield, we were told to remember where all the pubs were along the route. This wasn't for obvious reasons, but in case your train was in trouble. There were long block sections so signalboxes were few and far between. In the days when rural communities had few telephones, the local pub was a good bet if you needed to ring Control to report you'd 'stuck'.

Being in the spare link had potential advantages in terms of getting interesting jobs, providing you had good route knowledge. I made it my business to do a bit of freelance route learning when spare, rather than playing cards in the mess room. Some

Our own personal charabanc! The single-car unit waits at Griseburn Ballast Sidings, while some route-learners were busy mushroom-picking.

Our 'bubblecar' crosses Ribblehead Viaduct.

routes could be easily added, such as Preston to Blackpool, handy for seasonal specials and usually nice 'day jobs'. But the real prize was Carlisle and that needed several weeks of training. Interestingly, Blackburn men never referred to it as the S&C or the 'Long Drag', which were more 'enthusiast' terms by and large. It was always 'the Midland'.

The opportunity came in Autumn 1976 when a special 'route-learning train' was laid on to train drivers and guards from Preston and Blackburn in readiness for a series of diversions when the West Coast Main Line was to be completely shut. Those few weeks were some of the best of my railway career. We signed on at 07:30 and our little single car diesel (known as 'the bubblecar') set off, at an easy pace, for Carlisle. The instructor was Paul Jamieson of Preston, a knowledgeable and pleasant railwayman with a deep interest in railway history. He had started as a cleaner at Oxenholme.

We would arrive in Carlisle around midday, and the railcar would go to Kingmoor for fuel. Once we'd

familiarized ourselves with Kingmoor Yard most of us jumped off at Carlisle station and had a look round the city. I got to know Carlisle Cathedral, as well as a few of the pubs, intimately. Our journey back to Blackburn was again, usually leisurely. Sometimes we'd be put 'inside' if something needed to get past us, though by then there were few passenger trains left using the line. On one occasion we stopped near to Long Meg Sidings to raid a mushroom field. They tasted delicious!

Long Meg was a location well known to Blackburn men. In steam days, Lower Darwen crews worked the Long Meg–Widnes anhydrite trains, usually with a BR 2-10-0 9F heavy freight loco. Normally, Carlisle Kingmoor men worked the trains as far as Blea Moor and Lower Darwen relieved them, but sometimes they worked through.

It was over all too soon and I 'signed' the road to Carlisle at the end of October 1976. My first job 'over the Midland' was on Friday 29 October. I signed on at 14:00 to work the fully fitted 6M86 St Blazey–Carlisle.

This Blackburn driver has a good haul of mushrooms while the guard is looking a bit anxious about getting moving. Griseburn Ballast Sidings, c.1976.

Driver-trainer Paul Jamieson struggles with his mushroom haul.

It was loaded to twenty-five wagons, carrying china clay from the Cornish mines. The trailing load was 575 tonnes. It was running late so as 'spare guard' I fell for the job. The driver was former Lower Darwen man George Whittle with ex-Rose Grove secondman Tony Middleton; our loco was 47.455. They were both nice friendly guys with plenty of tales to tell and I rode in the front cab with them, arriving at Kingmoor Yard at 17:45. Our return working was a part-fitted train – 8K05 Carlisle–Stoke, a regular Blackburn job, which I worked on many occasions. It was a big train, with not much of a 'fitted head'. The thirty wagons equalled forty-five in 'standard-length units' with a weight of 973 tonnes. Our loco was one of the heavy English Electric workhorses, 40.110. We left Carlisle as it was getting dark and the journey was uneventful, arriving in Blackburn at 22:05.

I often 'swapped' for the Carlisle–Stoke job. Most guards preferred an early turn, whereas I liked 'lates' as well as the pleasure of working over the S&C, even in the dark. Sometimes my driver, secondman and myself would sign on and travel 'as passenger' to Carlisle only to find the train was cancelled – or 'caped' to use railway terminology. This happened on 6 December, when the three of us turned up at Carlisle to be told it was caped and we should get the next available train home to Blackburn. Three men's pay

for doing nothing! A couple of weeks later I worked the same job with driver John Mike McManus and his secondman Geoff Dore. John was ex-Rose Grove and very involved in the railway staff club movement. This time our train was running and we had early series English Electric Class 40 400.16, with '37 equal to 47' wagons, totalling 782 tonnes. It was running as a Class 7 train, so I was in the back, in my nicely prepared brake van. We had a long stop at Long Meg – 50 minutes – owing to some engineering works ahead. We then had to wait another 10 minutes at Settle Junction to let a passenger service off the branch from Carnforth. Despite the delays we got home to Blackburn in reasonable time, 21:45.

My next job over 'The Midland' wasn't until 12 January when I booked on at 12:00 to work 6Z23 Winsford to Millerhill (Edinburgh). It was a bitterly cold day with flurries of snow. It was another '40', no. 40032 which we took as far as Blea Moor. My driver was ex-Bolton man Bill Haddock with my good friend (and talented musician) Raymond Watton as secondman, though he was driving on the outward trip. This was the notorious 'salt train' taking rock salt from the Cheshire salt pits to Scotland. It was notorious for its habit of 'running hot' – in other words getting a hot axle box. The ancient wagons leaked badly and when it rained the water mixed with the salt to drip down onto the wheelsets and axle boxes. So you had to constantly be on the look

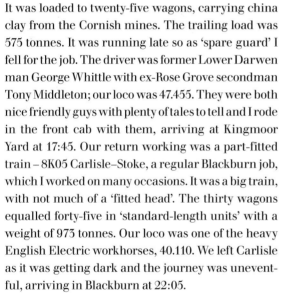

View from the brake van veranda towards Pen-y-ghent, 9 February 1977.

Train 7M86 St Blazey to Carlisle works its way north towards Ribblehead, 9 February 1977.

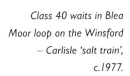

Class 40 waits in Blea Moor loop on the Winsford – Carlisle 'salt train', c.1977.

Driver Bill Haddock and secondman Raymond Watton on the 'salt train'. Winsford–Carlisle at Blea Moor, c.1977.

Looking back down the line near Selside. A local platelaying gang working on the line.

out for tell-tale signs of running hot: usually a trail of smoke, or sometimes an actual fire. On this occasion we got as far as Newsholme, south of Hellifield, when I noticed the smoke. We told the signalman at Hellifield to put us 'inside' while we detached the offending wagon. It was the thirty-seventh wagon of forty, which meant a long walk back to do the shunting moves. By now it was snowing and bitterly cold. I got off the loco after we'd come to a stand in one of the sidings and unhooked the wagon. For some reason Raymond thought I'd got out and given him the signal to draw forward – but I hadn't. I was still in between the wagons when the train started moving. In that situation there's only one thing you can do, and that is to lie down in the 'fourfoot' (the gap between the tracks – actually 4ft 8½in . The alternative is to risk losing a leg, or two, trying to get out. Eventually the train came to a stand and I went to the loco to remonstrate with my friend, who was mortified at what he'd done. I went back down the train and uncoupled, then signalled to Raymond to draw forward, put the 'cripple' down another siding and then come back for the rest of the train. Remarkably it only took half an hour, though it was 30 minutes I'll always remember.

We were relieved by Carlisle men who had worked south to Blea Moor with 7L93 Carlisle–Warrington with Sulzer diesel 25.064. We arrived at Blea Moor at 15:05 with just 20 minutes to make a brew and admire the snowy landscape around Barry Moss and Ingleborough. While inside the loop

the Nottingham–Glasgow express passed us with a Class 45 'Peak' at the head. The journey back, in a nicely warmed brake van, was uneventful. I was booked to work the 'salt train' 6Z23 a couple of weeks later (overtime, on my rest day), signing on at 11:35. The train didn't even manage to get as far as Blackburn and was reported running 3 hours late due to another 'hot box'. The job was cancelled and I signed off at 16.40.

One of the most delightful runs I had over the line as a guard was on 8 February 1977, working 7M86 St Blazey to Carlisle, headed by a Class 47. It was a very heavy train, with fifty-four equal to sixty-eight wagons totalling 1062 tonnes. I signed on to work the 'salt train' but it was cancelled yet again. We left Blackburn at 13:10, with a short delay at Wilpshire owing to reports of sheep on the line. The weather was bright and sunny, though cold. I'd brought my camera and took quite a few photos from the brake van as we made our slow progress up the 'Long Drag' to Blea Moor. We arrived at Kingmoor Yard at 16:40 and took the loco to get fuel. Then it was a bus back into Carlisle and 'home pass'.

The following day I signed on to do the same job with 6Z23 and we ran as booked, with no hot boxes. Our loco was 40.036 with driver Jack Lightbown and secondman Norman Heap. It was a big train, with forty wagons and 933 tonnes behind the Class 40's drawbar. We were told we were changing over at Garsdale, where we arrived at 14:58. We were away south in just 2 minutes with 40.024 on 7F893

View from the brake van as 7M86 runs through Ribblehead station, with the viaduct looking ahead, 9 February 1977.

View from inside the brake van crossing Ribblehead Viaduct, with Ingleborough beyond, 9 February 1977.

Carlisle – Warrington, with fifty-six equal to fifty-nine and 712 tonnes. We did a similar move the day after working 7Z75 Severn Tunnel Junction–Carlisle with 47.474 as far as Appleby where we swapped with Carlisle men to work 7F93 back, with 40.123. We had forty-five equal to forty-nine wagons, totalling 756 tonnes. The pattern repeated itself the following day, this time changing over at Long Meg.

I was enjoying life as a guard on the Settle–Carlisle but the combination of travelling from Adlington to Blackburn, and the unsociable hours, made me think of a change. At the end of February I noticed a signalling vacancy in the Bolton area – Bullfield West – and decided to go for it. I didn't get the Bullfield West vacancy, which had already been filled. But I was told I'd been appointed signalman 'Class

A' at Astley Bridge Junction, and my training would start on 12 April. This was even better as the box was a single turn, opening at 07:20 and switching out at 16:20, with an hour's booked overtime each day. I was already competent on basic railway operating procedures and the Rule Book, so my training period was relatively short. I started at Astley Bridge Junction on Wednesday 1 June to train the box with relief signalman Bob Lawson – and took over on 8 June.

My last job as a guard was, appropriately, a Carlisle turn. I was teamed with driver Ken McDonagh on 6L46 – so fully fitted – and the journey was uneventful. But my years as a guard at Blackburn were anything but uneventful and I'll never forget the men I worked with, even when they occasionally tried to kill me!

CHAPTER 7

A Line Under Threat: 1963–1989

Beeching's impact

The Settle–Carlisle Line was proposed for closure in the Beeching Report (*The Re-shaping of British Railways*) published in 1963. The report suggested that Settle and Appleby were 'borderline' in terms of economic viability; Appleby had some traffic northwards and Settle similarly had a fairly healthy business for southbound passenger traffic. Beeching's proposal was to close the central section between Settle and Appleby, retaining 'stubs' from Carlisle to Appleby and Settle Junction to Settle. There was a major outcry in Dales communities and the closure proposals were resisted by local MPs and councils.

Whilst the Beeching proposal did not proceed in its entirety, all local stations were closed in May 1970, leaving only Appleby and Settle open. The service was down to three trains a day, one of which ran in the middle of the night. The Skipton to Colne line closed in January 1970. Services from Blackburn to Hellifield had already ceased as far back as 1962 though the line remained open for freight and diversions. In 1977 the through trains from London to Glasgow were replaced by a Nottingham via Leeds to Glasgow service.

Steam ended on BR in 1968. The Settle–Carlisle Line was chosen as part of the route of the 'farewell special' on 11 August 1968. The train ran from Liverpool via Manchester and Blackburn, using Black 5 45110 for the Liverpool to Manchester leg, handing over to Britannia Pacific 70013 *Oliver Cromwell* for the remainder of the run to Carlisle via the S&C. Returning from Carlisle the train was hauled by a pair of Black 5s, 44781 and 44871, as far as Manchester, where 45110 took over for the final stage. Thousands of enthusiasts turned out to watch and photograph the so-called 'Fifteen Guinea Special'. Roads in the Dales ground to a halt with the weight of traffic! Most of us who were out that day assumed we'd never see steam on the Settle–Carlisle again. How wrong we were proved to be.

The line develops as a diversionary route

Despite the loss of the local stations, which caused considerable hardship to many small communities, the 1970s were a period of mixed fortunes for the line. Electrification of the West Coast Main Line north of Preston meant that a large amount of freight was diverted via Settle, with electric-hauled trains branching off the main line at Farington Junction, just south of Preston, where diesel locos replaced them for the gruelling journey via Blackburn, Hellifield and Settle to Carlisle. At the same time, the West Coast Main Line was frequently closed for

Traffic chaos! The last day of steam, 11 August 1968, saw thousands of enthusiasts heading to the Settle–Carlisle line to see the last trains. VERNON SIDLOW

A Class 25 heads a diverted Stranraer–Euston empty van train, near Armathwaite. April 1983.

entire weekends while electrification work took place, necessitating diversion of many passenger, parcels and fast freight services.

Yet behind the apparent vitality, a major threat was looming. The passenger service was unattractive to local passengers. The electrification work wouldn't last forever, and once completed the line's role as a regular diversionary route would be lessened considerably. However, although electrification was completed in 1974 the Settle–Carlisle was still required for unfitted, and slow, freight trains as BR had removed all catch-points on the route over Shap as part of the modernization process. It was to be several years before partially fitted trains became a thing of the past on BR. I was still working them as a guard at Blackburn, over the Settle–Carlisle Line, in the late 1970s (Chapter 6). However, by the early 1980s partially fitted freight trains had become largely a thing of the past. Would closure be back on the agenda? As we've seen, the Beeching proposal to close the line north of Settle Junction was successfully resisted. Instead, a process of 'closure by stealth' took place, with services reduced, stations closed, and trains diverted to other routes.

The Ribblehead Viaduct issue

Rumours began to grow that Ribblehead Viaduct was in poor structural condition and would require millions to be spent to maintain its ability to carry trains. During the 1970s BR's bridge engineers had begun to raise concerns about the condition of the structure and went as far to develop four alternative options, three of which involved a completely new structure (the designs are on display in the Ribblehead Visitor Centre). A high-level meeting took place at The London Midland Region's Euston headquarters on 18 May 1980 to discuss the line's future. Minutes of the meeting make fascinating reading. They note that the object of the meeting was 'to review the future of the Blackburn–Hellifield and Settle–Carlisle Lines and discuss the action to be taken in respect of Ribblehead Viaduct which is difficult and expensive to maintain and is now in urgent need of major repair or replacement.'

The minutes record that the representatives of all the different sectors, including planning, freight, operations, chief civil engineers and finance 'all emphasized the need for the lines to be kept open'. A key issue was the requirement for the line to be used as a diversionary route but also for what was then seen as a developing market for freight.

The meeting spent a considerable amount of time discussing the future of Ribblehead Viaduct, which was regarded by the chief civil engineer's team as 'life expired'. The favoured solution would be a new single line structure engineered for speeds of up to 60mph, though other options would be considered including refurbishment of the existing structure and a new two-track viaduct. If a new structure were the chosen option, the original viaduct would be retained as an ancient monument. The meeting also considered re-signalling of parts of the route, between Kirkby Stephen and Horton-in-Ribblesdale.

Yet a year later it was becoming clear that the tide of opinion within BR had changed. Whether this was a voluntary shift of opinion or one forced on a reluctant BR by Government remains an unanswered question. Yet the remarkable unanimity amongst senior managers from all key sectors of the London Midland Region, just a year earlier, suggests that BR was an unwilling actor in the developing closure saga. In the previous year Mrs Thatcher had been elected, heading a Conservative government determined to bring public sector finances under control. It seemed highly likely that loss-making routes, such as Settle–Carlisle, would have little future in the new free market environment which Thatcher was determined to develop.

DalesRail begins and steam returns

It wasn't all bad news: in 1975 a new initiative led by the Yorkshire Dales National Park saw the introduction of DalesRail trains, operating at weekends. They proved remarkably successful, thanks to the energy and enthusiasm of people like Colin Speakman. DalesRail had effectively been kick-started

One of the first 'DalesRail' trains stops at Dent, 1975.
SCRT

by the initiative of the Ramblers' Association a year earlier, when they chartered a train to take nearly 600 walkers from Leeds into the Dales, calling at Garsdale, Kirkby Stephen and Appleby (see 'The Ramblers' Railway' by Colin Speakman, in the *FoSCL Journal* August 2018). Volunteers, many from the Keighley and Worth Valley Railway, sold tickets on the train and provided a refreshment service in the guard's van.

> So successful was the initial project, with packed trains in both directions – ninety-nine people were recorded catching the second Saturday southbound service at Kirkby Stephen – that the experiment had to be extended for three further weekends.
>
> Colin Speakman, 'The Ramblers' Railway', *Settle & Carlisle Railway Journal*, August 2018

The success of the charter train led the Yorkshire Dales National Park Committee to fund BR to allow trains to call at Horton-in-Ribblesdale, Ribblehead, Dent, Garsdale and Kirkby Stephen. The national park contributed £5,000 with Cumbria adding a further £500 for Kirkby Stephen, which was outside the park boundary. For this remarkably small

figure, the stations were brought back into use for a series of special trains beginning in May 1975. A feature of the service – branded as DalesRail – was that local people were able to use the service to go south to Skipton and Leeds on the Saturday service. The following year saw more stations brought back into service – Langwathy, Lazonby and Kirkoswald and Armathwaite, thanks to the support of Cumbria County Council.

A further boost to the line and its communities came from the growth of steam-hauled charter trains, the first running behind LNER V2 *Green Arrow* in 1978. The Settle–Carlisle was hugely attractive; the combination of steam traction and the rugged Dales landscape was a winner for the growing number of charter train operators. For some years trains stopped at Appleby for water, giving passengers the chance to look round the pretty Westmorland town – and spend their money. Ironically, as the closure issue became more centre-stage, so did the attractiveness of the steam specials, with people anxious to ride over the line behind steam, before it was too late.

A short-lived increase in the number of Notting-ham–Glasgow trains via Settle gave the line a temporary boost before their withdrawal in 1981.

Preserved Southern Pacific City of Wells *takes water at Garsdale on a southbound 'Cumbrian Mountain Express', March 1983.*

LMS Pacific 46229 Duchess of Hamilton *heads north on a 'Cumbrian Mountain Express' near Selside in 1983.*

Yet while the success of DalesRail, the steam charters and a slightly improved through service gave campaigners a feeling that they were achieving results, there was a sense of an underlying threat which could result in all the gains of the mid-70s being lost.

The threat emerges

The most palpable sign of BR's intentions came in 1981 when it was announced that the three daily trains from Nottingham to Glasgow would be diverted via Manchester and the West Coast Main Line. This came into effect the following year, leaving the Settle–Carlisle with a basic service of two trains in each direction, weekdays only. Many rail campaigners claimed that this was the start of the run-down of the line that would lead to eventual closure – 'closure by stealth', as services were reduced and passenger numbers would inevitably decline. BR spokesmen at the time denied this was the case, though the evidence suggests that they

were being 'economical with the truth'. As early as August 1981 BR had prepared an internal document called *The Case Study for the Closure of the Settle–Carlisle Route*, though it wasn't discovered, through an internal 'leak', until nearly two years later. James Towler (*see* below), in *The Battle for the Settle–Carlisle*, makes the point that all the reassurances made by BR to the local authorities and Transport Users' Consultative Committees in the early 1980s were based on deception, or, in his words, 'were lacking in candour'. It is very hard to disagree with that assessment.

By the autumn of 1981 the only surviving intermediate stations, Appleby and Settle, were handling tiny numbers of passengers. Appleby averaged a mere fifty. Settle was similar, with many local people choosing to use the nearby Giggleswick station on the Skipton–Morecambe route, changing at Lancaster for the north.

At the same time, the amount of freight over the line dwindled to virtually nothing. The last scheduled through freight ran in 1983. As Martin Bairstow

A 'Peak' Class diesel pulls into Appleby in the late 1970s with a northbound train.

CURRENT SITUATION ON CLOSURE

3.1 The LMR Report has been circulated to Headquarters Chief Officers and the General Managers of the Eastern & Scottish Regions. There is general agreement that closure of the line must be progressed.

3.2 The view of the London Midland Region is that the proposal should remain confidential until the through passenger services have been diverted in May 1982, as otherwise this diversion could be barred until the completion of statutory procedures. After May 1982, the closure proposal would go to consultation and the region will initiate the closure procedure.

Whilst continuing to deny they intended to close the line, it was clear that BR was determined to get rid of the Settle–Carlisle when the opportunity arose, as this note of an internal meeting shows.

comments in *The Leeds, Settle and Carlisle Railway*, 'the line appeared doomed'. And as far as BR was concerned, it was. A highly confidential internal note of a meeting in December 1981 confirmed that BR's firm intention was to close the line.

Friends of Settle–Carlisle (FoSCL) is formed and the campaign gathers momentum

The formation of Friends of the Settle–Carlisle Line (FoSCL) in June 1981 was a direct response to growing fears that BR was about to issue formal closure notices, despite their public denials. Its first secretary was the energetic Graham Nuttall of Colne, to whom we shall return later.

Shortly afterwards, the Friends joined forces with the Railway Development Society and Transport 2000 to create the Settle–Carlisle Joint Action Committee. It had the backing of local authorities along the line led by Cumbria County Council, supported by North Yorkshire and Lancashire, with the West Yorkshire Passenger Transport Executive. In addition, its work was backed by James Towler, chairman of the Yorkshire area Transport Users' Consultative Committee (YTUCC).

The Joint Action Committee brought together not just three organizations but also a powerful combination of individuals whose combined talents

SETTLE/CARLISLE
Joint Action Committee

The **CLOSURE** of the **SETTLE-CARLISLE RAILWAY**

BR has now published a closure notice for the above line as is required by the 1962 Transport Act. The fight to save the line must now re-double its efforts and it is up to each and every one of us to object and produce arguments as to why the line should not be closed.

THE NOTICE OF CLOSURE HAS BEEN PUBLISHED, YOU MUST OBJECT IN WRITING

NOW.

BEFORE FEB.4TH

YOU SHOULD SEND YOUR OBJECTION TO ONE OF THE ADDRESSES LISTED OVERLEAF:

Some early publicity material from FoSCL.

More early FoSCL publicity.

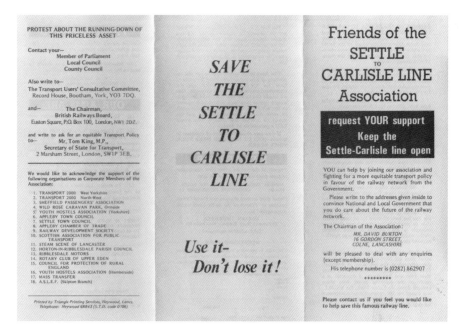

resulted in one of the most effective transport campaigns the UK has ever seen. John Whitelegg and Peter Horton of Transport 2000 were seasoned campaigners who understood the importance of mobilizing people. Richard Watts of the Railway Development Society was a highly knowledgeable railway enthusiast and campaigner who could rebut many of BR's technical arguments. Within the Friends of the Settle–Carlisle Line was a range of talented individuals including Brian Sutcliffe (who went on to become chairman of FoSCL) and legal experts such as Edward Album.

Alongside the voluntary campaigning, the importance of the formal procedures could not be overestimated. The TUCCs had been established under the Transport Act of 1948 and were often criticized for being 'toothless'; however, James Towler had sharp teeth and a forceful personality. He wasn't going to sit back and see the Settle–Carlisle Line close without a fight. He had become chairman of YTUCC in 1979 when it was becoming clear that, after a period of relatively few closures after the Beeching era, a new phase of cuts was on the way. From 1981 onwards, Towler was advising the anti-closure lobby on procedural issues, though as yet no formal intention to close the line had been announced.

FoSCL leaflet from early days of the campaign.

BR puts its cards on the table

The tensions within BR over the closure proposal, and other wider policy issues, make for a fascinating story. By 1984 the official BR position had hardened and in June 1984 BR prepared an outline of their case for closure to the North West and Yorkshire Transport Users' Consultative Committees (TUCCs). In its introduction, the paper states:

> The section of line between Settle Junction and Carlisle (Petteril Bridge Junction) is expensive to operate and maintain and requires heavy expenditure on essential renewals to Ribblehead Viaduct and four other bridges. Essential track renewals are required to maintain the line to passenger standards. It is therefore proposed that this section of line be closed for passenger trains by re-routing the existing through regular passenger service between Leeds and Carlisle via Giggleswick, Carnforth, Oxenholme and Penrith, thereby avoiding this considerable financial expenditure.

The document indicates that the existing weekday service was down to two through trains each day between Leeds and Carlisle, in each direction, with an additional morning service from Settle to Leeds. There was no Sunday service. Each of the through trains would be re-routed via Carnforth and Penrith and the morning commuter train from Settle to Leeds would start from Skipton.

The first clear indication that BR was going to proceed with closure of the line had come a year earlier, in August 1983, when BR published its five-year corporate plan. The Settle–Carlisle did not feature on the map of the future network.

Yet in one of the quirks of a very quirky story, later in 1983 BR appointed a manager to handle the Settle–Carlisle issue who was to become legendary. He was career railwayman Ron Cotton, who was highly respected by his colleagues. Whether this move by BR was coincidental, or whether some subversive elements within BR had their own agenda, it's still difficult to say. Ron Cotton suggests (see below) it may have had more to do with internal politics. While Cotton's brief was to manage the

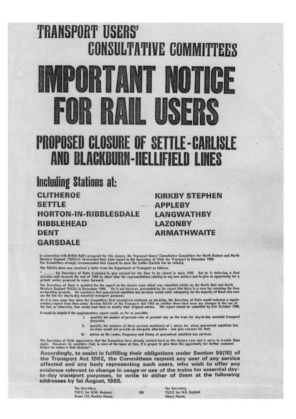

Transport Users' Consultative Committee poster asking for representations regarding the proposed closure.

run-down and closure of the line, he actually did the opposite. Through energetic marketing and promotion, usage of the line grew four-fold. If Cotton's job was to close the line, he was going about it in a very odd way.

Now BR played their card by appointing a manager to oversee the closure. I don't know if this was a Wild Card or a Joker, because the manager they appointed was a man with a track record based on marketing. This was Ron Cotton, a maverick manager who was nearing the end of his career. At this time there were only two trains each way over the line, no more than five coaches and loco hauled, but within a short period of time Ron Cotton's marketing skills had increased the train frequency to three each way, with up to ten coaches. On summer Saturdays it was not unusual to have a relief morning train from Leeds. This impacted on the *Friends* who by now

Discover Leeds–Settle–Carlisle! An example of BR publicity promoting the line, from the early 1980s.

were travelling on the trains collecting pro forma objections for the TUCC closure hearings from a captive audience. We also did local leaflet distributions for each new offer which Ron Cotton generated. At this time some members of the committee did not trust Ron Cotton, this sometimes left me in a minority on the Committee, but I believed you could not look a gift horse in the mouth, fortunately time was to confirm my belief.

Brian Sutcliffe, former Chairman of FoSCL, in
FoSCL newsletter, August 2011

'England's Greatest Scenic Route' – or a suitable case for closure? BR publicity in the early 1980s.

Ron Cotton took early retirement from BR (*see* Chapter 10) and has kept in touch with groups such as FoSCL. In an interview with the author he explained that his appointment to oversee the closure of the line was effectively an act of spite by a BR manager who wanted him 'out of the way' and thought that

giving him a particularly uncongenial task would temper his commercial enthusiasm. It had the opposite effect, with Cotton determined to do his best to promote the line. If that made the case for closure more difficult, so be it. Ron Cotton mentioned that throughout his time on the Settle–Carlisle, where he oversaw additional services, station re-openings and a range of marketing promotions, nobody in BR told him to stop! So he carried on... and the manager who gave him 'the poisoned chalice' only survived a few months after Cotton's transfer, when he was effectively dismissed – leaving Ron with a completely free hand, which he used to remarkable advantage.

Railway closure proceedings are nothing if they are not highly formalized; professionally informed rail campaigners have succeeded on more than one occasion in at least temporarily halting a closure on a technicality. By the 1980s, the main legislation guiding railway closures was the Transport Act of 1962 (successor to the Transport Act of 1948) which laid down procedures for establishing TUCCs and also the grounds for approving closures, which boiled down to 'hardship'. The Settle–Carlisle Line was, so it was thought, covered by two TUCCs – the Yorkshire and North-West committees. But, as we shall see, this assumption was to be proved incorrect as the closure campaign gathered pace.

Closure notices issued – and objections sustained

The official blow came just before Christmas, 1983. BR issued a notice to close the railway between Settle Junction and Petteril Bridge Junction (Carlisle), and to close Settle and Appleby stations. Trains would be diverted via Carnforth with stops at Giggleswick and Penrith. A seven-week period was allowed for objections. Surprisingly, the total number of objections received by the Yorkshire Transport Users Consultative Committee (YTUCC) came to only 2,369, slightly less than the proposal to close Goole to Gilberdyke, which had been issued at the same time.

Early in 1984 the secretary of the YTUCC noticed a discrepancy between the wording of the notice and that of the 1962 Act. Closure notices invited objections from 'any user of the service which it is proposed to discontinue'; the Act said, 'any user of any service affected'.

The implications of this were that users of stations outside the 'core' route proposed for closure, i.e.

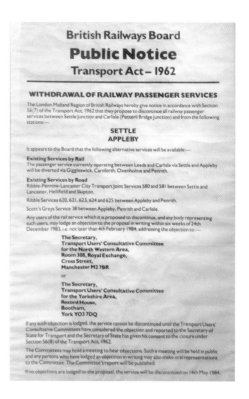

The official closure notice. MARK RAND

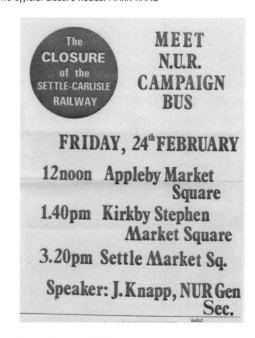

The National Union of Railwaymen played a key part in the campaign. Their general secretary, Jimmy Knapp, spoke at a well-attended meeting in Appleby during the campaign.

DalesRail leader Howard Hammersley with Northern's Matt Beaton look at some early DalesRail publicity at the naming of Northern Class 156 train Lancashire DalesRail. RICHARD WATTS

A group of S&C campaigners at Appleby. Councillor Bill Cameron (far left) and Ruth Annison (far right).

Settle Junction to Petteril Bridge Junction, were 'affected' by the closure. These included Long Preston, Hellifield and Gargrave. The 07:39 'morning commuter' train from Settle to Leeds would clearly be affected by the closure and the users of the three stations would lose their service to Skipton and Leeds. In addition, users of DalesRail and the growing number of steam excursions had been denied the opportunity to object, as users of services that clearly were 'affected' by the closure.

Further anomalies in BR's case appeared later in the year, as campaigners pointed out that the eight 'DalesRail' stations that had re-opened for the ramblers' specials should have been included in the closure notice.

BR's case was increasingly tenuous and campaigners racked up the pressure through MPs, local authorities and the media. As Martin Bairstow records,

> Reluctantly BR conceded, announcing in April 1984 that a revised notice would be issued widening the scope for objections and including eight DalesRail stations plus Clitheroe on the Blackburn to Hellifield which was used on about six days a year.
>
> Martin Bairstow, *The Leeds, Settle & Carlisle Railway*

This applied to both the Settle Line and also Goole to Gilberydyke, which had used the same, incorrect, wording.

A further seven-week period for objections was given, from May to July 1984. The number of objections to the Goole Line closure increased modestly from 2,485 to 2,570. However, the number of objections to the Settle–Carlisle closure shot up from 2,369 to 11,117.

Whilst the pool of objectors had widened the Friends of the Settle–Carlisle Line had become much better organized and there was a greater public awareness that the line was under threat. The Friends had been busy handing out information leaflets and pro formas on regular scheduled trains and specials for immediate completion, collecting them on the spot for bulk delivery to the TUCCs.

The anti-closure campaign had developed with a twin-track strategy. On the one hand there was the formal process channelled through the TUCCs, with particularly strong support coming from the Yorkshire TUCC under James Towler. On the other hand there was the much more spontaneous campaign of The Joint Action Committee, which owed much to the example of contemporary community campaigns beyond transport. There were differences of emphasis within the TUCCs, particularly between the two main committees, covering Yorkshire and the North-West. The latter, under the chairmanship of Mrs Olive Clarke, tended to take a more conciliatory approach towards BR and interpreted its role more narrowly than its Yorkshire counterpart, with Mrs Clarke stressing her role as an impartial chairman.

The Government smelt a possible weakness in the campaign and proposed to redraw the TUCC boundaries so that the Yorkshire and North-East committees would merge, losing any responsibility for the Settle–Carlisle Line. Although the merger went ahead, with Towler as chair of the combined body, he made sure that he hung on to the Skipton to Ribblehead section, which had previously come under his jurisdiction.

Whilst having two objection periods for the same closure was unusual but not exceptional, another legal technicality forced a third objection. It was realized that a short section of the line near Ais Gill, despite having no actual stations, lay within the territory covered by the North-East TUCC, which had not been officially consulted about the closure. BR conceded on the technicality and allowed a further seven weeks for further objections. Any objection received during the first and second objection periods were treated as valid with no need for the signatories to re-submit. However, it was a further opportunity for the campaigners to re-double their efforts and collect yet more objections to the closure, from any part of the line and from any users affected.

The revised proposals, issued early in 1986, clarified BR's intentions. Their proposal was to discontinue services between Settle Junction and Carlisle (Petteril Bridge Junction) and between Blackburn and Hellifield. This would result in the

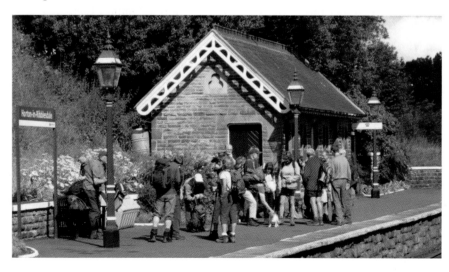

Walkers at Horton-in-Ribblesdale, 1980s.
RICHARD WATTS

BR plans to close railway are 'utterly incoherent'

BRITISH Rail's arguments for closing the scenic Settle-Carlisle railway line were described as "utterly incoherent" yesterday.

Robin Sisson, a teacher at Bradford Grammar School, was giving evidence at the Appleby inquiry into reasons against closure of the route.

He said he had used the line for 30 years and had often taken parties of schoolchildren on it.

"Life will be incomparably poorer without the Settle-Carlisle and the service now operating is the best since World War Two," said Dr Sisson.

"It is not just a simple heritage matter, but an important transport consideration and I cannot understand why a clear distinction is not made between operating balance sheets and the maintenance costs of this line. BR's arguments are utterly incoherent."

Alice Palmer, a retired history and careers teacher from Appleby Grammar School –

now a large comprehensive serving a wide area on the line — said further education was now a very viable option through the increased number of trains.

"Without the Settle-Carlisle as a part of the BR network, our children will become more disadvantaged in their job opportunities," Miss Palmer said.

by NWT Correspondent

Peter Simpson, chairman of Eden District Council's policy and resources committee, also emphasised that bus routes to connect the stations would lead to extended journeys with great problems in harsh winter weather.

"It is essential to keep the line open as a regular means of communication and part of our wider economic future. It has a key role as a diversionary route and as part of the Channel Tunnel network, which we must be part of to gain its advantages," he said.

He added that the number of users had increased nearly tenfold since 1985, but it was extremely difficult to get any figures and information from BR on the costings.

James Towler, a former chairman of the North East Transport Users' Consultative Committee, said the whole closure procedure had become such a "dog's breakfast" that the only logical and just solution was that British Rail should publish a new closure proposal after all concerned had decided what they wanted to do.

The hearing will continue at Appleby today, then move to Settle next Friday and Saturday. It is being held jointly by the North West and North East Transport Users' Consultative Committees.

It is understood that two major concerns are interested in buying the line, but 10,000 users and supporters have written to the committees, urging that the line should stay open.

HOWARD BARLOW

Press cutting from North West Times.

closure of stations at Settle, Horton-in-Ribblesdale, Ribblehead, Dent, Garsdale, Kirkby Stephen, Appleby, Langwathby, Lazonby and Kirkoswald and Armthwaite. There would be three direct services between Leeds and Carlisle, routed via Giggleswick and Carnforth. As a sop to the people of Appleby there would be two additional bus services between Appleby and Penrith, 'assuming the Secretary of State makes such a service a condition of his consent to close the line.' All three TUCCs, including the North-East as well as Yorkshire and the North-West, were charged with handling the objections.

The third period of objections gave more opportunities for the campaigners. As it turned out, only 69 objections were received by the North-East TUCC but the total number of objections to all three TUCCs increased to 22,150, including one dog. This was an all-time record for the number of objections received to a rail closure proposal and a huge testament to the hard and determined campaign put up by the Friends and their allies. The dog in question – Ruswarp – was the faithful friend of Graham Nuttall, first secretary of Friends of the Settle–Carlisle Line.

The press had a field day, with the national media full of stories about the '22,000 and a dog' protesting over the closure. It had the feeling of an Ealing comedy to it and the campaigners were savvy enough to exploit the opportunities as much as possible.

BR itself continued a dual strategy of arguing that the line was 'uneconomic' whilst doing all it could, through Ron Cotton, to promote it. The publicity surrounding the closure proceedings had created huge interest in the line, bringing out a natural sympathy for the 'underdog'. Special fares offers were introduced and additional trains were provided, with trains being strengthened to cater for increased demand.

The public hearings took place between March and April 1986, held in Appleby, followed by Carlisle, Settle, Skipton and Leeds. BR was represented at each of the hearings by Ron Cotton, Michael Harrison QC and a solicitor. The chairing of the hearings was split between James Towler and Olive Clarke of the North West TUCC.

A total of 392 objectors spoke or had their objections read to the hearing. The procedure raised questions as to what constituted 'hardship'. Would the loss of the train service and consequent leisure opportunities count as hardship? Many objectors highlighted the historical heritage of the line and spoke of the many people who died during its construction. While this appealed to the public, it was not pertinent to the tightly drawn criteria for refusing consent to closure.

James Towler, in The Battle for the Settle–Carlisle, gives us a stirring account of the hearings and some of the objectors' arguments. The local authorities had formed a joint lobby and Councillor Bill Cameron of Cumbria Country Council gave a powerful defence of the line and condemned BR's 'wanton neglect' of the route. As Towler records:

> He summarised Cumbria's objection which was on five main grounds: hardship to those living or requiring access to the region, particularly Appleby; the termination of DalesRail; the increase in journey times between Leeds and Carlisle via Carnforth; loss of jobs in Cumbria with little prospect of alternative employment; and the loss of the diversionary route for the West Coast Main Line, the alternative via the Cumbrian Coast or the use of buses would result in hardship.

BR's Ron Cotton responded to Councillor Cameron's comments, suggesting that the Coast route would be an acceptable alternative. It was known that this line required upgrading and Cumbria County Council had been lobbying for investment in the line. Towler records what he described as a 'bombshell' when Cameron said, 'I [i.e. the County Council] was offered £7 million if my council would not object to the Settle–Carlisle closure at a meeting with BR in 1981'. To their credit, the councillors rejected this crude bribe and continued to lobby strongly for the retention of the Settle–Carlisle Line *and* investment in the Coast Route.

The final hearing took place in Leeds Town Hall, starting on 26 April. By the time the 'Leeds Marathon' (as Towler described it) had ended, the TUCCs had heard 290 objections. They had come from a remarkable range of organizations and individuals. As well as the polished and carefully crafted submissions from the local authorities and Joint Action Committee, groups such as the Youth Hostels Association, Council for the Protection of Rural England, Yorkshire Wildlife Trust, Friends of the Earth, business groups and trades unions added their objections. MPs from all sides of the political spectrum spoke against the closure, highlighting the impact it would have on their constituents. The campaign received support from MPs across the whole of the country.

The business community gets engaged

An important feature of the Settle–Carlisle Line is the high dependence on the railway for the survival of many small businesses – pubs, cafés, guesthouses and a wide range of ancillary businesses. As well as bringing visitors into the Dales community, the line provides an important means of getting to larger towns and cities for business and leisure. Many small business people took the decision to relocate to the Dales because they knew there was a rail link to the outside world. Their contribution to saving the line could not be over-estimated.

The key figure in galvanizing the business community was Ruth Annison, co-proprietor (with her late

husband Peter) of the W.R. Outhwaite Ropemakers at Hawes (see Chapter 10). The Settle–Carlisle Business Liaison Group (BLG) was formed in 1985 by which time the threat was very clear. In January 1987 the BLG organized a delegation to No. 10 Downing Street, taking along a basket of local produce to demonstrate the breadth of the Dales local economy that was at risk from the railway's closure.

> Our basket of local produce included Wensleydale cheese, biscuits, cake and face cream. It was deemed a 'security risk' and we had to pay a visit to Cannon Street Police Station to explain that we weren't dangerous terrorists!

> Ruth Annison, interview with the auhor, August 2018

During the public hearings, many of the local authority objectors spoke of the importance of the Settle–Carlisle Line to their local economies. Councillor Beth Graham, a North Yorkshire county councillor and also chairman of Settle Town Council, told the hearing about two surveys they had conducted, which demonstrated the importance of the railway to Settle. Some 13 percent of all visitors to the town came by rail and a further 36 percent of visitors to Settle used the railway during their stay. She said that 32 percent of visitors to the town said their main reason for visiting Settle was the railway.

Local authority support

During the hearing period, the local authorities capitalized on the huge public interest in the line and announced that they were willing to offer financial support to improved services on the line. BR co-operated in the venture and in addition to a new twice-daily service from Skipton to Carlisle, eight stations – closed in 1970 and at the time only used by DalesRail services, were re-opened for regular traffic. The new service performed better than expected and by May 1987 the additional trains were extended to and from Leeds and fully integrated into the timetable. Initially, they had been run as 'charter' services and did not appear in the public timetable.

The 'Joint Councils' group of local authorities brought together the key public bodies along the line, presenting strong evidence-based arguments to keep the line open on social and economic grounds, much of the detailed research being done by the late Peter Robinson, of Cumbria County Council. He was assisted by local economic development officers from Cumbria as well as Rural Development Commission and National Park officers.

After the hearings

The members of the TUCC committees must have felt an enormous sense of relief at the end of the hearings – they had heard many more objections than any other previous enquiry in the history of railway closure proposals. They needed a rest, but though it was to be short-lived. There was the Herculean job of collating the evidence and preparing a report that would be agreed by both TUCCs. Interestingly, the views of the two committees – at one point diametrically opposed – had come much closer during the hearing period. The wars of the roses had come to an end!

The Yorkshire committee met on 11 June to consider the next steps, under the chairmanship of James Towler. The members were unanimous in their opposition to the closure. Difficulties arose once more with the North-West TUCC, which took a more conciliatory approach than that adopted by their Yorkshire neighbours. A lengthy process of negotiation ensued, which led to a report with which both committees were comfortable.

The TUCCs finalized their joint report in December and held two concurrent press conferences to announce their findings, on 17 December. The North-West committee held theirs in Appleby with the Yorkshire TUCC holding their conference in Settle.

Their recommendation was to refuse consent to closure 'strongly and emphatically'.

> On the basis of the undoubted hardship that closure of the line would cause, together with the strength of the commercial case presented for its retention, the committees strongly and emphatically recommend that consent to British Rail's proposal to close the Settle–Carlisle Line be refused.
>
> North-East and North-West TUCCs Joint Report, 12 December 1986

As the TUCCs published their case against closure, a few days later BR produced its own justification for abandoning the line and re-routing Leeds–Carlisle trains via Carnforth. Martin Bairstow made the acid comment:

> Speaking as a chartered accountant I can say that this read like nonsense. Costs of maintaining a Leeds to Carlisle service via Settle were weighted heavily by depreciation on Sprinter DMUS (diesel multiple units)... but if the service were routed via Carnforth, these trains were apparently free.
>
> Martin Bairstow

The key issue in favour of abandoning the line was the alleged condition of Ribblehead Viaduct. BR quoted a figure of £15 million for infrastructure work, most of which was the repair of the viaduct. These estimates were challenged by independent civil engineers. One, speaking at the closure hearing, suggested the cost of repairing the viaduct would be less than £1 million. On 11 February 1987 David Maclean MP initiated an adjournment debate in the House of Commons and called on the Government to commission an independent study of the condition of the viaduct.

The following year, 1987, would – or so all sides expected – see a final decision reached on the line's future. It didn't happen. The initial assumption, following publication of the TUCC's joint report, was that the Secretary of State would reach a decision on the line's future within 'three or four months'. Everyone waited, and waited. The delay might have not been unrelated to expectations of a General Election that year. What campaigners didn't know was that behind the scenes in the Government – at the highest levels – there was growing concern about the political fall-out from closing the line. An

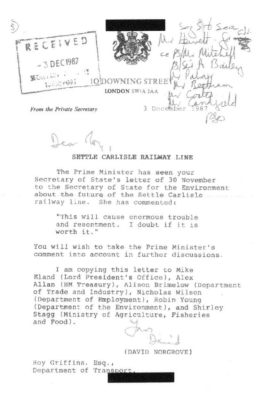

Internal note from the Prime Minister's office in December 1988 raising political concerns about the closure. EDWARD ALBUM

internal note from the Prime Minister's office (dated 3 December 1987) suggests that Mrs Thatcher was unconvinced of the case (see below).

Meanwhile, the line continued to flourish; in large part thanks to BR's attempts to close the line, combined with their own marketing efforts and those of the line's supporters, trains were full. BR's manager for the line, Ron Cotton, announced his retirement early in the year. Before his departure in February he allocated two eight-coach sets of coaches with powerful Class 47 locomotives, for use on the line. This gave the route a major boost in capacity, which was desperately needed.

Setbacks and challenges

The departure of Ron Cotton was a blow to the line, even though he had done his best to faithfully reflect the views of his employer, BR. He went on to play a very positive role in the future development of the line. Only a few weeks after Cotton's departure, James Towler's period as chairman of the TUCC was coming to an end that year. At the time, it was normal for the chair's tenure to be renewed, but on this occasion, it was not to be, and Towler's contract came to an end on 31 March. This caused a furore amongst the committee members and the anti-closure campaigners. It also reached the national media including *The Times*.

BR improved the timetable in May 1987, with five through trains in each direction. A General Election took place in June 1987, with the Conservatives re-elected. A new Secretary of State for Transport, Paul Channon, was appointed, although David Mitchell retained his ministerial portfolio for railways. In July the House of Commons Transport Select Committee recommended that the Government should safeguard the line's future by making a one-off grant to BR for repairs to Ribblehead Viaduct. However, David Mitchell told campaigners that the money would not be forthcoming.

While BR's case looked increasingly flimsy, with politicians swayed by the huge tide of opposition to the closure, victory was still not within the campaigners' grasp. However, they had a fairly sympathetic minister in the House of Commons, David Mitchell, who was under huge pressure from the highly professional lobbying of both the local authorities and the Friends of the Settle–Carlisle Line. He responded to the local authorities' pressure by asking how much they would be willing to invest in the line were it to be saved. Cumbria County Council and several of the district councils along the line took the lead, aiming for a target of £500m. West Yorkshire Passenger Transport executive contributed, followed by North Yorkshire County Council. Friends of the Settle–Carlisle Line made a commitment of £15,000, a huge contribution from a purely voluntary body. The National Union of Railwaymen contributed £10,000.

A major setback to the campaign came on 16 May 1988. Despite David Mitchell's apparent sympathy for the campaign, he announced to the House of Commons that he was 'minded' to give consent

The ultimate in train sets!

By TONY LIVESEY

But buyers will need £millions to keep line open

FOR SALE: A train set, track, engines and stations, complete with scenery.

WANTED! Anybody. But must have spare cash — £millions of it.

Yes, the search is on. The Government has signalled the railway sale of the century and up for grabs is the picturesque Settle-Carlisle line.

Not surprisingly, potential buyers' reaction has been as warm as a traditional British Rail pie.

Now the sellers have tossed in another incentive to multi-millionaires who may be mulling the deal over. And the carrot on the stick is . . . Blackburn.

British Rail say if a new owner is found before May, they can run trains into East Lancashire, direct from Carlisle, as the Evening Telegraph revealed yesterday.

But what else will they get for their money?

Dotted

For a start there are 10 stations dotted along the 71-mile line. Throw in a series of buildings and breathtaking bridges — including the notoriously "dodgy" Ribblehead Viaduct — and the package really does form the ultimate possession.

There are snags though. Certain structures, in BR's own words, are "causing concern." Annual maintenance bills are costly to say the least.

There are even a couple of seismic detectors at Long Marton to test for subsidence from nearby abandoned workings!

Centres

BR are prepared to sell two diesels, 20 coaches and even three hopper wagons for use on the line!

But steam buffs are in for a disappointment. BR point out that there are no water tanks or facilities for loading coal along the route.

They add that there are already steam enthusiast centres nearby, at Haworth and Carnforth.

Besides, running steam trains into Carlisle "would create problems" say officials.

That could be a stumbling block for any buyer. Over half of the line's passenger are on "leisure" trips while another 14 per cent are on holiday.

BR say: "There is scope for developing the potential of the line by exploiting opportunities in areas which lie outside British Railways Board's mainstream operations."

Historians

They add that besides appealing to ramblers, rail enthusiasts and people who want a "day out" on the line, they could offer road and rail packages to show travellers areas they can't see from the train alone.

Perhaps, BR also suggest, historians could be treated to tours to towns dating back to the 12th century. County councils will be co-operative, they suggest.

Not for sale, and BR are adamant, are the staff. Seventeen men are required to operate the line with over 50 men to carry out maintenance.

Apart from finding his own men, however, the major obstacle to any deal is straightforward cash.

Is anyone prepared to gamble on the future popularity of this grand old line — and possibly throw Blackburn a tourism lifeline too?

The new owner will have to discuss his rate bill — with FIVE separate councils!

How the press saw it: cutting from North West Times regarding the attempted sale of the line.

to closure but would delay a final decision for six months pending supplementary reports from the TUCC and BR. He also announced that he would then consider transferring the line to the private sector. The Government's argument seemed to be that the Settle–Carlisle Line was a delightful piece of 'heritage', which provided 'pleasure rides for railway archaeologists'.

This proposal was the first attempt to consider privatization of part of the national rail network. It did excite some interest and a company was formed to take over the line. Yet hard economic reality kicked in. The liabilities facing any standalone operation would be huge, far greater than for any existing heritage railway. The large number of tunnels and viaducts, to say nothing of the vicissitudes of the weather, would make any attempt to run the Settle–Carlisle as a commercial venture absurd. Bob Cryer, Labour MP for Keighley and a founder of the Keighley and Worth Valley Railway, told the minister in no uncertain terms that the proposal was unviable.

However, it was a novel proposal that took some of the wind out of the campaigners' sails. BR followed up Mitchell's announcement by saying that it would be willing to sell the Settle–Carlisle Line as a going concern. Lazard was appointed to manage the sale. A prospectus to potential buyers was published by Lazards, which was rather light on detail. It said that trains would be allowed to run on BR infrastructure beyond Settle and Petteril Bridge Junction but under conditions that were regarded as onerous in the extreme. It was suggested that a charitable trust could run the line, though whether a charity or a private business, there would still be major costs involved that could not be met from the farebox. Two Yorkshire businessmen formed 'Cumbrian Railways Ltd' to take over the line but their proposals lacked substance. Eventually, the proposal quietly died.

> People asked whether a privatized Settle and Carlisle would be allowed to link into the national network. Speaking on radio, David Mitchell said there should be no problem as BR and a 'private' railway already shared tracks at Alton near his constituency. This was nonsense. I told him face to face on Garsdale station, that the tracks are as segregated as those at Keighley.
>
> Martin Bairstow, historian

James Towler, in his new role as spokesman for the Railway Development Society's Yorkshire branch, lobbied the TUCCs for a fresh hearing that would take account of the impact on users of new services introduced since 1984. It fell on deaf ears. On 18 June a steam excursion ran from Leeds to Carlisle with what Towler described as 'local MPs, civic dignitaries, media representatives and several hundred ordinary enthusiasts'. The entourage included David Mitchell. Mitchell came under considerable pressure from both the local authority representatives as well as from members of the public who challenged him on his decision to be 'minded' to close the line. Suggestions had been made that he had wanted to issue a reprieve but had been overruled by 'Number 10'.

A few months later, during Mitchell's six-month stay of execution, the British Railways Board (Provincial Sector) issued its 'Financial case for the closure of the Settle–Carlisle railway line (updated)'. This was in response to a request from the Secretary of State for the BRB to submit an updated case for closure. By this time, David Mitchell had left his ministerial post and was replaced by an up-and-coming MP, regarded as an ardent Thatcherite, by the name of Michael Portillo.

The paper presented outline figures covering operating costs and revenue, additional costs for re-signalling, redundancy and infrastructure work. Closing the line would bring an operating profit, based on diversion of trains via Penrith, of £182,000. Retention of the line, with associated investment in renewals, would result in a loss of between £297,000 and £997,000, with additional losses of around £500,000 each year. This did not include redundancy costs of £427,000 and immediate repairs to Ribblehead Viaduct of £200,000 as part of the closure option, nor singling and some redundancy costs of £1.1 m and further costs of Ribblehead Viaduct totalling £2.7m, less contributions from English Heritage and local authorities.

The six-month stay of execution period came and went, with the new minister putting back the final date of 'offers' for the line to 31 October. The TUCCs organized a further round of 'joint meetings in public' during September. The remit of the meetings was criticized by campaigners as being restrictive and biased in favour of BR, whose representatives refused to take questions from the public. Subsequently the TUCCs issued a report which, while reaffirming that they strongly objected to the closure, said little that was new. At about the same time, the 'Joint Councils' group of local authorities along the line issued its own report, which was far more hard-hitting, pointing out the significantly improved performance of the line since closure was first proposed in 1983 as well as inadequacies in BR's own case for closure. The line was now carrying 450,000 passengers a year compared with 93,000 in 1983.

As 1989 dawned, the mood of the campaigners was ambivalent. The arguments had been won,

BR had been made to look mean and incompetent. Yet the mood music coming from Government still suggested that if a private buyer could not be found, closure was inevitable. Councillor Michael Simmons suggested to Portillo that in the absence of a private buyer emerging, a charitable trust could be formed which would involve BR, local authorities and other interests.

What happened on 11 April 1989 was remarkable – a red letter day in the history of rail campaigning. Michael Portillo (then Railways Minister) announced that the Secretary of State for Transport had refused consent to closure.

The statement makes very strange reading. It begins by seeming to accept the logic of BR's case argument, with the final coup de grace about to be made. But it doesn't happen; the line was to be reprieved. The letter says that whilst the Secretary of State accepted that closure of the line would cause 'some hardship to local residents who now rely on it for day-to-day essential transport purposes', he considered that 'provision of guaranteed substitute bus services could adequately cater for many travellers'. The letter continued in a similarly negative vein, giving the impression that it had been prepared by civil servants acting on the assumption that consent would be given to close the line. Only at the end, when the Secretary of State says that he has 'carefully considered all relevant factors and has decided to refuse consent to the Board's proposal' does the reader realize that the campaigners have actually succeeded in stopping the closure.

The response amongst the campaigners was one of jubilation. They had achieved what seemed to be nearly impossible in the dark days of the early 1980s. They had not only stopped the closure of a significant part of the rail network, they had effectively swung Government policy away from further line closures. Never again, in the UK, would any serious threat emerge to close a major railway.

One positive suggestion in the letter was that the Government wanted to see BR working with local partners including councils, businesses user groups and others 'to ensure that the line has a successful future and so the case for closure will

PRESS NOTICE

THE DEPARTMENT OF TRANSPORT

RECEIVED

PRESS NOTICE NO.   166

DATE   11 April 1989

SETTLE-CARLISLE LINE TO STAY OPEN

Paul Channon, Secretary of State for Transport, today announced that he had refused British Rail consent to close the Settle-Carlisle line and the associated Blackburn-Hellifield line to passenger traffic. He has taken account of new evidence on the financial case, passenger traffic and wider social and economic considerations.

Replying to a Parliamentary Question from David Curry MP (Skipton & Ripon), Mr. Channon pointed out that:

- BR are now to seek the cooperation of the private sector and local authorities to promote and develop the line.

- New evidence sought last May leads the Secretary of State to think that the financial case for closure is weaker. More people are using the line. Ribblehead Viaduct will cost less to repair than was first thought.

- The line may still operate at a small loss but there is an opportunity to improve revenue through new marketing initiatives.

The Department for Transport's press release announcing the reprieve – 11 April 1989.

DEPARTMENT OF TRANSPORT
2 MARSHAM STREET LONDON SW1P 3EB

My ref:

Your ref:

J C Album
n House
4 St Bride Street
on
4DL

11 APR 1989

r Mr Album

will be pleased to hear that the Secretary of State is today uncing that he is refusing consent for British Rail to close Settle-Carlisle railway line. I enclose a copy of the rtment's Press Notice and the formal decision letter.

ok to the Friends of the Settle-Carlisle Line Association to perate vigorously in supporting and promoting the line, as you promised.

Yours sincerely

Michael Portillo

MICHAEL PORTILLO

Letter from Michael Portillo to Edward Album about the reprieve.

THE HERALD, SATURDAY, 15th APRIL, 1989

JUBILATION — AND SURPRISE AS SETTLE LINE IS SAVED ...

By JENNIFER MAUGHAN

JUBILANT campaigners in the long and arduous battle to save the scenic Carlisle to Settle rail line were toasting a famous, if somewhat surprising, victory this week.

Mr. Paul Channon, Secretary of State for Transport, shocked all those involved in the years of struggle to retain the route by suddenly announcing on Tuesday that the line would remain open and part of the nation's British Rail network.

Rumours had been rife earlier in the week that the line was to be partly privatised in a deal between BR and two Hull-based industrialists. Line supporters were therefore expecting any announcement to be "gloomy" news.

However, in a reply to a question from Skipton and Ripon MP David Curry, Mr. Channon said new evidence led him to believe the financial case for closure to be much weaker.

More people were using the line and the repairs to the picturesque Ribblehead Viaduct would cost less than first estimated by BR.

When BR first proposed closure in 1983 they said that the 93,000 passenger journeys brought less than £3.5 million to revenue and the repairs to Ribblehead Viaduct would cost £4.3 million.

Since then the position had improved dramatically with 450,000 passenger journeys

in 1988 and a decrease in the estimated costs of repairs to the Viaduct to £2.4 million.

Penrith and the Border MP Mr. David Maclean said he had been "quietly confident" that the Government would ensure the line remained part of the BR network.

He warmly welcomed the decision and said it was a marvellous victory for the Eden Valley, for the tourist industry and for all local rail users.

"I am delighted at the Minister's decision, but not at all surprised.

"I have always said that the line would survive and have backed every option to save it.

"For the last few months I was quietly confident that the Government would keep it open. We were right to explore the privatisation option and we are right now to order BR to keep running trains on the line," he said.

Mr. Bill Cameron, the chairman of Cumbria's Economy and Environment Committee, who also chaired the Joint Councils' Steering Committee, said: "Mr. Channon's statement vindicates entirely everything we have said about BR's case for closure.

"The line is vital to the economy and tourist industry of Cumbria and we are confident that with proper investment and marketing

Mr. Peter Walton, of Kirkby Stephen, a founder member of the Friends of the Carlisle-Settle Line told the "Herald" that he was delighted common sense had prevailed.

ESTABLISHED

"Now that the line's immediate future has been secured, I look forward to seeing the route becoming firmly established as part of the national rail network.

"I would like to see all parties concerned, BR, local authorities and Friends, all working together to improve and extend existing train services and facilities," he said.

Mr. Pete Shaw, secretary of the Friends, said: "My immediate reaction on hearing the line had been saved was one of relief. After working on the campaign for over six years, it is very rewarding to know that all our arguments have been vindicated."

Appleby Mayor Mr. Keith Morgan said the news was a great relief to all those who had battled long and hard to save the line.

He hoped that BR would ensure the route was not run down again and that everybody would continue to use the line to its full purpose.

In the future, a whole range of marketing ideas had to be tapped to run alongside the line's main role of serving the Eden Valley communities.

Mr. Carl Bendelow, speaking on behalf of the Settle-Carlisle Business Liaison Group, said he believed their recent meeting with Mr. Michael Portillo, in which they stressed how vital the line was to the area's social and economic development, had been paramount in producing the right decision.

"As a group we will continue to put forward to BR our ideas for improving services," he said.

CRUCIAL

Mr. Bendelow said the crucial thing was to see if BR

up some kind of consultative body, incorporating councils, chambers of trade, individual bodies and organisations, to work together for the line's future development.

Eden councillor Mr. Peter Simpson said he was "absolutely over the moon" about the news. He said the decision justified the tremendous effort over the past six years.

"Eden Council have fought for the line on behalf of the people, but we have been fortunate to have the big guns like the County Council behind us all the way and without them and others we would have been struggling," he said.

Westmorland and Lonsdale MP Mr. Michael Jopling said thanks to the stupendous efforts of many people this "incomparable railway line" was to be remain open, despite the machinations of BR.

He went on to say that BR had deliberately run down the service and convenience of various lines so they were ripe for closure and he challenged them to dare to "fiddle" the figures as they had clearly done over the cost of repairing Ribblehead Viaduct.

Rail enthusiast Mr. Ian Alletson, of Crosby Garrett, said the decision had come as a surprise, particularly bearing in mind the Government's current views on privatisation.

He hoped strong possibilities for marketing were followed up and that all promises of support were now put into action.

The Craven Herald *breaks the news.*

from   Dame Elaine Kellett-Bowman M.P.

HOUSE OF COMMONS
LONDON SW1A 0AA

12th April, 1989

Dear Tony,

I was absolutely thrilled to bits yesterday, when Paul Channon wrote to me (copy enclosed) telling me he had decided to refuse consent to British Rail to close the Settle-Carlisle Railway. I am sure you will be particularly gratified by paragraph two of the Minister's statement, in which he says "there have been changes in the financial case. For example, following the trial repairs to Ribblehead Viaduct that I requested last year, it now seems that it will be much cheaper to repair the whole structure than previously thought".

I vividly remember you explaining to me just how you were working out these very much more cost-effective repairs, and I know that you can take a great deal of the credit for the fact that this Line has been saved.

There will be tens of thousands of people who will owe you a considerable debt of gratitude now and in the years to come when they enjoy this lovely scenic route.

With many thanks and warm regards,

Yours ever,

Elaine

T. Freschini Esq.,
15 Sandown Road,

Letter from Lancaster MP Dame Elaine Kellet-Bowman to Tony Freschini on the reprieve.

The Westmorland Gazette

FRIDAY, APRIL 14, 1989

The Westmorland Gazette

ESTABLISHED 1818

THE NEWSPAPER FOR SOUTH LAKELAND

A famous victory

Whichever way you look at it, campaigners battling for the future of the Settle-Carlisle railway line have won a famous victory.

There have been times in the past year when it appeared the Government was simply playing for time before bringing down the axe.

But this week's announcement by Secretary of State for Transport Mr Paul Channon that the line is to remain open is an unqualified success for opponents of British Rail's closure wishes.

Mr Channon made it clear that his decision was the final word in the six-year-long battle to save the line and his insistence that it should remain in the hands of British Rail will end speculation that it could be transferred into full or partial private ownership.

Close cooperation with local councils and the private sector will be needed to market and develop the route - but as the feeling has long been held that BR was not doing the job properly, who can quibble about that?

It was, perhaps, typical of a prolonged debate which has generated much heat and emotion that even the announcement of the line's continued future was not without acrimony. MPs were angry that Mr Channon chose to break the news to journalists at his department's headquarters rather than to the House.

But it is doubtful whether the various local authorities and other organisations who have put up such an admirable fight for the line's retention could have given a hoot about where the announcement was made. To them, procedural niceties must have been largely irrelevant. All that really mattered was that the 72 mile route - a magnificent feat of Victorian engineering and still an important link in the national rail network - had been saved.

Now British Rail must bury its pride and wholeheartedly play its part in ensuring that the line's considerable potential is exploited to the full.

Craven Herald & Pioneer

Craven Herald & Pioneer

38 HIGH STREET, SKIPTON
Tel. 2577/2578
FRIDAY, APRIL 28, 1989

Settle-Carlisle line and the future

Euphoria at the Government decision to save the Settle-Carlisle railway line is understandable. For some it marks the successful culmination of six years of campaigning. That campaign was often quite magnificently conceived, though it has to be said that few organisations can have shot themselves in the foot with the frequency British Rail achieved. It is matched only by their ability to ensure that trains don't connect—and that might have been a quite deliberate ploy so far as this particular issue is concerned.

On what other issues, for example, would the likes of Coun. Beth Graham, a leading Liberal, and former Conservative agent for Skipton, Mr. Gerry Thorpe, speak with one voice?

A blend of hard facts, many of them obviously culled from within the innermost cloisters of BR's hierarchy, and clever gimmicks which have caught the attention of the media, have meant that the fight to save the line has caught the imagination of newspapers and television, and through them a wide public.

Yes, a brilliantly orchestrated campaign which has achieved the result its exponents required. We offer congratulations to all concerned. Their tactics could well become a blueprint for other battles on other issues.

Deliberately we have delayed a comment on the outcome. It would have been easy to have been swept along with the hysteria of the success. Now, however, there are other more serious long-term problems that need to be addressed. On at least one occasion we posed the question as to how many of those who have packed almost every train — especially if steam hauled — would travel regularly? Sure, in terms of the numbers game they made it seem as though the line was going from strength to strength. But will the camera and tape recorder brigade be there in such great numbers now that the line is no longer under threat?

The answer, we feel, is that they won't. If that is an assumption that proves correct, then some new attraction, added incentive to travel, will be required. The possibilities are there. People have more and more leisure. The great outdoors beckons, and the line can give access to some beautiful countryside, stimulating walks; to activities such as climbing and potholing. Yet even these activities create problems for our area as proved this week by yet another airlift of material to help halt erosion on one of the Three Peaks.

Now, having saved the line, what of the future? Mr. Paul Channon in announcing his decision, expressed the hope that circumstances would be such that closure would not arise again. To guarantee that, the line must continue to be used in great numbers. BR can help by planning its timetable to ensure that trains connect, but that won't be enough. If the line is not again to make the losses which first raised the spectre of closure, then those who toiled so imaginatively to save it, must now show the same qualities to ensuring its future viability. That will mean walking, not only the Dales, but a tightrope. Success in persuading people to continue to visit in large numbers, with possibly such things as circular walks, need to be sensitively planned if new problems are not to be created or existing ones exacerbated.

Westminster Report by David Curry M.P.

SENSIBLE DECISION

As far as I am concerned the new term got off to a good start with some good news — the decision not to permit closure of the Settle-Carlisle line. I am grateful to all those who lobbied for the line, and particularly grateful that it was done in reasoned, courteous and non-political terms. My aim in this campaign was not to back the Government into a corner, but to make sure that it had the information to make a sensible decision. I shall now seek talks with British Rail about how it is going to develop services on the line.

First, though, the Government will have to be convinced that their judgement was right. It might be necessary to do that without British Rail, unless they continue to show the dynamism they have demonstrated over the past eighteen months.

Yes, the campaigners deserve their spell of euphoria. The celebrations though, will have to end and a new realism emerge. Yesterday is history. Can they generate the same enthusiasm to guarantee the future as they did to create the present? Answering that question will prove whether the real intent was to beat British Rail and no more, or whether all the oratory about preserving this great piece of Victorian engineering was genuinely meant.

ABOVE LEFT: The Westmorland Gazette makes some telling points about the campaign.

ABOVE RIGHT: The Craven Herald reflects on the successful campaign.

LEFT: The campaigners celebrated with a grand party in Appleby.

not re-emerge'. This led to the creation of the Settle–Carlisle Railway Development Committee (see Chapters 8 and 9).

Why the U-turn from the previous March when the Government was 'minded' to give consent to the line's closure? James Towler suggests that one reason was the Government's concern about further legal challenges to the proposal. This was supported in a conversation with Edward Album more recently.

However, some fascinating information has come to light recently thanks to the efforts of Settle–Carlisle campaigner Martin Pearson. Using the Freedom of Information Act, Martin was able to gain access to a fascinating letter written on 6 April 1989 – days before the formal reprieve was announced, from Secretary of State Paul Channon to the Prime Minister, Margaret Thatcher. The letter sets out the changed environment in which the railway was operating and – crucially – the strong political outcry that would ensue should the line close. Channon recommended to Thatcher that the line should be reprieved, with efforts to encourage private sector involvement. A very interesting aside to the story is that Channon makes clear that the reprieve could be construed as a U-turn on its policy of 'bustitution' – closing railways and substituting buses – which was clearly very much on the Government's agenda at the time. He suggests that the policy would continue in relation to other lines, though in reality the reprieve led to a changed environment in which rail closures were off the agenda.

A number of factors were clearly at work in persuading Channon – with the Prime Minister's implicit support – to refuse closure. The hopes of privatizing the line were crumbling into dust, with a lack of a sufficiently robust proposal from any of the bidders who had shown interest. Before the line could be 'privatized' the Government would have had to consent to closure, allowing the railway to be transferred to the private sector.

Perhaps the most compelling reason was the powerful campaign mounted by the closure campaigners, including the Joint Action Committee, the local authorities through the 'Joint Councils' group, and the TUCCs. The campaign had won support across the board, from MPs and councillors of all political shades, from the business community, trades unions, churches and many more. Channon effectively acknowledges this in his letter to the Prime Minister.

It was a very inclusive campaign, thousands of people contributed to it in so many ways. The campaign was marked by real strength and resilience with a healthy dose of common sense. A key factor was a belief amongst many of us that you can affect your own future; we don't have to be passive bystanders.

Ruth Annison, former chair Settle–Carlisle Railway Business Liaison Group, interview August 2018

The campaign had combined formal legal nitpicking with broad-based campaigning of a sort that hadn't been seen before in a railway context. The campaign needed its James Towler and Olive Clarke – but it also needed its John Whitelegg and Peter Horton, Ruth Annison and Peter Robinson, each of whom brought different perspectives and approaches to the lobby. A special mention should go to Ron Cotton, BR's man charged with managing the closure, who became one of the railway's strongest allies. It is the stuff of fiction, but it happened. Whoever was transport minister or secretary of state at the time would have found it extremely difficult to consent to close the line given the scale of well-organized and cross-party opposition. Credit should also go to Michael Portillo for fronting the refusal of closure.

CHAPTER 8

Renaissance

The refusal of consent to closure was met with great rejoicing, perhaps more than had greeted the line's opening in 1876, after years of delay. The campaigners had every right to feel proud of their achievement. Not only had they saved the Settle–Carlisle Line from closure, they had achieved a seismic shift in Government transport policy. Whatever hopes Paul Channon had to retain his 'bustitution' policy, line closures were off the Government agenda, and have stayed off ever since, despite the occasional temptation by Government ministers, perhaps encouraged by some bean-counting civil servants, to revive cuts. Ironically, one effect of privatization has been to make rail closures more, rather than less, difficult to implement through the sheer bureaucracy involved.

BR responded to the announcement in a positive way. New rolling stock was introduced and further efforts were made to promote the line. Far from passenger numbers dropping off after the reprieve was announced, numbers continued to grow. From October 1990, Class 156 'Super Sprinters', reliable trains with good window views, were introduced. The new trains were ideal for start-stop operations, much more so than the locomotive hauled trains they replaced. BR was able to introduce an accelerated timetable, offering end-to-end journeys from Leeds to Carlisle of around 2 hours and 45 minutes.

The controversy surrounding Ribblehead Viaduct was finally brought to an end. BR engineer Tony Freschini had developed a scheme to repair the viaduct that cost well below BR's original estimate of £10m. The reconstruction work, which took place during a full line closure in October 1989, cost less than £3m. Further investment included restoration of the northbound platform at Ribblehead, in 1993.

But perhaps the most notable development after 1989 was the transformation of what had been the UK's most effective anti-closure campaign into an entirely positive force, not only lobbying for improvements but in many cases contributing to the costs of them.

Friends of the Settle–Carlisle Line (FoSCL)

FoSCL has a very strong claim to being the UK's premier rail user and promotion group, with a membership exceeding 3,000 individuals drawn from the locality but also across the UK and beyond. As we've seen, FoSCL was formed at a meeting held on 27 June 1981, before the formal closure announcement had been made. Their campaign within the Joint Action Committee, together with the efforts of the local authorities (the 'Joint Councils' group) and the Transport Users' Consultative

A Northern Class 156 units pause at Ribblehead station, before Class 158 units were introduced on most services.

The campaigners organized a special train to celebrate the reprieve. Here it makes a special stop on Ribblehead Viaduct.

Works continue on the solum of the viaduct during 1990.

ABOVE: *The Keller contractors at Ribblehead.* TONY FRESCHINI

LEFT: *The Direct Labour Organisation (DLO) team played an important role in the viaduct's repair.* TONY FRESCHINI

Committees, ensured the line's future. It would have been understandable had FoSCL, flushed with its victory in April 1989, hung up its boots and retired gracefully. It didn't. FoSCL had already been active in promoting the line, together with the efforts of Ron Cotton in BR. Numbers using the line had grown from around 150,000 in 1983 to more

The membership renewals were done on a manual basis throughout the closure campaign, although by the mid '80s an embryonic system using an external computer company started producing labels. Although this was better than when I joined, the Friends still had some way to go before they would have fully computerized records and label production in-house. When I joined we had around 1,000 members and when the line was saved from closure, that figure had risen to nearly 4,500, with a fixed membership renewal date. Imagine processing so many renewals!

Brian Sutcliffe, former chairman, FoSCL

than 500,000 in 1989, but there was still scope to do much more. It's easy looking back to see 1989 as a turning point at which closure of the line was off the agenda for all time – but it wasn't so obvious then. The best way to ensure the line's survival, clearly, was to keep growing the business.

Already, FoSCL volunteers had been busy promoting the line across the North, distributing leaflets on charter trains and making sure every shop, pub and café in the Dales had literature about the railway. Society volunteers act as on-train guides on several services. At the local stations along the line, volunteers had been active since 1987 in restoring station gardens that had long been left to decay. This work continues, with every station along the line being a jewel, reflecting the pride in the line shown by the local community (Chapter 9).

A popular feature of the line is the guided walks programme, for many years co-ordinated by FoSCL volunteer Ruth Evans before David Singleton took over the job. Recently, David handed over respon-

When it was first mooted that the Settle–Carlisle Line might close, the Friends of the Settle–Carlisle Line came into existence and quickly gathered momentum and gained members. They promised a lot about what they would do if the line were saved. At the time, I was chairman of the Transport Users' Consultative Committee of NW England and adopted an impartial, independent position. So I thought, 'let's wait and see if they can deliver on these promises.' Of course the line was reprieved and I have to say that Friends of the Settle–Carlisle Line has more than achieved what it promised. I really admire that, because too often people make lavish promises and little happens. The FoSCL has done more than anyone could have expected. I say this with absolute sincerity.

Mrs Olive Clarke, former chairman
North-West TUCC

ABOVE: *Eric Bentley – an outstanding S&C volunteer – on one of the FoSCL music trains.*

BELOW: *Guided walks from the line: walkers alight at Kirkby Stephen.*

sibility to John Disney and John Carey. The walks have introduced thousands of people to the delights of the Dales and brought substantial extra passenger numbers to the line. In addition to the core walks programme, mostly taking place on Saturdays and Sundays, the society has been organising 'heritage' walks around the former shanty-town sites near Ribblehead.

After the Line was saved, the Committee somehow thought that our main job was done. This proved incorrect. There were numerous other activities for the Friends, including lobbying for improved services, sales of memorabilia, a station shop and sponsored walks. Then came the challenge of privatization, which involved a number of detailed memoranda from the Friends and our appearance at the famous Committee Room at the House of Commons. We opposed the proposals not for political reasons but on the grounds of cost and practicality. I still have the memoranda that I drafted at the time, with approval and additions from the Committee members, and these were distributed to MPs and the Department of Transport.

Edward Album, FoSCL newsletter, November 2011

FoSCL developed a remarkable range of activities, ranging from providing on-train volunteer couriers explaining the surrounding landscape and history of the line, through to members doing station gardens, promoting the line in the local community and maintaining the line's high profile. FoSCL continues to lobby both the train operator and Network Rail for service and infrastructure improvements. FoSCL has invested significant sums to complement other investments going into the line, including station waiting rooms, seating, lighting and signage.

The key post of chairman was held for many years by former police officer Mark Rand. He handed over the baton to Richard Morris in 2014 and Richard was succeeded by Douglas Hodgins in 2016. FoSCL keeps a substantial archive of materials at The Folly, in Settle. In addition it runs a joiner's shop (see Chapter 8) adjacent to Settle station for the production of station signage and furniture – another unique facet to a unique organization.

In July 2018 Michael Portillo became President of FoSCL, following the death of its previous President, Sir William McAlpine. In accepting the role, he told FoSCL, 'I will accept because I do indeed feel a strong connection to the line through our shared history' (FoSCL newsletter August 2018).

Mark Rand with Robert Handy in the 'Wonder of Wood' workshop at Stainforth.

Mark Rand with Ged Pinder in the FoSCL Joiners' Shop at Settle Station.

The Development Company

The Secretary of State's recommendation that BR should work with local partners to develop and promote the line was acted upon quickly, and has achieved great success. The Settle–Carlisle Railway Development Company was formed as a not-for-profit company in 1992. Joe Ravetz was the first general manager, followed by Rob Rimmer. Marion Armstrong worked for the company between 1993 and 2014, serving as general manager from 2009, and has retained a close involvement with the railway ever since. The focus of the company was and still is very much on promoting the line and the rail corridor, growing passenger numbers and making a significant impact on the Dales and Eden Valley economies. Estimates suggest that it has directly led to the creation of some seventy jobs.

> The beauty of the Development Company's structure as an independent business is that we can respond quickly and flexibly to commercial opportunities along the line, putting money back into the Dales economy.
>
> Drew Haley, General Manager, Settle–Carlisle Railway Development Company

The board originally included several representatives of the main local authorities as well as local entrepreneurs, and the train operator – BR until 1994 and then franchised train operating companies. Production of timetable and promotional literature was taken on by the company at an early stage, resulting in an attractive leaflet which both promotes the line and provides timetable information.

The Development Company initiated the Dales Railcard in 1995, offering residents within the railway corridor a one-third discount on fares between Leeds and Carlisle and on the Leeds–Morecambe line. It has proved a great success and now has around 5,500 users. There is no doubt that the railcard has stimulated local travel on the line enormously. The company worked with West Yorkshire Passenger Transport Authority to introduce low winter fares, which attracted a large new market for the line.

A radical development took place in 1999 when the company took on the direct employment of station staff at Settle and Appleby, to ensure those stations would be staffed when required. Whilst the trades unions were initially wary of the idea, it has worked well and the union has benefited from the addition

Drew Haley and Susie Arms, trolley assistant, at Settle.

The trolley service has proved popular!

Loading the trolley at Settle.

Occasional music trains from Leeds to Ribblehead have proved popular.

Service with a smile on the line. SETTLE-CARLISLE RAILWAY DEVELOPMENT COMPANY

of new members who are employed by the company. Currently the company employs five part-time staff at these two stations.

Another early project was to take over the group travel business, which was operated by the train company up to 2002. This involved liaising with coach operators to include a ride on the line as part of a coach trip. The group travel team at Appleby has developed a strong working relationship with group clients, highlighted in 2016/17 when bookings had to be rearranged following the agonising 15-month closure of the line following the landslip at Eden Brows near Armathwaite (see below).

In 2004 a trolley service was introduced, operated and managed by the Development Company, with the support and help of Arriva Trains Northern. The company worked with a local businesswoman who ran a small catering business 'Country Fayre' to supply the trolley service. This grew from a one-person business to a major enterprise employing dozens of local people. The Development Company also works with other local suppliers in sourcing products for the trolley service, including traybakes from Mallerstang, 'Settle–Carlisle' branded and locally produced beer, and locally made ice cream.

The Development Company has initiated a number of projects to improve facilities and help reduce carbon emissions. During a line closure in 2008 for major engineering work, the company examined ways to reduce energy costs. They partnered with Yorkshire Renewable Energy Co. to provide six biomass stoves at Settle and Appleby. They also introduced LED lighting at several stations.

A new toilet block was provided at Settle through a collaboration between Northern Rail, Network Rail, the Development Company and North Yorkshire County Council, with additional funding from FoSCL and The Railway Heritage Trust. The toilet block is fully accessible with baby changing facilities. It also includes enhanced facilities for station staff and, for the first time in its history, hot water! A similar project was undertaken at Appleby in 2011.

In 2008 the Development Company took over the café at Skipton station, establishing a stand-alone

business to run it and employ staff. Café Express has proved a great success, providing commuters with good quality refreshments and creating four jobs. In a novel experiment, the train company takes a 20 percent profit share in the business, instead of having a fixed rent.

Regular music trains have been a popular feature of the line, organized by a partnership between the company, FoSCL and the train operator, Northern. The events, using scheduled evening trains, have featured live music with a real ale bar.

The Development Company's role is to support the train operator and the services it provides, rather than replace them. However, always keen to explore new ventures, in 2017 the company ran its first charter train – the 'Christmas Comet' – which ran from Carlisle via Settle to York. It was a great success and the company is looking at further charter train projects aimed at people living along the route.

Along with its partners on the line – FoSCL, the Settle Carlisle Railway Trust and the rail industry – the Development Company is developing a future strategy for the line covering service enhancement aspirations, marketing initiatives to improve passenger numbers, station improvements, community involvement and supporting the local economy. One important aim, shared with Transport for the

Seasonal entertainment on the Development Company's 'Christmas Comet'.

North, is to bring back through links between West Yorkshire and Scotland.

To spend twenty years working for the Settle–Carlisle railway was a great privilege and on the whole lots of fun. This lasting legacy to the Midland Railway and the people who worked so hard to complete it needs to be cared for and taken into the future. Our greatest aim at the DevCo was to blend that heritage with the needs of the modern world in a way that complimented the route and the region. There's always more work to be done but we feel sure now that in 2018 this line has a secure and successful future.

Marion Armstrong

Our *raison d'être* is to attract more people to travel on this magnificent rail line both locally and over longer distances. This has the added spin-off of promoting local businesses and enhances our important relationships with the local communities along the line. There are challenges but working with Northern and our other partners in the Settle–Carlisle family I am optimistic about the future.

John Moorhouse, Chairman of the Development Company

The Settle–Carlisle Line Trust

The origins of the trust owe much to the work of Edward Album, a London-based solicitor who played an important role in the closure proceedings (*see* Chapter 10).

An important element of the Friends' closure campaign was an offer to set up a Trust to raise funds for the Ribblehead Viaduct repairs and future works. This offer was accepted by the Minister and mentioned in his reprieve statement. He said: 'It has been proposed that a trust fund be set up to care for the structures on the line of heritage importance. I support that proposal.' Substantial sums were then raised for the Ribblehead repairs and later for the acquisition and restoration of the three stations later acquired by the Trust at Ribblehead, Horton and Kirkby Stephen and also, much later, for the Station Master's House at Ribblehead.

Edward Album, FoSCL newsletter,
November 2011

The Trust now manages a number of former railway properties along the line, making them available as holiday accommodation. They include the former station master's house at Ribblehead and station accommodation at Kirkby Stephen and Horton-in-Ribblesdale.

The Trust is born: on a special train with commemorative headboard. SCRT

Horton-in-Ribblesdale lamp and station clock.

Ribblehead station in ruins, c.1980. RAILWAY HERITAGE TRUST

Ribblehead station visitor centre today.

The Trust's first major undertaking was the restoration of the station building at Ribblehead. Although Railtrack had renewed the roof of the building in 1997, the rest of the structure required major work to bring it back into use. The Trust has created a visitor centre in the former booking office and booking hall, and a small shop in the former porters' room. The former ladies' waiting room and gents' toilet block, together with new floor space created in the roof void above, have provided accommodation for the caretakers' flat. The Trust completed the acquisition of the building on a 125-year lease in September 1999, and work commenced on site later that month. Work was completed in six months and the visitor centre opened its doors in June 2000. The restored building was formally opened by Steve Macare, Chairman of the Yorkshire Dales National Park Authority, at an event to mark the occasion on 14 October 2000. The project was funded by the European Union Regional Development Fund, the Yorkshire Dales National Park Authority, English Heritage, the Railway Heritage Trust and Friends of the Settle–Carlisle Line. The building won the Trust a prestigious Ian Allan Railway Heritage Award in 2000.

Following the successful restoration of the Ribblehead station building, the Trust turned its attention to Horton-in-Ribblesdale. In August 2002 the Trust completed the acquisition of the building on a 125-year lease similar to that at Ribblehead and work commenced on site in September. Although the building was weather-proof and structurally sound, much was still required to make it habitable. Plans were drawn up to completely refurbish and convert the building for office use. Work was completed in January 2003. The offices have since been successfully let and there is a non-resident caretaker. Principal funding came from the Yorkshire Dales Millennium Trust, Yorkshire Forward and the Railway Heritage Trust, with other contributions from the Friends of the Settle–Carlisle Line. The work involved restoring and refurbishing the building, including many original features, to a high standard, creating office accommodation, a community room and improved passenger waiting facilities.

The next major project for the Trust was Kirkby Stephen. Like Horton, the main station building had been structurally repaired by Railtrack in 1998. However, much work was still required to bring the building back into use. Plans were drawn up to completely refurbish the building. The Trust completed the acquisition of the building on a 125-year lease in December 2003 and work commenced on site in March 2004. The works entailed restoring period features and refurbishing the building to a high standard, and improving passenger waiting facilities. Building work was completed in November 2004. The building won the Railway Heritage Trust Conservation Award for 2005. The building at Kirkby Stephen was much larger than those at Ribblehead and Horton, being of the Type 1 'large pattern' structure (similar to Settle and Appleby). The project was on a much bigger scale and budget than that of the previous two stations. The restored building was formally opened by HRH The Prince of Wales on 22 March 2005, when a slate plaque was unveiled to commemorate the event.

Funding for the project came from a variety of sources, including European Union Regional Development Fund, Northwest Development Agency, Railway Heritage Trust, The Clothworkers' Foundation, Friends of the Settle–Carlisle Line, Arriva Trains Northern and Network Rail.

The Trust has also been involved in smaller projects such as restoring some of the station clocks along the line. It was involved in restoring the unique railway 'weather station' at Ribblehead, which still functions today, albeit using modern technology. The Trust has also produced a Design Guide, which forms an essential reference for any work to develop buildings along the railway.

Settle–Carlisle Railway Business Liaison Group (BLG)

The BLG was a unique organization, bringing together small businesses with an interest in their railway, to ensure its future. The business people were not primarily railway enthusiasts, but people committed to their communities and wanting to

Horton-in-Ribblesdale station: a little gem.

Kirkby Stephen station – a good crowd of local people join the train for Leeds.

This Station Building was restored by The Settle and Carlisle Railway Trust and was declared open by H.R.H. The Prince of Wales on Tuesday 22nd March 2005

Plaque at Kirkby Stephen.

make a success of their enterprises. The BLG functioned as kind of linear development agency, providing the means for businesses to network, share ideas, and build commercial as well as friendly relationships with each other. It was responsible for at least one marriage! Alongside many other achievements, its 1991 report *Trains and Trade* is an outstanding example of creative but practical thinking, showing how a railway can invigorate the local economy and local businesses contribute to the line's success.

> After the reprieve many of us thought we could get back to our day job but it wasn't to be; there was still lots to do.
>
> Ruth Annison, Chair, BLG

The BLG organized a conference to pool ideas and look at ways of developing its activities. 'Linking communities – making a difference' took place in Kirkby Stephen in March 1997 and received funding from the Department for National Heritage and the Community Development Foundation. More than twenty businesses, and Kirkby Stephen School, took part. The event discussed a number of topics through workshops, including new technologies, tourism and trading, transport, countryside and community, culture, education, leisure and young people. The event led to two specific recommendations:

- that resources should be invested at grass roots level to promote connectivity through highly interactive workshops of this kind – linking communities subtly to make genuine partnerships possible for the greater good of generations yet unborn; and
- to establish a Regional Forum that should serve the communities to promote devolved responsibility, collaboration and grass roots initiatives.

It's debatable whether the BLG's aspirations were achieved. The proposed 'regional forum' never appeared, but what has happened has been the growth and maturity of relationships between businesses along the line. Around 2003 the BLG itself changed its name to 'Settle Carlisle Economic Network' – Scene. It continued into the new century but it became more difficult to resource the formal network. It closed down in 2013, though many informal networks of relationships between businesses continue.

The Countryside Networks

A key part of the fight to save the line was the active involvement of ramblers' groups. The Dales have always been one of the most-loved destinations of walkers in Yorkshire and Lancashire. The threat to the line mobilized thousands of walkers to join forces with other campaigners to lobby for the line's future – and to use it.

> In many ways the history of the Yorkshire Dales Society and the saving of the Settle–Carlisle Line are intertwined. The railway, one of the most spectacular in Britain, is now a huge tourist attraction in its own right, but also a local lifeline for communities in the Yorkshire Dales and the Eden Valley.
>
> Colin Speakman, 'Saving the Settle to Carlisle Line' in *Yorkshire Dales Review*, Summer 2018

The role of the Ramblers' Association in chartering the initial special train in 1975 has already been mentioned. The support of the Yorkshire Dales National Park is ongoing, both in funding initiatives such as DalesRail but also in linking the railway with the wider offer of this remarkably beautiful area. The Yorkshire Dales Society (now 'Friends of the Dales') was formed in 1918 as a voluntary organization to promote interest and awareness in the Dales. It has continued to work with Friends of the Settle–Carlisle Line and train operators to promote the line.

The Railway Partners

The rail industry has undergone massive change since the days of the closure campaign. Following

Walkers waiting for the train to the Dales, at Settle.

Northern's Paul Brown with FoSCL's Mark Rand.

a major re-organization, the line became part of BR's Regional Railways North-East in 1992. BR was privatized in 1993 and the Settle–Carlisle Line became part of a new franchise covering the North-East of England. The first franchise was won by MTL, a Merseyside-based transport operator, in March 1997. It was rebranded as 'Northern Spirit' in May 1998. In 2000 the franchise was purchased by German Rail-owned Arriva who re-branded the company 'Arriva Trains Northern'. The franchise (widened to include most local services in the North) passed to a joint venture of Serco and Netherlands Railways subsidiary NedRail (subsequently Abellio) in December 2004. In 2007 Northern named one of their Class 156 trains and provided Settle–Carlisle artworks, helping to promote the line across the network.

A new franchise began in April 2016 when Arriva was awarded an eight-year franchise, with services branded as 'Northern' operated by Arriva Rail North

(ARN). The Settle–Carlisle Line comes within ARN's Eastern regional directorate. Train crews are based at Leeds and Skipton, with ARN employing a small number of 'core' staff at Settle and Appleby, as well as all the station staff at Skipton and Aire Valley staffed stations.

The privatization of BR led to the separation of infrastructure from operations. Railtrack was set up in 1994 to own and manage the track, signalling and associated land and property. It was privatized in 1996 but was converted into a 'not for profit' company limited by guarantee called Network Rail in 2002 following the Hatfield accident. Network Rail itself was taken back into the public sector, under the umbrella of the Department for Transport, in 2014. The Settle–Carlisle Line now comes within Network Rail's London and North Western regional directorate. Network Rail employs staff at the remaining signalboxes along the line as well as track maintenance workers and signalling engineers.

CHAPTER 9

The Settle–Carlisle Line in the Twenty-First Century

The first two decades of the twenty-first century have been every bit as exciting and varied as previous years. The line entered the new century in good shape. The threat of closure had receded and the biggest challenge was accommodating growing freight traffic with a vibrant passenger market, stimulated by the efforts of the Development Company and Friends and their partners in Northern Rail. The franchise for the Northern network, won by a joint venture of Serco and Abellio (formerly NedRail, part of Netherlands Railways) was let in 1997. During the period of the franchise the line saw gradually rising passenger numbers and growing calls for a more frequent train service. A new franchise, this time won by Deutsche Bahn-owned Arriva, started in April 2016 with commitments to improving frequencies along the route. However, the positive momentum that had become a feature of the railway received a huge blow in February 2016 when part of the railway embankment at Eden Brows, between Armathwaite and Carlisle, collapsed. Had this happened in earlier years the future of the line could have been in serious jeopardy. As it was, Network Rail set to work to repair the embankment in a project that took 14 months and cost £23 million. No trains were able to run between Carlisle and Appleby, making a huge dent in the local economy, which has become more dependent on the railway for bringing visitors into the area.

During the closure, Network Rail used the suspension of services to carry out other works along the line including embankment strengthening at Baron Wood and improvements to the level crossing at Low House. The reopening of the line in April 2017 saw some amazing scenes as Northern operated a steam-hauled service using *Tornado* (see below), and a special train ran behind the world's most famous locomotive *Flying Scotsman*.

The Settle–Carlisle Line is now carrying significantly more coal traffic and diverted passenger traffic than it has in the past. The December 2008 timetable saw the WCML [West Coast Main Line] coal traffic pathed instead along the Settle and Carlisle (S&C), and then via Hellifield–Blackburn to accommodate capacity demands on the WCML. To facilitate this, work has been carried out in Control Panel 3 to improve the line's capability by installing intermediate block signals to reduce the headway between trains. This section now becomes the heavy freight route for the North–South daytime flows on the WCML. Longer term, this corridor will require additional capital expenditure to improve capacity.

Network Rail Route Plan 2009: North-West Rural

A busy time at Settle station.

Better passenger facilities

The line has seen significant improvements to passenger facilities at most stations. In several cases new waiting shelters have been provided, in a style in keeping with the heritage of the line. A major asset in the process of maintaining existing and creating new facilities has been the joiners' shop, sponsored by the Friends of the Settle–Carlisle Line (FoSCL) at Settle station. Ged Pinder, a retired joiner who had helped restore the former signalbox at Settle, has been the mainstay of the workshop. It has turned out signs, benches, doors, windows and other items that help to enhance the character of stations and the line. In 2018 new nameboards were provided at Settle, together with replacement doors on some of the station buildings. Ged is supported by local FoSCL volunteers.

By 2017, the 'down line' shelter at Ribblehead, provided in 1993, needed substantial repair and Ged's team worked with Network Rail to replace rotting timbers.

On 3 August 2017 a new waiting shelter was opened on Settle station. The 'new building', which can accommodate up to thirty people, was designed by local architect Stephen Craven and constructed by G.I. Copley Ltd of Settle. The cost of £28,000 was met from Railway Heritage Trust, a private trust (Oliver Lovell Legacy), Northern Rail, Settle–Carlisle Railway Development Co. and Friends of the Settle–Carlisle Line. Network Rail provided considerable support in kind, as did Craven Council. A team of volunteers led by Mark Rand helped to prepare the site.

A linear holiday resort?

The Settle–Carlisle Line has many local guesthouses and hotels within easy reach of stations. However, several stations now have holiday accommodation in former railway buildings. Kirkby Stephen and Ribblehead have holiday lets, the latter in the former station master's house. Elsewhere, such as at Garsdale, former railway workers' cottages are available

The station tearoom at Ribblehead.

to let. At Dent the main station building and the nearby former snow huts are holiday rentals.

Friends of the Settle–Carlisle Line (FoSCL) has organized walks from the line for many years. These continue to offer a popular and easy way to explore the magnificent scenery along the line and boost ridership. Some more specialist walks are now provided, including guided walks exploring the heritage of the line and particularly the human story behind the building of it. Capitalizing on the TV series *Jericho*, based on navvy life during the line's construction, FoSCL organizes 'Jericho Tours' using experienced and knowledgeable guides, who take the guests to some of the former navvy encampments around Ribblehead.

Ribblehead station's visitor centre, staffed by FoSCL volunteers, has been refurbished and extended. It now has a welcoming tearoom. A recent addition was 'The Hawes Junction Chimney'. The centre offers an interactive journey along the line called 'ExploreMore'. By clicking on particular features more information is provided, with galleries of photos and people's reminiscences. The guide can also be downloaded at www.exploremoresettlecarlisle.co.uk.

The former signal box at Armathwaite was restored by FoSCL in 1992 and is now a small museum, run by FoSCL and looked after by the local station adop-

tion group. The station itself is lovingly tended by the volunteers who have installed heritage-style benches and look after the original Midland Railway waiting room and the formerly neglected gardens.

Turning a journey into an experience

The Settle–Carlisle Line is one of a select number of lines in the UK which people travel on as much for the experience as getting from A to B. Others would include the West Highland and Kyle lines in Scotland and the Heart of Wales route between Shrewsbury and Swansea. What makes Settle–Carlisle really special is the added value from on-train guides and catering, the latter being provided by paid staff from the Settle–Carlisle Railway Development Co. The guides are volunteers from FoSCL who go up and down the train distributing information, answering queries and pointing out features along the route. The Development Company works with coach operators to include a ride on the line as part of a day out to the Dales. Typically, coach parties will join the train at Settle and ride through to Appleby or Carlisle where their coach is waiting for them.

The railway plays a central role in the annual ride2stride festival, promoting walking in the Dales.

Settle station: a large group of tourists awaits the arrival of the train.

As well as a selection of guided walks from the railway, the event supports a series of talks about the history and landscape of the area.

A 73-mile linear garden

Lovingly cared-for station gardens were a feature of rural railway life up to the Beeching era. The great days of the station garden have returned, mainly thanks to the work of community volunteers, supported by Network Rail and train operators like Northern. An outstanding example is Settle, once the pride and joy of station master Jim Taylor. In more recent years the gardens were brought back to life by FoSCL volunteer Eric Stanley, who died in 2016. The station garden work was taken over by a local community group, Cultivating Settle, on behalf of FoSCL. They have continued Jim and

Station master Jim Taylor at Settle looking after his prize-winning gardens.
SCRT

Horton station gardens looking a treat.

BELOW: **Tornado** *on one of its hugely popular 're-opening specials' in 2017.* BOB SWALLOW

Eric's work and have dedicated a small part of the station gardens to Eric's memory. Horton is another delight – it is cared for by local people, led by Dave Moss who has been actively involved since 1987.

Beyond Settle, most stations have delightful gardens, the next one heading north, Horton-in-Ribblesdale, being really special. Of the smaller stations, Lazonby, Langwathby and Armathwaite stand out. Appleby, the line's other main station, has long been a joy to behold with lovingly tended flowerbeds, hanging baskets and the station name picked out in white stone. Some stations beyond the core route, such as Bingley, have recently benefited from volunteer-led station garden schemes.

As well as the on-train catering, the railway benefits from several business activities that provide improved passenger facilities and support the local economy. Both Settle and Appleby Stations have shops staffed by volunteers. The catering trolley is stocked with as much locally supplied produce as possible.

Tornado hits the line

One of the most remarkable events along the line for many years happened during the celebrations to mark the re-opening of the line in 2017. RAIL magazine editor Nigel Harris came up with the idea of running some scheduled services using steam traction. The newly built *Tornado*, based on an LNER A1 design, operated several services between Skipton and Appleby on three successive days. The response from the public was amazing, with trains packed out and thousands waving to the train from the lineside. This was the first regular mainline scheduled service in England using steam for more than half a century. The service carried more than 5,500 passengers during its three days of operation. Since the re-opening of the line in its entirety, the demand for steam specials has grown, with an average of two steam-hauled trains each week during the summer months.

Another view of Tornado *crossing Ribblehead Viaduct on one of the re-opening specials.* SETTLE–CARLISLE RAILWAY DEVELOPMENT COMPANY

Banner promoting integrated transport links at Ribblehead.

Developing integrated transport links

The railway was built as a fast, modern 'Inter City' railway before the term was invented, and links to local villages and towns was not the main purpose of the line's creation, as we have seen. That said, the railway is close to many of the towns and villages in the Dales, such as Settle and Appleby. However, towns like Hawes and popular tourist spots like Malham are out of reach on foot for most people. The 'Little White Bus' provides a useful connection at Garsdale station for Hawes whilst on summer Sundays there is a bus link from Settle station to Malham. The 'Northern Dalesman' bus runs from Preston and Lancaster on summer Sundays and connects with trains at Ribblehead.

The tale of a chimney

The tragic story of the Hawes Junction accident of 1910 is told in Chapter 10. There has been a remarkable addition to the tale recently, involving part of one of the locomotives involved in the crash. The express that collided with the two coupled 'light engines' was hauled by two locomotives (a 'double-header'). The front loco, number 48, was damaged but not beyond repair. However, photographs of the

The mystery chimney, at Ribblehead station.

loco being rescued show it without its chimney. This may have been for ease of transport. Certainly the pictures of it immediately after the crash show it still with its chimney. In the 1970s, a locomotive chimney was discovered near Garsdale station, about a mile from where the crash happened but it was regarded as too heavy, and corroded, to warrant moving. A few years later, local railway enthusiast Terry Sykes decided it was worth rescuing and roped in his wife Helen and some friends to help. Some clever detective work narrowed the likely 'owner' of the chimney down to locomotive number 48. The chimney is now displayed at Ribblehead Visitor Centre.

Remembering Ruswarp

The first secretary of the Friends of the Settle–Carlisle Line, Graham Nuttall, was a much-loved railway eccentric. He met a tragic death whilst walking in the Brecon Beacons with his faithful border collie, Ruswarp (the one non-human objector to BR's closure proposal, using his paw-mark as a signature). Graham, aged forty-one, went missing on 20 January 1990. He and Ruswarp had bought day return tickets from Burnley to Llandrindod Wells to go walking in the Welsh mountains, but they never returned. Searches in the Elan Valley and Rhayader found nothing until 7 April when a lone walker found Graham's body beside a stream. The fourteen-year-old Ruswarp was nearby, having stayed by his master's body for eleven weeks in winter weather; he was so weak that he had to be carried down the mountain. His veterinary fees were paid by the RSPCA, which awarded him their Animal Medallion and collar for 'vigilance' and Animal Plaque for 'intelligence and courage'. He died shortly after Nuttall's funeral. A statue of Ruswarp was erected on the 'up' platform at Garsdale in 2009 and was unveiled by Mrs Olive Clarke and Ron Cotton. Today, it is a popular feature along the line.

> During the TUCC closure hearings one man I remember particularly well was Graham Nuttall, secretary of FoSCL, who was always there, with his dog Ruswarp. He nearly always had something to say, and I remember he always brought sandwiches with him, made by his mother, which he shared with his dog. He went missing and after some time it was realized that he had purchased a ticket at Burnley station to a station in mid-Wales, Llandrindod Wells. This enabled the mountain rescue to be alerted and his body was eventually traced after 77 days. As is well known, Ruswarp was there by his side but in a very poor condition – a bag of bones. The local vet resuscitated him and it was given to an elderly couple in Burnley. Having seen Graham at so many hearings I was moved to attend his funeral at Burnley Crematorium. Ruswarp, with its new owners, was there. I vividly remember that when the coffin disappeared behind the curtain, the dog let out a long howl. If anybody had told me this without me witnessing it, I wouldn't have believed them. But it happened. Years later, I unveiled the lovely statue of Ruswarp on Garsdale station, with Ron Cotton.
>
> *Mrs Olive Clarke*

The commemorative sculpture was funded by public subscription and made by sculptor Joel Walker and cast in bronze. When the heavy statue was being secured to its stone plinth on the up platform it was realized that Ruswarp's gaze was directed to a wooden bench on the opposite platform. This was the very bench that had been placed there years ago and dedicated to Graham Nuttall. The statue in part celebrates the saving of the line from closure and also is a tribute to the loyalty of Graham's companion.

The line-long conservation area: the SCRCA Project

At the beginning of 2012, a small group of volunteers launched a long-term project to identify, catalogue and create a comprehensive record of key railway-related structures and sites within (or associated with) the Settle–Carlisle Railway Conservation Area. They then began the job of researching and documenting the history of the most 'interesting' sites and structures. They identified a wide range of structures, which included 24 railway stations,

The famous 'Ruswarp' at Garsdale.

Milepost 254 (from St Pancras) near Newbiggin.

12 goods sheds, 17 cattle docks, 14 general loading docks, 23 yard offices/weigh-houses and 48 signalboxes. In addition, there are 362 bridges, 22 viaducts, 14 tunnels and 145 culverts. There are 232 former railway workers' houses (all now in private ownership) and 379 other lineside buildings (almost all of which are now disused and in various stages of decay). These include lamp huts, 162 platelayers' huts, 58 fog huts (some of which were probably used or re-used as toilets) and 111 other railway-related buildings (including 'stores', 'coal offices', 'blacksmiths' shops', etc.). Smaller items include 305 mileposts and 118 gradient posts.

There are aspirations that the SRCA Project can be extended to cover many more smaller structures ad sites of archaeological interest along the line.

Freight renaissance

In recent years, due to congestion on the West Coast Main Line, much rail freight traffic has been using the S&C once again. Coal from the Hunterston coal terminal in Scotland was carried to power stations in Yorkshire, and gypsum is transported from Drax Power Station to Kirkby Thore. Major engineering work was needed to upgrade the line to the standards required for such heavy freight traffic and additional investment made to reduce the length of signal sections. In July 2009 work to stabilize a length of embankment near Kirkby Thore and remove a long-standing permanent speed restriction was undertaken. Freight traffic is subject to big fluctuations but at the time of writing, freight traffic on the line is buoyant with quarry traffic originating on the line and through workings, including china clay from Wembley to Irvine, which originates in mainland Europe and arrives in the UK via the Channel Tunnel.

Reconnection to quarries

In July 2015 it was announced that the stone quarries at Arcow and Dry Rigg would be reconnected to the line via north facing points. Stone from both of these quarries is in demand for road building due to its high PSV (Polished Stone Value) and would be taken out of the Yorkshire Dales National Park by freight train instead of lorries. The work was undertaken during the last quarter of 2015 with the link opening to traffic in 2016. In 2018, the quarry was sending out most of its output by rail, with most weekdays seeing two trainloads departing from the quarry. Serious thought is being given to re-opening the nearby branch to Horton Quarry.

Celebrating the reprieve

In April 2014, the 25th anniversary of the line's reprieve was celebrated by the running of a special train from Leeds to Carlisle over the route. This conveyed many of the campaigners who fought to save the line and called at Settle station, where a ceremony was held to commemorate the announce-

The Irvine–Chirk timber train thunders through Settle, July 2018.

The new rail facilities at Arcow Quarry, north of Settle.

Michael Portillo chats with Olive Clarke on the 2014 anniversary special train.
SCRT

A Northern 158 heads north of Settle near Selside, with Pen-y-ghent in the background.

ment made on 11 April 1989 that the line would be kept open. Michael Portillo, the Minister of State with responsibility for railways in the Thatcher government of the time attended the celebrations.

New Northern franchise

In December 2015, it was announced that Arriva Rail North Ltd had been awarded the rights to operate the new Northern Rail franchise from April 2016 (replacing Serco and Abellio). As part of the new franchise agreement with the DfT, the new operator was obliged to run one additional return journey over the line on weekdays (leaving Leeds in the late afternoon and returning from Carlisle later in the evening than the current last train) and two extra services each way on Sundays.

The Eden Brows catastrophe

The winter of 2015–16 saw services over the route repeatedly disrupted by flooding and a serious landslip north of Armathwaite. Storm Desmond saw the line closed for several days at the beginning of December by flooding at several different locations, whilst the landslip at Eden Brows near Armathwaite resulted in the closure of the southbound ('up') line between Cumwhinton and Culgaith from 29 Janu-

ary 2016 to allow the damaged embankment to be inspected and stabilized. Problems had first been reported in mid-December 2015, but repairs were carried out and services resumed on 22 December. Single line working was in place for several days over the northbound ('down') line whilst the remedial work continued and an emergency timetable was in operation. Further ground movement at the site, due to the base of the embankment being eroded by the river, led to the complete closure of the line between Appleby and Carlisle on 9 February 2016, with buses replacing trains over this section. Repairs to the affected section entailed building a 100m-long piled retaining wall and support platform for the track and stabilizing the embankment beneath it; work began in July 2016 and was completed in March 2017. The line between Appleby and Armathwaite was reopened to traffic on 27 June 2016 on a temporary timetable, though the through route remained closed. In February 2017, to celebrate the forthcoming reopening of the line on 31 March, scheduled trains were hauled by 60163 *Tornado*.

Work on the piled wall and trackbed at Eden Brows was completed and the work site was handed back to Network Rail on 22 March 2017, allowing the infrastructure operator to re-commission and fully test the track and signalling system over the affected

Contractors get to work at Eden Brows following the catastrophic landslide in 2016. NETWORK RAIL

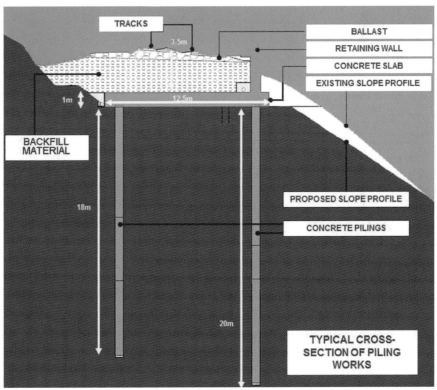

TRACKS

3.5m

BALLAST

RETAINING WALL

CONCRETE SLAB

EXISTING SLOPE PROFILE

12.5m

1m

BACKFILL MATERIAL

18m

PROPOSED SLOPE PROFILE

CONCRETE PILINGS

20m

TYPICAL CROSS-SECTION OF PILING WORKS

A diagrammatic illustration of the piling work. NETWORK RAIL

section of line ahead of the scheduled reopening date. LNER Class A3 Pacific 60103 Flying Scotsman operated a special trip to Carlisle and back to celebrate the full opening to traffic on 31 March 2017.

The line is always subject to extremes of weather and March 2018 saw some severe snow storms, which closed the line for several days. Network Rail teams went out in atrocious weather attempting to clear the line, assisted by DRS locomotive crews (*see* Chapter 3).

CHAPTER 10

Settle–Carlisle People

This chapter offers some short snapshots of some people who have played, in one way or another, a key role in the life of the Settle–Carlisle Railway. There are some obvious gaps – I would like to have featured a navvy, or perhaps the wife of one of the men who built the railway, but little personal information is available. There are many more people who have played important roles, but space prevents their inclusion, particularly those who have been prominent in the last forty years. My apologies for the omissions.

James Allport

James Allport was one of the nineteenth century's most respected railway managers. He was born in 1811 and was associated with railways from an early period of his life. He began his railway career with the Birmingham and Derby Junction Railway in 1839 as the traffic agent at Hampton in Arden. He became Chief Clerk and then General Manager. When the railway merged with the Midland Railway, he moved to the York, Newcastle and Berwick Railway, which became the North Eastern Railway.

In 1845 he assumed charge of the Manchester, Sheffield and Lincolnshire Railway (later renamed the Great Central Railway). In 1853 he was appointed general manager of the Midland Railway – an office he

James Allport.

held continuously, apart from the period between 1857 and 1860, until his retirement in 1880, when he became an honorary director. He was knighted in 1884.

Allport was a great entrepreneur and a pioneer of affordable railway travelling. In 1872 he introduced major improvements to the quality of Third Class passenger facilities. This was followed by the abolition of Second Class in 1875. Second-class was abolished by the Midland in 1875. He died at the Midland Grand Hotel, St Pancras, on 25 April 1892, from acute inflammation of the lungs, the result of a chill. He is buried in Belper Cemetery, Derbyshire.

John Crossley

John Sydney Crossley was a great Victorian railway engineer, famous for his work on the Settle–Carlisle Railway. He was born at Loughborough on Christmas Day, 1812. At an early age he was articled by his guardian to Edward Staveley, engineer to the Leicester Navigation Company, and in 1832 he was appointed a director of the company, a position he held until his death. He became involved on railway work in 1832 when he was employed on surveying the Leicester and Swannington railway, one of the first railways in the UK, and in 1835 he began his association the Midland Counties Railway.

His railway work developed during the late 1840s, involving surveys for the South Midland Railway and the Leicester and Swannington extension of the Midland railway, the construction of the line from Ashby to Coalville and projects in Leicestershire. In 1851 and 1852 he was engaged as engineer for the Leicester Waterworks Company and surbeyed of the Leicester and Hitchin branch of the Midland Railway. Due to the heavy workload, he suffered a stroke. In 1853 he was appointed resident engineer on the Leicester and Hitchin railway. This line was completed in 1857, when he was appointed resident engineer to the Midland Railway Company, becoming its engineer-in-chief the following year.

His greatest engineering work was the Settle–Carlisle railway. He was responsible for the design and construction of all the major features along it. He died at Barrow-upon-Soar on 10 June 1879. He is buried in Holy Trinity Churchyard; the lych-gate entrance to the Church was erected in his memory, and there is a dedication to him beneath the roof.

Charles Sharland

The story of the man who surveyed the railway, between 1865 and 1870, is a fascinating one. Charles Stanley Sharland was born in Tasmania in 1844 and travelled to Britain in 1862 with his brother William, who became a barrister.

When he arrived in Britain, Sharland worked as an assistant in the office of the Maryport and Carlisle Railway. He came to the notice of Crossley (above) for whom he worked. He was recruited into Crossley's small team that surveyed the line and walked the entire length of the proposed route. Their work was held up for several days when their accommodation in The Gearstones Inn, near Ribblehead, was snowed up. Sharland is credited with having devised the route that the Midland adopted as their high-speed railway to Scotland.

The harsh weather took its toll on the young man; he fell victim to tuberculosis and was forced to resign from the project in the autumn of 1870. He retired from the railway to live in Torquay, but shortly afterwards, at the age of just 25, he died. Members of his family came together at a ceremony at his graveside in Torquay on 14 April 2018 when a new headstone, highlighting his contribution to the Settle–Carlisle railway, was dedicated.

Samuel Caudle

Samuel Caudle was part of the Carlisle railway community in the second half of the nineteenth century. He was born in 1854 at Avening near Stroud in Gloucestershire and probably joined the Midland Railway in Gloucester Barnwood shed before he moved to Carlisle (Durran Hill). His main work was over the Settle–Carlisle Line. Caudle was a well-respected member of the railway community, which made his subsequent treatment all the more unacceptable to many railwaymen. After the horrific crash at Ais Gill, Caudle was 'reduced in grade' and spent the rest of his railway career on shunting duties. He died in 1922. He was subjected to what many described as a 'show trial' at the Cumberland Assizes in Carlisle where even the Judge was critical of his own sentence of two months' imprisonment. The Home Secretary intervened after Caudle had spent some days in prison and he was given a Royal Pardon.

Ritson Graham.

Ritson Graham

Ritson Graham was an exceptional person, a classic working-class intellectual who was largely self-taught. He was born near Wigton in 1896. His first job was as a farm labourer, but was then called up during the First World War and served as a machine-gunner in Italy. He had no intention of returning to farm work and saw a railway career as offering better prospects. The local vicar had to stand as guarantor, even for a lowly post as engine cleaner! He started his railway career as a young man at Durran Hill sheds, Carlisle. He rose through the footplate ranks and became active in his union, ASLEF, and was heavily involved in local Labour Party politics. He became a keen student of natural history and often went off into the Pennines on his rest day to explore the countryside.

> Although it was a hard and long slog up to Ais Gill on the Pennines, every time out, it was through some of the finest scenery in the country. I had special and personal reasons to be concerned and was deeply interested in the countryside we passed through,

for I was familiar with most of it from my natural history wanderings.

When he was exploring the surrounding countryside on foot, his mates would often sound a friendly whistle if they spotted him nearby. Ritson went on to become a ward councillor on Carlisle City Council, then Mayor. He was appointed a Freeman of the city.

He served as a lay union representative and also became president of the city's natural history society. Talking to historian Frank McKenna in the early 1980s, he had fond memories of Durran Hill shed:

> I shall always regard as maturing years those spent as a fireman at Durran Hill depot.... This, though we may not have realized it at the time, was one of the best run engine sheds in the country, a model of efficiency where both men and machines were respected and where decency and order prevailed.

Frank McKenna, *The Railway Workers 1840–1970*

Ritson Graham's memory is immortalized in his book *A Border Naturalist: The Birds and Wildlife of the Bewcastle Fells and the Gilsland Moors, 1930–1966* (published in 1993).

Jim Taylor

James Taylor began his railway career in the Dales, employed as a porter. He took on the post of station master at Horton-in-Ribblesdale where he took to his role with gusto. The station gardens became a showpiece, regularly winning 'best kept station garden' prizes. He transferred, with promotion, to Settle where he continued his horticultural activities to good effect. The London Midland Region's staff magazine for 1961 records:

> Station master J.M. Taylor took the garden shield from Aspatria. Mr Taylor is no stranger to honours in gardening for it was his earlier efforts at Horton-in-Ribblesdale that made the station a showpiece

Jim Taylor.

Ron Cotton.

on the Settle–Carlisle Line. Settle scores a double victory by also winning, along with Shap, a first class award for tidiness and cleanliness.

Mr Taylor lobbied hard to ensure that BR served Settle when it introduced an augmented service between Nottingham and Glasgow. He was an energetic promoter of the railway, a real pillar of the local community.

Ron Cotton

Ron Cotton began his railway career at Marylebone Goods Depot in 1950. His parents wanted him to go to university but he was determined to pursue a railway career. He got a junior clerk's job in the Eastern region's freight office and then moved to Hamilton House, Bishopsgate, a few months later. He was called up for national service and after a tussle with the authorities ended up with the Royal Engineers 'Operations Department'. He was stationed at Farnborough and then worked on the Longmoor military railway. He returned to BR in

1952 and worked at the Central Timing Office (Eastern Region) at Bishopsgate. He then moved up the promotional ladder to become Assistant Controller in the Eastern's Stratford Control Office. He became Controller at Knebworth, covering the southern end of the East Coast Main Line, before moving on to work at Great Northern House in central London. Like many BR managers, he lived a nomadic life with moves to the Western region at Birmingham Snow Hill then to Manchester Control where he became District Controller. The next move was to the Southern Region's HQ at Waterloo in charge of the region's freight business. In 1965 he moved to Edinburgh then back south to Newcastle in 1968.

He was promoted to Divisional Passenger Manager that year, and moved to a similar role in Liverpool in 1971. It was during his time in Liverpool that Ron's skills as a dynamic and creative railway manager really blossomed. He developed the 'Merseyrail' brand and introduced high frequency services with cheap tickets. He used the model of the London Underground to develop strong line 'brands', starting with the Wirral Line, followed by 'Northern' and 'City' lines. In 1983 a series of internal wranglings led to the departure of the Liverpool Divisional Manager and Ron came under the wing of the Manchester equivalent. There was friction between the two men and Ron was given what seemed like the poisoned chalice of managing the closure of the Settle–Carlisle Line. Whilst remaining the complete professional, Ron stimulated the use of the line and oversaw the reopening of eight stations for the DalesRail services. Privately, he admitted, 'I was determined I wasn't going to close it', though in public Ron represented the British Railways Board at the TUCC hearings, presenting the BR case as best he could. He developed a strong and positive relationship with the anti-closure campaigners and has remained friends with many of them to this day. He took early retirement from BR in February 1987 and worked for the Football Trust (now the Football Foundation) for several years.

John Whitelegg.

Professor John Whitelegg

John Whitelegg played a key role in the fight to save the line, along with his colleague Peter Horton. The two brought a strong community-based campaigning approach to the anti-closure campaign and helped galvanize support for the line's retention.

From 1990 to 1993 Dr Whitelegg was Head of Department of Geography at Lancaster University and Director of the University's Environmental Epidemiology Research Unit. He has authored ten books including *Transport for a Sustainable Society: The Case for Europe*, and *Critical Mass: Transport, Environment and Society in the Twenty-first Century*, and is founder and editor of the journal *World Transport Policy & Practice*.

His most recent book is *Mobility: A New Urban Design and Transport Planning Philosophy for a Sustainable Future*. In this book he strongly advocates a 'joined-up' approach to achieving three zeroes, all of which need the same set of measures and interventions, to achieve zero carbon, zero death and injury in the road traffic environment, and zero air pollution.

John is a Visiting Professor in the School of the Built Environment at Liverpool John Moores University (UK). In addition to a PhD in Geography he has a Law degree (LLB). In recent years he has held professorial appointments at Lancaster University (Geography), Roskilde University in Denmark (Transport), Essen University (Geography) and York University (Sustainable Development).

He is a member of the International Advisory Board of the Wuppertal Institute for Climate, Energy and the Environment (Germany), appointed by the state government of North Rhine Westphalia, and a member of the Advisory Board of the Chandradeep Solar Research Institute (CDSRI) in Kolkata (India) and a member of the Board of Directors of the US organization *Transportation Choices for Sustainable Communities Research and Policy Institute*, a nonprofit corporation.

He has worked on sustainable transport projects in India, China, Australia, Germany, Sweden and Slovenia and on the same subjects with the European Parliament and European Commission. He is the author of the world's first technical standard on reducing demand for private motorized transport, published by the British Standards Institution. He is a member of the World Health Organization expert group on physical activity, which has produced a global strategy for improving health (reducing non-communicable diseases such as cardio-vascular disease, diabetes and obesity) that gives strong support to walking, cycling, spatial planning and urban design.

In China and India he has worked on transport strategies for Kolkata and Beijing. His main interests are in innovative demand management strategies, spatial planning to reduce the demand for transport, walking and cycling strategies, travel plans and road pricing. Recently he has given advice to the Australian Greenhouse Office in Canberra on the potential of travel plans for reducing carbon emissions and to the Swedish government on its 'fossil-fuel free' policy. He has also advised the Australian Federal Government on a national transport investment model to deliver economic and climate change objectives.

He was a Green Party local councillor in Lancaster (2003–11) representing Bulk ward in the city including a period of time as a member of the Lancaster City Council cabinet. He is a former chair of the North West (of England) Green Party and has been the party's Sustainable Development Spokesperson.

Colin Speakman

After an early career in teaching and lecturing, Colin spent five years as a Principal Officer of the Yorkshire Dales National Park, before serving three years as a Countryside Commission Recreational Transport Officer. This was followed by a year as County Tourism Officer for West Yorkshire. Between 1986 and 2012 he was Managing Director of his own company, Transport for Leisure Ltd, which specialized in developing new green travel opportunities – walking, cycling and public transport – in the countryside, especially to and through protected landscapes such as National Parks and areas of outstanding natural beauty (AONBs).

Colin Speakman.

Colin was also the Founder-Secretary and is now a Vice-President of the Yorkshire Dales Society, established in 1981. He is also the Chairman of the Dales Way Association, Vice-President of the West Riding Ramblers' Association and the Vice Chairman of Friends of DalesBus. In 2015 he became National Transport Campaigner of the Year, awarded by the Sheila McKechnie Foundation for his work for public transport in the Dales and beyond.

A keen walker and writer about the countryside, he is the author or co-author of over fifty books, mainly about Yorkshire, including *A Portrait of North Yorkshire*, *Walking in the Yorkshire Dales*, *The Nut Brown Maid and other Dales Stories*, *Adam Sedgwick – Geologist and Dalesman* and several other books, including walking guides in both UK and mainland Europe, poetry, biography, transport history, and two literary anthologies. In 1997 he was awarded the Honorary Degree of Doctor of Letters at the University of Bradford in recognition of his literary and environmental work, and in 2007 received the first Dalesman Rural Lifetime Achievement Award. His most recent publications include *Walk!*

A Celebration of Striding Out – a history of the literary origins of walking as a leisure activity and its profound impact on our perceptions and concerns for the countryside, *The Yorkshire Dales National Park: A Celebration of 60 Years*, and in 2017 (with Fleur Speakman), *The Yorkshire Wolds: A Journey of Discovery*.

Colin has a growing regional reputation as a poet. His fourth collection *People in a Landscape* was published in 2016 to some excellent reviews.

Richard Watts

At the time of the Settle–Carlisle campaign, Richard Watts was a teacher in Blackpool and Chairman of the North West Branch of the Railway Development Society (RDS). Rumours that the Settle–Carlisle Line was going to be closed had been circulating for some time and the RDS wanted to ensure that there was a vigorous campaign to oppose it. As its opener in the campaign, Richard wrote a leaflet in early 1983 called 'Settle Carlisle is Threatened'. Shortly after that he met with Transport 2000 (North Lancashire and Cumbria) which resulted in the formation of the Settle Carlisle Joint Action Committee (JAC) Ltd. This brought together the RDS, T2000 and the Friends of the Settle–Carlisle Line. The JAC soon became an effective campaign organization arranging public meetings, meeting local and national politicians and once closure was announced ensuring as many people objected to the closure as possible.

The JAC also looked to the future of the line and published a number of books including 'New Life in the Hills' (1986) which led to Richard setting up a campaign group on the Blackburn to Hellifield line. In 1986 he organized a very well-attended public meeting held in Clitheroe which led to the formation of Ribble Valley Rail (RVR). RVR took an active role in the campaign and Richard assisted them in operating a number of very successful and high profile Ribble Valley Rail Days. Trains ran from Clitheroe to Blackburn, Preston and Skipton. This helped promote the value of the line to the local community, which was a great support to the overall Settle Carlisle campaign and of course ensured more objections to closure!

Richard was also Chair of the Ormskirk–Preston Travellers' Association. Like many groups, OPTA ran a well-filled charter train from Ormskirk to Carlisle over the Settle–Carlisle Line. The funds raised were donated to the Joint Action Committee. He took an active role in the closure hearings, preparing evidence on why buses couldn't replace trains. The evidence on bus replacement that Richard amassed from across the country led to the RDS publishing a booklet called *Bustitution – The Case Exploded*.

Richard Watts (right) with Matt Beaton and Howard Hammersley (left).

Following the line's reprieve in 1989, Richard joined Lancashire County Council in 1990 as their Rail Officer. His work resulted in Lancashire being recognized as one of the country's foremost local authorities in railway development. One of his first projects was the return of regular rail services to the Ribble Valley line. This culminated in 1994 in the opening of three new stations, the refurbishment of Clitheroe and the introduction in May 1994 of an hourly service from Clitheroe to Manchester Victoria. Richard has also supported the popular DalesRail service which played such a key role in the Settle–Carlisle campaign. He played the key role in getting the 'Todmorden Curve' reopened in 2015, allowing direct passenger services to operate from East Lancashire to Manchester.

Richard is a director of the Association of Community Rail Partnerships and a member of Northern's Community Rail Executive Group. He chairs Community Rail Lancashire.

Howard Hammersley

Howard Hammersley played an important role in promoting access to the Dales by rail, particularly from the North West. In 1989, when the BR-sponsored 'Rail Rambler' excursions ended it seemed very probable that the Rail Rambler organization would slowly drift into obscurity. Salvation came when Richard Watts, of Lancashire County Council, asked if the organization could deliver the Lancashire DalesRail walks programme and Howard's enthusiasms found a new lease of life. He rose magnificently to the challenge of planning one of the largest rail-based guided walk programmes in the UK. To extend the reach of the programme the Rail Ramblers have organized dedicated connecting coach links to places such as Dent Dale, Hadrian's Wall and Wensleydale.

Howard used to split the work of drawing up the DalesRail walks programme, with Howard planning the walks and Craig Ward, Chair of the Rail Ramblers, organizing the leaders. It's still done this way although it is now Geoff Sherrocks who draws up the programme with Craig sorting out the leaders.

Howard kept detailed logs of each DalesRail service right down to whether the train had been 'tanked' or the toilets cleaned. The logs also contained full details of passenger numbers; how many bikes and prams; who went on a guided, unguided or no walk at all; the weather; any incidents on the day and each log was beautifully hand written. Being a statistician, Howard maintained comprehensive statistics that charted the fortunes of the service and helped target the marketing campaigns.

Howard was passionate about promoting DalesRail as a means of getting people out of urban areas and into the countryside for walking and learning something about the area, from local history to the flora and fauna. His planning, expertise and infectious enthusiasm gathered round him a team of similarly committed and enthusiastic people who travelled thousands of miles in pursuit of their shared interest.

Bill Cameron

Councillor Bill Cameron was a much-liked figure in Cumbria politics and, as leader of the Joint Councils' Campaign against the proposed closure, played a key role in saving the Settle–Carlisle Line. He was born in Maryport and worked as a coalman and then a foundry worker before standing for Maryport Town Council, representing his home town for forty-three years. He first went into local politics in 1967 and stood down in 2010. He died in March 2014, aged 87.

At the 2008 community rail festival he had a Class 156 train named after him, number 156.444, to his great surprise. He described it as the proudest moment in his political career.

> I thought I was going to a function to mark the centenary of the Carlisle railway station. When I got there I discovered that it was a function to name the train. I was thrilled. I believe I am the only councillor to have a train named in their honour.

Bill said he was overwhelmed by the tributes paid to his work by people including former railways minister Michael Portillo, former Rail Freight Group

Bill Cameron, with model of Class 156 train named in his honour.

John Moorhouse.

chairman Lord Tony Berkeley, and former Carlisle MP and chairman of the Parliamentary West Coast Main Line group, Eric Martlew.

He was a chairman of the West Coast Rail 250 pressure group, which campaigned for a West Coast mainline upgrade, and took on Margaret Thatcher when she tried to close the Carlisle–Settle Line. A committed Methodist and life-long socialist, Bill was also a fine rugby player and an accomplished wrestler, a noted Cumberland sport.

John Moorhouse

Following a career in railway operations, John joined the Transport Users' Consultative Committee (TUCC) for Yorkshire as secretary in December 1983, just as the closure notices for the Settle–Carlisle Line were being issued! He spent a very absorbing five-and-a-half years at the forefront of these proceedings (including a discovery that led to the closure notice being re-issued) before the last-minute reprieve of the line in 1989.

He continued to work with the TUCC (later the Rail Passengers Committee) in Manchester until taking early retirement in 2004. He has since worked with the consumers group, TravelWatch NorthWest and became chairman of the Settle Carlisle Railway Development Company in 2005. Apart from one brief period he has remained with the Company as chairman ever since. During this time the Company has prospered and expanded, focusing on its major objective of promoting the line. John feels privileged to work with many dedicated volunteers and professionals alike and to give something back to this magnificent railway line that he has known intimately since growing up in Skipton in the 1950s and '60s.

Olive Clarke

Mrs Olive Clarke played an extremely important role in the fight to save the Settle–Carlisle Line in the 1980s, when she was chairman of the North West Transport Users' Consultative Committee (TUCC). However, her contribution to public life has gone well beyond railways.

Mrs Clarke attended Kendal High School for Girls before marrying farmer Arthur Clarke, with whom she raised a family on Kaker Mill Farm in Preston Patrick. She achieved many 'firsts' including becoming the first female president of the Young Farmers' Clubs and the Country Landowners' Association. She is the County Federation of Young Farmers' longest-serving member and took the role of Westmorland chairman in 1959 and Cumbria president in 1980. She has played a remarkably active role in public health in education, in country affairs, as well as in her local church. She was made 'temporary' treasurer of her local village hall committee fifty-one years ago, and recently retired!

In 2013, Mrs Clarke became the first person to be made an 'honorary life vice-president' of the Cumbria Federation of Young Farmers, after seventy-five years of being part of the organization. She joined the Hutton branch of the Federation in 1938 and won its first public speaking contest that year.

Her role as chairman of the TUCC for North West England during the closure hearings had a very different character to that of her Yorkshire and North East counterpart, James Towler (see below).

> The chair of the TUCC was expected to be impartial; having been a magistrate for many years, and chairman of the Inland Revenue commissioners, this wasn't a problem for me!

She worked assiduously behind the scenes, preferring to persuade and cajole politicians and railway managers whilst maintaining a clear position of impartiality. Arguably, it needed a combination of Towler's assertiveness and Mrs Clarke's more subtle tactics to win the day.

Currently she is a Deputy Lieutenant of Cumbria, a Fellow of the Royal Agricultural Society of Great Britain, the president of the Witherslack Horse Show and patron of Cumbria in Bloom. She was also the Westmorland County Show's first female chairman in 1986 and has since been made a life member. Since then she has been a tutor and adjudicator of public speaking competitions in a bid to empower the farming industry.

In 2018 she was made vice-president of the Friends of the Settle–Carlisle Line as a tribute to her part in saving the line. She has had a life-long

association with the Women's Institute movement. 'I strongly believe in the W.I. principle that you build Jerusalem on your own home ground'. Mrs Clarke's life's work is a clear confirmation of that.

W. R. (Bill) Mitchell

Bill (W. R.) Mitchell has become synonymous with the Settle–Carlisle Line, having written dozens of books and articles about the line and the people who worked on it. He was born in 1928 at Skipton, North Yorkshire. His family worked in the local textile industry and were staunch Methodists, a faith that played an important part in his own life in later years; he was a Methodist local preacher for over forty years.

In 1943, aged fifteen, Bill Mitchell joined the *Craven Herald* as a junior reporter. After national service at Royal Navy air stations, he returned to the newspaper, but in 1948 was asked by Harry J. Scott, editor of *Dalesman*, to join the staff of the magazine. From 1951, in addition to his work on *Dalesman*, he began editing *Cumbria*. In the course of his journalistic work, he met and interviewed many people involved with the Settle–Carlisle Line and developed a great affinity for the railway.

W.R. Mitchell.

In 1969 he took over as editor of *Dalesman*, a post he held until his retirement in 1986. Yorkshire Television marked his retirement with a programme about his life, narrated by Alan Bennett. In 1996 Mitchell was awarded the MBE for his services to journalism in Yorkshire and Cumbria, and was made an honorary Doctor of Letters by the University of Bradford. In the same year Mitchell became an honorary member of the Yorkshire Dales Society, later becoming president and the Society's first patron.

In September 2009 he was voted 'greatest living icon' for the Yorkshire Dales National Park in a poll by this organization to mark the sixtieth anniversary of the National Parks. In May of the following year, 2010, he won the Lifetime Achievement Award at the Dalesman Rural Awards Ceremony in Harrogate for his work in recording the history, heritage and wildlife of the Yorkshire Dales and Moors. He died at Airedale General Hospital on 7 October 2015, aged 87.

The University of Bradford Library has a substantial archive of Bill's material, including scrapbooks, correspondence and audio tapes. In 2011 the W.R. Mitchell Archive was established and is managed by the charity, Settle Stories, based in Settle. The aim is to make a selection of these tapes accessible to the public. In January 2012, Settle Stories received a £50,000 Heritage Lottery Fund grant to digitize a selection of the cassette tapes. This will enable all interested to research, read and listen to these oral histories online.

Bill's books on the Settle–Carlisle Line include *Settle–Carlisle Railway: The Midland's Record-breaking Route to Scotland* (1966), *Settle–Carlisle Railway* (1969), *Settle–Carlisle Railway: A Centenary Edition* (with David Joy, 1976), *Seven Years Hard: Building the Settle–Carlisle Railway* (1976), *Footplate Tales of the Settle–Carlisle Railway* (1990), *The Settle to Carlisle: The Middle Route to Scotland, and Settle to Carlisle: A Railway over the Pennines* (with David Joy, 1994), and many others. He is credited with having written over 200 books on all aspects of Yorkshire Dales and Cumbrian life.

A plaque commemorating Bill was unveiled on Settle station on 21 March 2018; what better location could be found for a man who did so much to promote this railway?

Mark Rand.

Mark Rand

Mark Rand was chairman of FoSCL during the Noughties during which years the line was closed for almost total renewal of the track and some structures during summer peak seasons to make it capable of carrying increased freight – power station coal especially. This disruption was treated as short-term pain for long-term gain.

A former police officer, eventually Chief Superintendent, his career kept returning him to Bradford whose City Police he had joined in 1966. He was for some years chairman of Bingley Civic Trust when the then highly controversial Aire Valley trunk road was planned to go straight through the middle of the town. There was fierce opposition – but not from Bingley Civic Trust which recognized the route as the least bad among few options. At the same time the Settle–Carlisle Line was under threat of closure Bingley Civic Trust became corporate members of FoSCL. He later had the privilege of digging the first sod of the Aire Valley trunk road.

As FoSCL chairman he worked closely with the railway bodies to increase the line's public profile during a difficult patch. Garsdale station underwent a massive refurbishment, FoSCL adopted a 'Five Year Vision' for the line, the statue of Ruswarp was commissioned and unveiled and two public walks over the temporarily closed Ribblehead Viaduct attracted thousands of visitors. He was FoSCL's point of contact during the re-connection of Arcow Quarry and track renewals at Kirkby Thore. In 'retirement' from FoSCL he is an S&C on-train guide and recently rescued No. 48's chimney from being sent for scrap (see Chapter 9).

He has taken part in many TV programmes about the line – not least the S&C episode of *Great Rail Journeys* where he first met Michael Portillo and the pair of them hit it off. He made a big and permanent commitment to the S&C's future when he and his wife bought and restored the then derelict Settle station water tower eventually 'opened' by S&C saviour, now FoSCL President, Michael Portillo.

Mark has seen the line go from almost certain closure, through reprieve and renaissance to what he sees as renewed threats yet opportunities. The coal traffic has gone and passenger train diversions via the S&C have ceased. Even so he sees a bright future for the line, given pragmatism and a willingness to embrace progress, whilst remaining respectful of its precious heritage.

Paul Brown

Paul started work at Settle in August 2011 as station supervisor, part-time, for the Settle Carlisle Development Company. He got his first full-time job working for Northern in July 2013 at Burnley Central (Bank Top) until Settle became available as a full-time post in December 2014. When he left high school in 1991 at sixteen years of age, he became a volunteer on the Keighley and Worth Valley Railway. He became the youngest member of the society council at eighteen years old then progressed to vice-chairman of the society then ultimately chairman for seven years.

During that time he volunteered in the Railway's Carriage and Wagon department undertaking restoration and examinations of rolling stock. He was also a diesel driver, secondman, guard, station foreman, booking clerk, level crossing keeper,

Paul Brown in Settle booking office.

signalman at Damems passing loop and signals, and filming coordinator. Paul is an author and was the first coordinator of the Railway's Beer and Music Festival. Other roles on the K&WVR have included chairman of Santa Specials group, coordinator of Wine and Dine operations and Interim Catering chairman. Since retiring from K&WVR activities in 2011 Paul has helped the Development Company in various ways, including hosting a bar for the Settle–Carlisle 'Beer and Music trains'. Paul is a friendly and familiar face at Settle station. In May 2019 he was elected chairman of The Friends of the Settle-Carlisle Line

Marion Armstrong

Marion has been a constant thread in the story of the renaissance of the Settle–Carlisle Line since the early 1990s. She started her career on a three-year training programme at Coutts' bank in London, but travel and the more unsettled (and poorer) life beckoned until after two children and a move to Yorkshire made her realize she needed to get back into some sort of meaningful work.

She embarked on a two-year IT applications college course and found she was required to do a

Marion Armstrong.

Tony Freschini

Tony has spent a lifetime on the railways, starting as a goods porter in a temporary job during the school holidays firstly at Bradford and then two summers at Thornton Goods yard on the former Bradford to Keighley line. In October 1960 he obtained a permanent position as a technical assistant in the BR District Engineer's office based at Mount Street in the centre of Manchester working mainly on bridge renewal and repair works. In 1963–64 he became involved in the electrification of the Macclesfield Branch, working on many of the bridges in that area. In 1964 he moved south to Ipswich and continued to work on bridge works. Following a major reorganization resulting in the closure of the Ipswich office he was transferred to Stratford for a short time before gaining a post in the Derby and Nottingham Divisional Engineer's office continuing to gain experience of larger civil engineering bridge works.

After leaving Nottingham in 1966 Tony moved to London as an Assistant Resident Engineer working on the complete rebuilding and modernization of the station. The rebuilding of Euston was a major project with about 750 people working on the site at its peak in 1968. The nature and variability of the works enabled Tony to gain the experience and knowledge needed to fulfil the duties and legal responsibilities of a Resident Engineer supervising contractors undertaking railway works. In 1968 Tony was appointed Resident Engineer.

After Euston Tony moved to Lancaster to supervise bridge works being undertaken by contractors as a part of the West Coast Main Line Electrification Scheme; on completion of electrification he continued to work supervising new bridges and structures works in Cumbria and Lancashire.

Tony's first involvement with the Settle–Carlisle Line occurred in 1976 when he became responsible for the supervising the construction of a new bridge to carry the line over the Appleby bypass. The project was completed in 1978.

In 1978 concerns were arising about the deteriorating condition of Ribblehead Viaduct and the high maintenance costs being incurred annually in order to resolve this. Tenders were invited with the aim of

week of work experience. A week at the Settle–Carlisle Railway Development Company was enough to get hooked and she then spent the next twenty years delivering projects and building up the company. In 1994 the DevCo had one and a half employees on their books and when Marion left the company in 2014 as General Manager the company was proud to employ nineteen people.

Numerous projects were delivered, huge sums of funds were applied for (some successful and some not) and important contacts and partnerships were made in that twenty-year period. All of that ultimately aided the line in its transformation; a line rescued from the brink of closure and dilapidation transformed into what we see today.

Marion retains an involvement with the line, as a volunteer gardener with the 'Cultivating Settle' group, which looks after the station gardens. She has served as a town councillor and plays an active role in many local voluntary groups.

Tony Freschini.

continued to have a personal interest in the line, and loved to walk in the Dales landscape. He took retirement from Network Rail in 2005 and often gives talks about the line and the 'saving of Ribblehead Viaduct'.

Ruth Annison

Ruth Annison grew up in the village of Wensley in Derbyshire but has lived in Wensleydale in North Yorkshire since 1975, when she and her husband Peter – a textile chemist – moved to take over the traditional rope-making business in Hawes from Tom Outhwaite on his retirement.

During the 1980s, when the Settle–Carlisle railway was under long-running threat of closure, thousands of people were involved in a vigorous campaign to save the line, which became a national and international news story. Meanwhile, three years earlier, Garsdale – 6 miles (10 km) from Hawes – was one of eight small stations

completely refurbishing the structure and giving it a twenty-five-year life. The costs were deemed too high and no one was prepared to give a twenty-five-year guarantee. BR's own engineers then came up with proposals to build a new viaduct alongside the old; however, these also proved too costly and with a reduced amount of traffic on the line BR could not justify further major expenditure.

Meanwhile, closure of the line was formally proposed, with the condition of the viaduct cited by BR as a major factor. Tony became involved in a scheme part-funded by English Heritage (see Chapter 8), which involved a full refurbishment of two arches, to demonstrate the feasibility, as well as cost, of repairing the original structure. The results were sufficiently positive to let a contract for the refurbishment of the entire structure, and Tony was in overall charge of the job. This was given the go-ahead shortly after the line's reprieve in 1989. The project was completed in February 1992. Tony

Ruth Annison.

that were re-opened by BR after sixteen years' closure. The immediate need for public transport between the remote station and the market town of Hawes led to the setting up of a minibus link, whose successor today is the renowned all-year round Little White Bus service. From 1986, when Ruth first became involved in the Settle–Carlisle campaign, she rallied hundreds of local business people along the line (including leading a deputation to 10 Downing Street, accompanied by members of the cast of *Starlight Express* in full costume) and mobilized a very effective lobby that politicians would listen to. This led to the formation of the Settle–Carlisle Railway Business Liaison Group (later the Settle–Carlisle Enterprise Network) – which for twenty-seven years championed the line and its role as a catalyst for local development – and organized a range of events to develop the line's potential.

Reprieve of the Settle–Carlisle provided the trigger for a campaign to bring back passenger services to Wensleydale. Ruth called the first meeting, held in Hawes, on 23 May 1990; her Churchill Travelling Fellowship in 1994 provided international evidence of the benefits of considering and promoting rural bus and rail services as an integrated network. In 2003 passenger trains returned to the surviving 22 miles (35 km) of the Wensleydale line, with the long- term goal of reinstating the full 40-mile (64 km) railway through the dale in stages, to re-connect the East Coast main line at Northallerton with the Settle–Carlisle at Garsdale. In August 2018, Ruth called an initial public meeting – again in Hawes – to raise the tantalising possibility of re-building the 6-mile (10 km) branch line from Garsdale station to Hawes. 2019 will be the sixtieth anniversary of the last train!

Drew Haley

Drew Haley, a railwayman from the age of nineteen, is the manager of the Settle–Carlisle Railway Development Company (the 'DevCo'). He has been involved with the line since 2003, when he was the area manager for Northern, working with commu-

Drew Haley.

nities and stakeholders. This was at a time when the community rail movement was really starting out and railways were keen to be more inclusive. Drew embraced this way of working and when the Northern franchise was let with only minimal investment, it became more important to work with supportive bodies to source rail improvements collectively.

Working with the Friends and the DevCo, the stations of Appleby and Settle were fully refurbished with modern toilets, hot water (for the first time in living memory), eco heaters, low-energy lighting and customer information screens delivered by Wi-Fi. Station staff finally got hot water, a kitchen and their own toilet too, much to the delight of the union! Improvements were not limited to the stations, though; after many years of campaigns the line's first trains finally went through from both ends, instead of the strange operation of starting from Ribblehead and Kirkby

Stephen after running empty from Skipton and Carlisle. The Sunday service was increased from three to four trains, which has proved to be so popular there are now six in either direction.

With these improvements it became important to promote the route; improvements for Dales Railcard holders drove sales, and finally they could travel from either end of the line to and from stations north of Skipton, and members of the Friends could also purchase a railcard. Popular offers were run in winter with Metro to entice passengers out of the city and these proved to be so popular that overcrowding issues had to be addressed in winter!

Drew says:

> The S&C really was a line where working with the community and the railway companies bore fruit. When they had eighty days of engineering work over a year to slate twenty-six speed restrictions, Railtrack painted the bridges, gave compensation to the trolley service to ensure its future and paid for a 156 to be fully liveried with table tops inlaid with line maps (the first in the UK). One of the more unusual developments was the iPhone Audio Guide, which is like having your own personal guide to the Settle–Carlisle, telling the story of the line's construction and giving you fascinating insights into the unfolding landscape in real time. A first on a mainline railway we believe.

Drew and Marion Armstrong were instrumental in setting up Skipton café, which has a very different lease from normal, with 20 percent of the profit being the annual charge. This new way of working ensures risk is managed for small enterprises but also can be a driver for stations to be occupied rather than empty, especially in areas where the large franchised operations don't see enough profit for them. Drew's proudest moment was actually putting the fares down in 2007, when all others were rising across the company; he remembers very little press coverage was given to this!

In his work as manager of the DevCo, Drew is now working on getting through services to Glasgow with regional bodies and looking at a totally new venture to revamp the retail and café offer at Settle station. 'Heritage the line may be but it never stops moving forward'.

Edward Album

Edward played a key role in saving the line, through skilful deployment of legal and financial skills as a company and commercial lawyer in the City of London. He was born in London in 1936 and was educated at the Primary School at Frizinghall, Bradford, then Emanuel School, London and Christ Church, Oxford. He did his National Service (1954–6) in the Army and then served for nine years in the Territorial Army. He is a member of the Honourable Artillery Company. He played rugby as a prop forward for fourteen years with Old Emanuel (B's), Christ Church and Finchley Rugby Club. 'A few punches thrown but never sent off' is his proud record.

Edward Album.

His legal career began with a BA in Jurisprudence at Oxford. He then was appointed by the University of Chicago as an Instructor in the Law Faculty 1959–60. After Articles in London, he became a qualified solicitor in January 1964, and still practices as a company and commercial lawyer and arbitrator in London.

His involvement with the Settle–Carlisle Line dates from 1985 when he was appointed a committee member of the Friends of the Line with the brief to represent the London end of the campaign to save the Line from closure. In that capacity, he liaised with Ministers, MPs and the Department of Transport. He was heavily involved with the anti-closure campaign from 1985 onwards, and represented the Friends at TUCC hearings. He worked with Cumbria County Council in preparing for a judicial review in the event of a decision by Government to close the line. He also prepared financial reports giving a true position of the performance of the Line. In the end, the Government refused British Rail's closure request and it is believed and recorded that the substantial funds raised (to come through the Trust) for the Ribblehead Viaduct repairs, with also the threat of a judicial review, were significant factors in the reprieve decision.

After the reprieve, Edward founded The Settle and Carlisle Railway Trust in 1990, serving as a trustee (including chairman from 2000 to 2009). He is a Vice-President of the Friends and the Trust.

Edward continues to work on Settle–Carlisle issues on behalf of the Friends and the Trust and has assisted in the creation of a substantial archive of materials on the line's history, particularly during the campaign against closure.

Douglas Hodgins

Douglas was born and brought up in Bishopbriggs on the north side of Glasgow; weekends and school holidays were earmarked for train spotting and visits to loco sheds. On leaving school he found a job as the 'office junior' in a firm of stockbrokers in the centre of Glasgow. Several mergers later, and many years on, he was made a director of a large

Douglas Hodgins.

stockbroking concern in Glasgow with branches throughout the UK.

His interest in railways had not diminished, however. He was a member of the Scottish Railway Preservation Society at Bo'ness, and for several years ran their railtour operation. Highlights were footplate trips from Appleby to Garsdale on 'No. 9' on a tour to the Keighley and Worth Valley Railway, several trips on what he describes as 'our old favourite *Maude* in central Scotland' and on various locos on the Fort William–Mallaig service.

Work suddenly changed and he found himself working in a large office, which was 'very demanding'. He was able to transfer to the firm's office in Carlisle: 'much better, with only three colleagues for company'. Such were the benefits of computers that one could work anywhere as long as you could

200

'log on' to the company files. As a result of his office move, Douglas and his wife Margaret moved house to Church Brough, just outside Kirkby Stephen, some twenty-seven years ago. He retired in 1990.

His love for the S&C had developed over the years, through many forays on a Saturday from Glasgow to photograph steam and diesels, 'much easier living on the doorstep', and then he joined the FoSCL Committee. He was Chairman of the S&C Railway Development Co for a time and also a Trustee of the S&C Railway Trust for a number of years. Douglas said:

> How the railway has changed, sometimes, it seems, not for the better. My real ambition as Chairman is to see the restoration of through trains from Nottingham to Glasgow via Leeds, giving the S&C the ideal mix of express and local services coupled with a reasonable amount of freight.

Ken Harper

Ken is a career railwaymen who started in 1965 as a 'box lad' in Penrith No. 1 signalbox. He was promoted to signalman and briefly worked as a guard in 1993, as the manual signalboxes on the West Coast Main Line were being closed. He returned to signalling at Appleby North and joined the supervisory grade in 1975 at Carlisle. He became Traffic Manager for the Carlisle Area for thirteen years, covering his hometown Penrith as well as the northern end of the Settle–Carlisle. Amongst his most vivid memories are of the hard winter of 1979 when the Settle–Carlisle was blocked for several weeks. He worked on the snow plough attempting to clear the line.

As BR reduced its staff, he gradually took on more of the Settle–Carlisle, covering as far south as Dent Head from Carlisle. Further parts of the network

Ken Harper.

came under his wing including the Windermere branch. Ken became closely involved in the efforts to promote the line in the early 1980s, after closure notices had been issued! He worked with Ron Cotton to organize shoppers' specials from the small stations that were officially closed.

Ken became Traffic Manager (Carlisle) and his final job was Operations Manager, before retiring in 2007. He remains very active in the Friends of the Settle–Carlisle Line.

Conclusion: Personal Hopes and Dreams

The Settle–Carlisle Railway has become a national treasure. The threat of closure has long abated but the line still needs careful nurturing to develop its potential. There's a balance struck between the needs of a modern railway and conserving the superbly restored stations, and other infrastructure, along the line. The line plays an important, and increasing, role in the economy of the Dales and makes a major contribution to the National Park objectives of encouraging the use of public transport. Can it do more? Most people involved with the railway would give a definite 'yes'.

The Settle–Carlisle Railway can look forward to an assured future. Passenger numbers remain buoyant and freight traffic, despite the loss of most of the coal operations, is doing well. Many rail campaigners see it as a mainline 'Cinderella' railway waiting to come back into its own. After all, it was built (albeit reluctantly) as part of a fast, direct route from London and West Yorkshire to Scotland, for the Midland's London to Glasgow and Edinburgh expresses.

What does the Settle–Carlisle Line have to offer in today's society, with more leisure time available, the building of HS2 increasingly likely and growing freight potential for rail? Perhaps a starting point is to consider the existing markets served by the line. The passenger market splits several ways. Firstly, is used by people living between Skipton, Settle and Carlisle to go about their business – to work, shops and for longer distance leisure purposes. They are dependent on what is 'their' railway, and its loss would be a disaster. Then there are the leisure travellers who use the line to access the magnificent Yorkshire Dales and North Pennines. Without the line, they would be forced to use the car, or not come at all. The impact on the local economy, as well as the environment, would be catastrophic – as campaigners back in 1983 pointed out. There are some through passengers, typically from West Yorkshire travelling to Scotland, who use the line and change at Leeds for onward journeys to Glasgow and Edinburgh. It isn't a big market, but could be developed.

Finally, there is the charter market – mostly, but not exclusively, steam operated. The actual benefit of charters to the Settle–Carlisle Line is debatable; it could almost be a negative. The days when charter trains stopped at Appleby, and to a lesser extent Settle, bringing business to local pubs and shops, are long gone. The best one could hope for from a charter train journey is that people are so impressed with the line that they want to come back on a scheduled service. And there's no doubt that some do. The down side is that the charter trains take up precious line capacity and also attract large numbers of car-borne enthusiasts to photograph the trains (and I have to plead 'guilty' to being one of those in the past!).

So the main passenger markets are locally originating travel to Leeds, Carlisle and beyond, some through journeys beyond Carlisle to/from Leeds, and incoming visitors. It's the visitor market that must have most potential and the railway is well suited to serve that market, including new markets in the North West, which are not currently served other than by circuitous journeys via Leeds or Lancaster and Hellifield.

The other important traffic is freight. As a through route the line has always had its value, not least for diversions or slower-moving traffic that would cause delays on the West Coast Main Line via Shap. Currently, the amount of through freight isn't great. However, there is the very welcome revival of aggregates traffic originating on the line at Helwith Bridge and hopefully before long at Horton-in-Ribblesdale. To that could be added the cement traffic from Clitheroe (Horrocksford) to Gunnie in Scotland. Whilst freight is a nuisance to passenger operators, reducing the number of paths and sometimes causing delays in the event of failures, few people could argue against the huge environmental benefits of locally originating rail freight taking hundreds of lorry movements off the roads.

From a railway operating perspective (recognized by BR in the 1970s and early 1980s) the line has an important role as a diversionary route. Whatever happens with HS2 north of Preston, the line will continue to have a value for both planned engineering work on the West Coast Main Line, as well as in the event of emergencies. Campaigners are right to argue for more services to be diverted via the Settle–Carlisle Line during weekend engineering work, rather than shepherding passengers onto coaches at Preston and Carlisle.

Line capacity is key to the argument about the future of the line. It seems unlikely that the line would ever return to its original status as a fast InterCity route (today's 'fast' is 125mph or more). But there is a half-way house between having the current all-stops service between Leeds and Carlisle and an

The author aged 13, Ribblehead.

InterCity service that would be of little benefit to people living on the route, or wanting to visit, since a true 'InterCity' service would be unlikely to stop anywhere other than Skipton. But the line could manage more semi-fast services, some of which could be extensions of Northern's current Nottingham–Leeds service, which will form part of its 'Northern Connect' network of premium services. Trains could call at Shipley, Bingley, Keighley, Skipton, Settle, Garsdale (for Hawes), Kirkby Stephen, Appleby and Carlisle. That isn't an 'inter-city' operation but it's a potentially valuable 'inter-regional' operation. Extending that service beyond Carlisle, in co-operation with ScotRail, would make sense, particularly if it served the more populous route via Dumfries and Kilmarnock. For the longer term, if and when – surely it must be 'when' – the Waverley Route is extended south from Tweedbank (Galashiels) into Carlisle, a new service from West Yorkshire to Edinburgh and the Lothians via Carlisle would be possible.

For freight, the real prize is more originating traffic from along the line, above all aggregates. Through freight may be good in terms of helping guarantee the line's future, it takes away capacity and knocks the stuffing out of the track. If more 'originating' freight can be developed, that's good news but the right infrastructure must be in place to avoid potential delays to other services.

So infrastructure investment is vital to the development of the line. The current signalling arrangements, with the delightful Midland Railway signalboxes and semaphore signalling, look great for a heritage railway but are a drag on the line's future development. Better to turn the boxes (like those at Settle and Armathwaite) into small museums and convert the line to modern signalling, with line speed upgrades to 75mph or more.

An often forgotten aspect of the railway is the importance of its feeders. The route from Manchester via Bolton to Clitheroe and Hellifield has a passenger service as far as Clitheroe. There must be a strong market for travel from Greater Manchester to the Dales, with the possibility of trains combining at Hellifield for the onward journey to Carlisle, or timed to connect. Having local bus services integrated with trains at Settle, Ribblehead, Garsdale and Kirby Stephen is a further vital part of the jigsaw. In the longer term, it would be wonderful to have a heritage rail service from Garsdale taking tourists into Hawes and Wensleydale.

The Leeds–Settle–Carlisle service is part of a much bigger network – the 'Northern' franchise, specified by the Department for Transport and Transport for the North. Its fortunes are, to a considerable extent, tied in with success of the parent franchise. There have been suggestions in the past, which I have a great deal of sympathy for, of having Leeds–Carlisle (and Lancaster/Morecambe) as a single 'mini-franchise'. As the rail industry seems increasingly intent to strangle itself with bureaucracy, freeing up the 'S&C' as a separate business unit with a degree of commercial freedom could bring benefits. If it began within the parent franchise and developed its own independence (within the overall network) it

The author aged 65, Ribblehead.

could be the best of all worlds, particularly if it could have dedicated staff including a Route Manager.

The Settle–Carlisle Line has a great future ahead. Travel patterns will change but the lure of a day out in the Dales will never wane and what better way to get there than by train? For people living in the Dales and Cumbria, the line is an essential part of life and will continue to be so, for journeys to school, college and work and for access to the wider world. We can thank the determination of those Midland Railway pioneers who, albeit reluctantly, forged a railway through this most wild and beautiful landscape, but perhaps even more the men and women who fought so hard to save it from closure in the 1980s. Not forgetting that dog!

Bibliographical Essay: A Much Written About Railway

I am very conscious of travelling in the tracks of many previous authors, each of whom has brought their own distinctive approach to the railway's history and contemporary operation. This essay hopes to do justice to all of them and encourage the reader to explore further.

The first writer to give substantial attention to the Settle–Carlisle Railway was Frederick S. Williams in his classic work *The Midland Railway: Its Rise and Progress*, subtitled *A Narrative of Modern Enterprise*. The book was published before the line's completion but contains fascinating insights into the construction period and life in the shanty towns.

The first book specifically on the railway itself was Frederick W. Houghton and W. Hubert Foster's *The Story of the Settle–Carlisle Line*, first published in 1948, well before a widespread interest in railway history had developed. It is an important work, written for a post-war readership. Whilst written for the general reader it has a good grasp of both railway history and contemporary railway operations. The 'human factor' is not neglected.

The acknowledged classic work on the line is Peter E. Baughan's *The Midland Railway – North of Leeds*, sub-titled *The Leeds–Settle–Carlisle Line and its Branches*, first published in 1966 with a new edition in 1987. It has rightly been described as monumental. It is a detailed history of the line,

which nobody with a serious interest in the Settle–Carlisle can afford to neglect.

The late W. R. ('Bill') Mitchell wrote a huge amount about the railway, often in articles and pamphlets. His book, co-authored with David Joy, *Settle–Carlisle Railway*, first published in 1966 and revised up to a fifth edition in 1979, is a very good general introduction which covers all aspects of the line's history. Another joint work with David Joy was *Settle–Carlisle Centenary: 100 years in Pictures of England's Highest Main Line railway*, 1976. Bill wrote a fascinating account of life in the shanty towns, with Nigel Mussett, in *Seven Years Hard*, published in 1976. A sequel was *Shanty Life on the Settle–Carlisle Railway*, published in 1988. A particularly interesting local study by Bill, published in 1999, is *Garsdale: History and Traditions of a Junction Station (on the Settle–Carlisle Railway)*. His book *Thunder in the Mountains: The Men who Built Ribblehead* (2009) was his last major work, covering the social history of Ribblehead Viaduct and its surroundings. Bill's recent death (2018) has deprived the railway community of a great character and a learned historian of both the railway and the Dales as a whole.

David Jenkinson's *Rails in the Fells* (1973) is a most unusual railway book, with a strong focus on landscape, architecture and the impact of the railway on the local economy and Dales communities.

My good friend Martin Bairstow, who has the unenviable task of doing my yearly accounts, has written extensively on the railways of the North of England (as well as Ireland). *The Leeds, Settle and Carlisle Railway: The Midland Route to Scotland* was first published in 1994 and a new edition appeared in 2012. It is an excellent general account of the railway from its building up to its current operation in the early part of the twenty-first century.

Several accounts have been produced on the closure campaign. A very good personal account, and highly readable, is James Towler's *The Battle for the Settle–Carlisle Line* (1990). Alan Whitehouse and Stan Abbott wrote the classic account of the campaign, including its wider national context, in *The Line That Refused to Die*, published in 1990. The most recent book on the closure is Martin Pearson's *The Settle–Carlisle Railway 1850–1990: The Building and Saving of a Great Railway – a Line of Critical Decisions*, published in 2016. Martin's work includes the discovery of an all-important letter from Paul Channon to Margaret Thatcher outlining his reasons for refusing consent to the closure. Martin places the attempt to close the line, and the reasons for its reprieve, in a wider theoretical context.

Bob Swallow's book on railway life on the line has some delightful stories. *Against The Grade: Working on the Settle–Carlisle Railway*, was published in 2016. Dick Fawcett's *Ganger Guard and Signalman: Working Memories of the Settle & Carlisle* (1981) is a great account by a working railwayman.

Photographic books on the Settle–Carlisle Line abound, but a good general 'picture book' with informative text is T.G. Flinders The Settle & Carlisle Route and its sequel The Settle & Carlisle Route Revisited, 1985. Donald Binns has written several informative pictorial histories relating to the line, with an emphasis on locomotives, including The Settle–Carlisle Line: Railways in the Northern Dales, 1989. Anthony Lambert's large-format book Settle to Carlisle (1995) not only has some excellent images of the line but also has a useful outline history of the railway.

More general works of interest include Terry Coleman's classic *The Railway Navvies* (1965) and Dick Sullivan's *Navvyman* (1983). David Joy's *Rails in the Dales* (2017) is a scholarly and highly readable account of eight railways in the Dales, including the author's beloved Settle–Carlisle Line.

To keep up to date on developments along the line, the Friends of the Settle–Carlisle Line's quarterly magazine, *The Settle–Carlisle Railway Journal*, makes indispensable reading. It comes free with your annual membership – a very good reason in itself to sign up! www.foscl.org.uk.

Index